OLD SEVILLE

SEVILLE

- The City of Eternal Youth -

MARK COLENUTT

*When a hedonist is tired of Seville
they are tired of their youth,
for there is in Seville
all that life's passions
can desire.*

This book is dedicated to Borja, Concha, Howard, Jorge, María del Mar, Pablo and Paco (el muricano), without whom my time in Sevilla would have been half the glorious experience that it was.
Thank you, ¡y e'to va pa' ustedes!

Copyright © Mark Colenutt 2012
All rights reserved

The moral right of the author has been asserted

This book is sold subject to the condition that it shall not, by way of trade or otherwise, be lent, re-sold, hired out, or otherwise circulated without the publisher's prior consent in any form of binding or cover other than that in which it is published and without a similar condition including this condition being imposed on the subsequent purchaser

Also by the same author

A Vision of Seville

- in images -

Handbook to the Legacy & Odyssey of Don Qvixote

- Everything the armchair academic needs to know about the greatest novel ever written -

Spanish Bull

- A Provocative Guide to Bullfighting -

CONTENTS

UNO
1492 AND ALL THAT *p.1*

DOS
LANDMARKS & LEGENDS *p.33*

TRES
¡AY, TRIANA! *p.99*

CUATRO
TUNA NIGHT *p.113*

CINCO
THREE 'MAGIC' KINGS *p.119*

SEIS
A FLEMISH FLAMINGO *p.125*

SIETE
SUN & *SOMBRAS* *p.153*
- Everything you wanted to know about bullfighting but weren't sure you should ask -

OCHO
HOLY WEEK *p.181*

NUEVE
VANITY FAIR *p.199*

DIEZ
LIDS & OTHER APPETISERS *p.223*

ONCE
PRIMAVERA *p.235*

DOCE
SEVILLIAN SUMMER *p.239*

TRECE
'WINE, WOMEN AND SONG' *p.253*

CATORCE
OIL MASTERS & PAPER MENTORS *p.267*

QUINCE
EXCURSIONS: *¡VÁMONOS!* *p.277*

DIECISÉIS
FIRST IMPRESSIONS *p.295*

DIECISIETE
HASTA LUEGO *p.303*

INTRODUCTION

"He who does not travel does not know the value of men."
Moorish proverb

Byron once notoriously stated, *"I am so convinced of the advantages of looking at mankind instead of reading about them, and of the bitter effects of staying at home with all the narrow prejudices of an Islander, that I think there should be a law amongst us to set our young men abroad for a term among the few allies our wars have left us."*

If such a law were passed then Parliament would do well to ensure that England's youth spent a year in the capital of the Spanish south. One may of course prefer to travel abroad and head off for coastal areas or the deep hinterlands, but if it is the urban skyline that beckons you, then there are few cities, if any, that can offer the inspiration-seeking disciple more colour, culture and stirring experiences than Seville. Your first year there will be like none other.

We all have the same desires, but disparate cultures go about them in very different ways. If you think that the customary 9 to 5 is more or less the same wherever you turn your attention in Europe then you are about to change your mind, as Aldous Huxley well-knew: *"To travel is to discover that everyone is wrong about other countries."* Not all will be to your liking but then *"...a foreign country is not designed to make you comfortable. It is designed to make its own people comfortable."* However, Samuel Johnson hoped that, *"If the passenger visits better countries, he may learn to improve his own"*, and the author also anticipates that this book will effect a similar transformation on the reader.

In a globalised, standardised planet the people of Seville, *los sevillanos* (pronounced se-vi-YA-nos), remain true to their roots. They see things in a different light under their southern sun and are pro-active in seizing the day. More importantly for the outsider though, they welcome all who wish to share their vision and join them in celebrating life. In this brief existence then, one must have a child, plant a tree, write a book but also... visit Seville.

- UNO -
1492 AND ALL THAT

'Out of chaos God made a world, and out of high passions comes a people.'
Lord Byron (1788–1824)

This is the story of how Sevilla, pronounced se-VI-ya, emerged from the prehistoric soup and became its present day *gazpacho*.

A long, long time ago before there was anything much good on telly peoples tended to roam about a bit. In fact, they roamed all over the place. This was, of course, long before someone came up with the not so bright idea of passport controls. Then you could roam just about anywhere you wanted and that was exactly what happened when Spain's first inhabitants turned up and found, to their delight, that there were no officials to tell them to go back where they had come from. They liked the place so much that they decided to have it for themselves.

The rich discovery in the Sierra de Atapuerca near Burgos in 1997 of human remains and fossils created a stir in the archaeological world. The corpses discovered in a cave date back a million years and are thought to be our earliest known ancestors in Europe. The find has lead to the dubbing of a new species in the evolutionary chain: *Homo Antecessor* and was recognised by UNESCO in 2000 as Europe's oldest ancestors to date.

However, in 1982 in Orce in Andalucía, 70 miles east of Granada an even more sensational discovery of human remains and tools had been made, which almost re-wrote the prehistory books. It put man's earliest descendants back to 1.7 million years, but the authenticity of this claim has been disputed ever since. The small piece of bone on which such extrapolations were made, has been dubbed in typical Andalusian jest as *la galleta* – the biscuit.

After that, the oldest human remains found in the region of Andalucía are those of a Neanderthal woman on Gibraltar dating back to 50,000 BC. Gibraltar made its find eight years before a similar skull was unearthed in the Neander Valley, Düsseldorf. It was not to be for Gibraltar though whose bone was stuffed in a draw and forgotten about, leaving 'Gibraltar Woman' to be outdone by 'Neanderthal Man'.

Settlers after this time wandered right up to the Pyrenees

bordering France and decided to give the climb a miss making good where they were. They left their indelible mark nearby in some of the world's best prehistoric cave paintings at Altamira in the medieval town of Santillana near Santander, on the northern shore of Cantabria. However, as they didn't sign their work, we don't know much else about them apart from the fact that they arrived some 13,000 years ago.

The first cave paintings left by Homo Sapiens in Andalucía date from 25,000 BC in Málaga province at the *Pileta* cave in Benaoján near Ronda. There are other prehistoric paintings in Nerja and the cave of *Tajo de las Figuras* in Medina Sidonia. There are megalithic constructions such as the biggest dolmens in Europe at Romeral and Menag in the province of Málaga as well as Viera in Antequera and Trigueros in Huelva province. There are around 20 examples in the small town of Valencina de la Concepcíon just outside Sevilla alone, dating from 2,000 BC. The most popular one at Valencina is the 32m *Matarrubilla*. There is also the necropolis of *Los Millares* with its fortified site in the province of Almería going back to 2,700 BC.

The Iberians, whose name, and probably infringing copyright, was given to the peninsular by the Greeks. They were a people that emerged from these early groups. Their origins, however, are not quite clear. One theory says they arose around the Ebro river basin. Another points to the idea that the autochthonous population of southern Europe emigrated there from Africa, although close study has revealed that there is little similarity between the two groups of people. They did, however, start their days as wild tribes gradually civilised by their contact with the arriving Phoenicians who introduced them to writing and the decorative arts. The Iberians came to leave behind them a collection of objects in *Ilirturgi*, their most important city, now modern day Andújar. A fourth century terracotta statue of a woman known as the *Dama de Baza* was also found in Baza in the province of Granada.

Next on the scene was the kingdom of Tartessus in 1,200 BC whose culture lasted about 600 years and was rooted in the Guadalquivir basin. The Tartessians are the first known inhabitants and founders of Sevilla and they fused the dual influences of the Iberians and Phoenicians. The Phoenicians, as their exotic name implies were a resplendent race who struck up trading outposts along the Andalusian seaboard. They were from Lebanon and lay claim to having established Europe's oldest city:

Gadir meaning 'castle', modern day Cádiz - pronounced **KA**-dith, in 1,100 BC. They also founded *Malaka* - 'royal town', now named Málaga. Both cities were staging points on the pewter route. The Phoenicians also stopped off in Ibiza building the city walls which still stand to this day making them the oldest in Europe. They also left to Spain the legacy of their musical influence.

So, what made them and other subsequent civilisations found their capital on the same spot as modern day Sevilla? Why not by the sea or further inland still? The city was erected at the highest navigable point by seafaring vessels up the Guadalquivir river, 50 miles inland, similar to London. From this point in, further navigation would have to be undertaken in smaller craft.

Excavations in the centrally located street of *La Cuesta de Rosario* have revealed that the earliest settlement started in 9th century BC, the same time as the Guadalquivir basin takes on its present shape after being subjected to extensive cultivation.

The southerners had had a bite of the cherry and now it was time for some northerners and easterners to come in and see what was pulling in all the punters into Iberia. They came in the form of Germanic tribes and the Celts around 1,500 BC. However, they kept very much to themselves within the northern territories not wanting to mix much with them down south. There was a distinctive racial divide in Spain with the Ebro river acting as a natural barrier between the two groups. (*Ebro* coming from the Iberian word meaning river.) Nevertheless, there were one or two cheeky rascals on either side of the river banks that couldn't keep their eyes off the blonde bombshell to the north and the beautiful brunette to the south. So, when in the South you come across conspicuous blonde-haired and blue-eyed people in Andalucía, they may notnecessarily be tourists. They have been around a little longer than that, so don't go up to them asking for directions.

Three hundred years later and the Greeks thought they'd give it a bash and came by the boat load, no doubt getting their package tours in before their own islands were given the same going over. They made the trip to the south from their northern settlements in Catalunya with more merchants than warriors on board, hoping to capitalise on the trade opened up by the friendlier Phoenicians and the ever-growing fame of the mines at Ríotinto. The Greeks founded what is present day Écija just 94km to the east of Sevilla, and like the Phoenicians before them, they also left their musical instruments behind them. Unfortunately, their architectural legacy in the south got nicked over the years and nothing has been left standing to tell their tale. More interestingly though, for the land of Andalucía, they left in their wake as they sailed out of port their classical mythology. Greek writers make mention of Atlantis some way out towards southern Spain and a good case has been put forward for its location being near Cádiz.

However, the really lasting myth, which has become part of the regional identity, was the arrival of Hercules. At one time the land masses of Africa and Europe were joined at the hip and it was Hercules, according to legend that separated them. A legend that Phoenicians paid homage to by constructing their temple of Melkart on the islet in Sancti Petri near Chiclana de la Frontera soon on arrival. Looking at the flag of Andalucía you will also notice a half-naked figure flanked by two lions and two columns. Here he is: the greatest and strongest of them all. The symbolism couldn't have been any better, because he was a hero of the ancient classical world. But what of his significance to Andalucía? The story laid down by the Greeks went that Heracles, Greek for Hercules, came to this region and erected two columns – the promontories of British Gibraltar and (across the Straits) Spanish Ceuta. On the columns he inscribed the words *Non Plus Ultra* - 'Do not go beyond here'. (Don't ask why an ancient Greek wrote it in Latin). The legendary beginnings of the region and the province of Sevilla speak of Melkart the Semitic deity that founded the city by marking out its boundaries with six columns.

Melkart was believed to be the Greek God Heracles. He was, in actual fact, a real person in Greek history and the first to sail beyond the Straits of Gibraltar and out into the Atlantic. Maybe he put up the columns because he didn't want anybody following him. Too much of a good thing perhaps. Christopher Columbus was a logical extension of how a discoverer could become world famous – though times had changed when he took to the high seas and he never quite became part of mythology.

Hercules stands flanked by his columns in the centre of the Andalusian flag on a background of a green and white horizontal triband. The green is the colour of Islam and was taken from the standard of the Umayyads (*Omeyas* in Spanish) who dominated the region from 711-750 AD. The white is from the standard of the Almohads who ruled the territory until 1269. In heraldry white represents peace or parliament. *La*

Junta de Andalucía says the following about the symbolism of their flag:

"Throughout all its history the spirit of the Andalusian flag has always been the same, the white and the green, the peace and hope of a country, that which is Andalusian."

'Andalucía for herself, for Spain and Humanity'

After the Greeks, it was the turn of the Carthaginians who at that time could very well have gone on to be the predominant power house in the Mediterranean and not, as it later turned out, the Romans. They had just been routed by the Romans in the First Punic War. Dispossessed of Sicily and Sardinia they had nowhere else to expand into. So, in 238 BC they decided to try their luck in Spain where their competitors had yet to set foot. They named the land *Ispania* – meaning 'land of rabbits'. They obviously turned up around Easter. Under the leadership of Hamilcar Barca (who, generously on his part, gave his name to Barcelona) the Carthaginians founded their Iberian capital in what is now Cartagena, naming it *Cathargo Nova* 'New Carthage', on the south eastern coast. Their overpowering influence took its toll on the Tartessan culture breaking its power base and fragmenting its society forever. This had been preceded by a brief inter-marital period between Iberians and Carthaginians under the rule of Hasdrubal the Fair. However, when he was murdered things soon returned to their old war-like self under Hasdrubal's father-in-law, Hannibal, Hamilcar Barca's eldest son, who had been busy elsewhere until then. He promptly crossed the Ebro and set about conquering Iberia's southern territories. His effect on Sevilla wasn't much brighter either, which he sacked on entering it.

We all know the Romans came from Rome, the Greeks from Greece and the Phoenicians from Phoenix, but where did these Carthaginians show up from? Well, Carthage, of course. It was a Phoenician city based in Tunisia across from the current city of Tunis.

It was not long before the Romans eventually followed Barca's son Hannibal, 'the elephant man', back into Spain after he had made the famous crossing over the Alps taking the Romans by surprise in the Second Punic War. The eventual defeat of Carthage by Rome owed to the fact that Hannibal had miscalculated Rome's allies defecting to him, which they never did. And so the fateful battle of Zama, where Hannibal ironically faced many of the tribes he had been convinced would come over to him, changed European destiny radically giving us a Greco-Roman culture based on the Roman code of law as opposed to that of a Punic-Carthaginian legacy. Rome's allies, although subdued, perhaps felt things would be worse under Carthage.

Commanded by the young general Publius Cornelius Scipio Africanus in 206 BC the Carthaginians were crushed at the battle of Ilipa where the town of Alcalá del Río now stands, only a few kilometres from Sevilla. It would take the Romans a further two centuries to complete their conquest of the Iberian Peninsular but now the tables had turned and there was only one master left on Spanish soil, which was soon to be top dog in the Med. Up until then it had been the Carthaginians waging war on the Romans, the moment had come for the Romans to take the initiative and lay siege to Carthage. When the final blow fell their vengeance was so complete that they boasted that no stone was left upon stone. Even today the city was so thoroughly erased from the map that tourists, a stone's throw away from the great city, were largely unaware of its presence. Carthage was declared a UNESCO World Heritage Site in 1979.

After the Romans had had time to take a breather and a good look around, they actually liked what they saw and decided to take the place lock, stock and wine barrel with no questions on the asking price. As in every region they touched, the Romans were literally enlightened years ahead of the civilisation that they had conquered. The newly invaded must have found it impossible to trust their eyes when they saw the new cities going up and the farming techniques being employed. A section of Publius Cornelius Scipio's army established a permanent settlement where their field hospital had been, beyond the boundary of contemporary Sevilla. It was set well back from the promontory that overlooks the city where the Phoenicians had first weighed anchor and the Roman general named the town *Vicus Italicenses* to commemorate their recent victory. Later it became known simply as *Itálica* and the city grew into the most prosperous and powerful centre in the Roman Empire after Rome herself. Its city walls had a perimeter of 3,150 metres and it was laid out in five parallel streets. Today much of the treasures that survive are to be found in Sevilla's Archaeological Museum or in *La Casa de la Condesa de Lebríja* mansion in *calle Cuna*. Many of the mosaics were lifted whole-piece and into the spaces of private homes in Sevilla.

Itálica soon began supplying the whole Empire with wheat, oil and wine. It was nurtured by Rome and later produced two of its greatest Emperors: Marco Ulpio Trajan (53-117), the first emperor to come from a province, and his great-nephew and adopted son Publio Aelio Hadrian (76-138), both born within its walls. Two of Rome's greatest writers and thinkers: Seneca (b. Córdoba) and Lucan (b. Córdoba) were also from the region. *Baetica*, the southern area of *Hispania*, lived a golden age of influence, affluence and cultural development as the Latinisation of their land was made complete. Unlike the Celtic north which proved difficult to overcome and fell behind in its sophistication.

The old part of the Roamn city is situated beneath the town of Santiponce. An original section of Itálica is still above ground and open to visitors is and is reputed to have one of the best preserved amphitheatres outside Italy with a seating capacity of 25,000 people.

In 60 BC at the age of 41 Gaius Julius Caesar was promoted to Governor (*Praetor*) of Hispania Ulterior – 'Further Spain', the area to the south and west. It was the second time he had been in Hispania. Three years before he had been in the province as *Quaestor* and is said to have wept at a statue of Alexander the Great in Cádiz (*Gades*). The Macedonian had conquered the known world by the age of 30 while Caesar was only known for having squandered his wife's fortune. Anecdotes about the great Roman abound. Even Shakespeare was suitably impressed to pen him an entire piece. The Roman historian Suetonius wrote:

He was embarrassed by his baldness, which was a frequent subject of jokes on the part of his opponents; so much so that he used to comb his straggling locks forward from the back, and of all honours heaped upon him by senate and people, the one he most appreciated was to be able to wear a wreath at all times...

At the battle of Munda in 45 BC, just east of Sevilla near the town of Osuna, he brought to an end a protracted conflict for the control within the Roman state. He renamed Sevilla *Iulia Romula Hispalis* and raised the settlement to the rank of a Roman Town in honour of his victory over Pompey. The name *Hispalis* adapted the previous Phoenician name of *Spal*, in reference to the poles used to shore up the foundations of the city's buildings, which had to be kept at a safe height above the level of the frequent flood waters, as the city is a mere 6m above sea level. Little changed to the name of the peninsular either, renaming it *Hispania* – meaning 'land of *Roman* rabbits'. The city reached its height at the same moment that Rome reached hers by which time it had become the 11th largest *urbs* in the Empire. Even so, Córdoba – *Corduba*, was used as the capital of the southern Hispanic province of *Baetica*.

Next in were the Vandals and like their contemporary package tour counterparts they headed straight for the sun and the *costas*. They had arrived here after being pressurised by the expanding Mongol population in the Russian Steppes. This pushed the Germanic tribes and the Franks to the frontiers of the Roman Empire which they eventually breached in 410 AD. The Vandals settled predominantly in Andalucía. In 409 AD they sacked, one could say vandalised, Hispalis, when they arrived from the old Roman town of Mérida to the west. They renamed Sevilla *Spali*. The Silingian Vandal King Rekhila took the city in 411 but was soon ousted by another Vandal, Gonderic in 426. Three years later and another Vandal tribe the Sueves arrived in their place. The Vandals stay in the region was a brief one and they were promptly moved on as the next wave of invaders came in from the cold.

In 415 AD, the barbarian Visigothic leader Ataulf 'Father-wolf' crossed the Pyrenees and entered Spain, first under the banner of Rome until they later broke away and went it alone. *"I hope to be acknowledged by posterity as the initiator of a Roman restoration."* He was eventually slain while bathing near Barcelona at the hand of a servant of a noble he had killed. The Visigoths had been enlisted by Emperor Honorius to displace the Vandals. The Goths had not come to visit but to stay. Partly Romanised and fully Christianised, it was their leader Euric who broke their agreement with Rome and established Home rule for their people and a unitary control over a great part of the Iberian territory. The civilising effect of their religion saw them establish a two hundred-year rule and their capital at Toledo.

They arrived in Spali in 531. During this time two of Spain's greatest minds found themselves in the same place at the same time and they became known throughout Europe. The Bishop Leander (d.600) and Bishop Isidore (d.636). Both men made Spali a European centre of scholastic Latin learning. Isidore 'of Seville', as he was called, was one of the great scholars of the Early Middle Ages. He wrote the acclaimed books of *Etymologiae* or *Origenes* as they were also known in Spanish and are regarded by some as Europe's first dictionary and a repository of all knowledge handed down to us by Antiquity. The work comprised all the learning of the epoch into one volume comprising History, Natural Science, Cosmology, Grammar and Literature, which had a great influence throughout Medieval Europe and was the forerunner of the encyclopaedia.

Christianity also drove a wedge between the Arian Christian King Leovigild and his son Hermenegild, recently converted to Catholicism. One result of this conflict was the changing of the river route away from the city centre where it had come in through what is today *Plaza Nueva*. The rerouting was necessary to stop his son from landing an army smack bang in the town centre. The confrontation and the refusal of the son to renounce his religion led to a civil war which culminated in his arrest and subsequent execution in Valencia. He became Sevilla's third Christian martyr and was later canonised.

Once again history repeated itself and the Visigoths, like the Romans before them, had grown soft with the good life and unaware that there was someone else waiting in the wings ready to take it away from them. This time the new kid on the block was the Moor and by Allah was he up for it! The Moors crossed the straits of Gibraltar in 711 AD under the leadership of Jabal Tariq Ibn Ziyad who roused his troops with the words: *"My brethren, the enemy is before you, the sea is behind; whither would ye fly? Follow your general; I am resolved either to lose my life or to trample on the prostrate king of the Romans."* He was responding to the invitation by the family of the late Visigothic King Witiza. The family had made the offer after much in-fighting had resulted in the throne being usurped on Witiza's death by Roderic the Duke of Baetica. The Viceroy of North Africa, Musa Ibn Nusayr, under the authority of the Umayyads based in Damascus, had sent his deputy Tariq on ahead. Tariq summarily defeated the Gothic king at the battle of Guadalete. However, he didn't stop there and went on to conquer the rest of Iberia, incorporating it into the wider empire of the Caliphate of Damascus as a dependant Emirate. All bar one small kingdom nestled in the lush green hills of Cantabria under the leadership of the Visigothic King Pelayo resisted the African invaders. (Maybe he was the inspiration for Asterix and Obelix.)

In 712 Musa Ibn Nusayr joined the rout and conquered the city of Spali. Once more the new occupants decided that they too would make their base in Andalucía, which they named *al-Andalus*. Spali changed its name to the arabised version of *Hispalis* to *Isbiliya*, also written *Ixbilia*, *Sbilia* and even *Isbiliyyah* and أشبيليّة in Arabic as one imagines it was actually written at the time. (*Sepharad*, incidentally, was the Hebrew term for Spain.) The river *Baetis* was changed to the Arab name *wadi al-kabir* or Guad al-Quivir which means *Rio Grande* in Spanish, 'Big River' in English and 'Mississippi' in Amerindian. It is the name that has survived to the present day - *El Guadalquivir*.

Musa arrived as far as southern France and was in the process of undertaking a wider invasion of Europe when he was summoned to appear before the court in Damascus. According to the writer Washington Irving in his 1835 *'Legends of the Conquest of Spain'*, a feud had begun between the Emir Musa and his deputy Tariq as to whom belonged the greater glory for having taken possession of the peninsular. It was Musa that was eventually stripped of rank and riches and then imprisoned. Tariq's name lived on through history, not only for his role in the conquest but also in the name 'Gibraltar' from *jebel el Tariq*, meaning 'the mountain of Tariq'.

In 750 Abd al-Rahman was the only surviving member of the

Umayyad dynasty - direct descendants of the prophet Muhammad - to have survived the Abbasid takeover and subsequent massacre at the Damascan court. The Abbasids were angered at the Umayyads' favouritism shown to Arabs, in direct contradiction to the teachings of the Qu'ran. They set up a new Caliphate in Baghdad. While Abd al-Rahman arrived in al-Andalus in the same year, 750 and just six years later he had created a separate Caliphate in Córdoba with himself as Caliph. Al-Andalus had split the Arab empire. By 800 all of Spain and North Africa comprised a distinct Caliphate. In 868 Egypt had also decided to go its own way from Baghdad.

In 844 the Guadalquivir basin as well as Lisbon and the port of Cádiz were visited by pillaging Normans who wreaked havoc on the region for almost a year and a half before finally being repelled. Forces from Córdoba had to go to the aid of Isbiliya and save the city from being sacked, but not before the Vikings' ancestors had razed the central mosque to the ground.

By 929 Córdoba, *Kurtuba* in the Arab voice, had become a rival to Baghdad consolidating the independence of the Spanish state of Islam, now firmly set under Abd al-Rahman III, who maintained Córdoba as its capital. During the 10th century, *'The great century of lights'*, the city saw its peak of glory, as did the rest of the Moorish civilisation in al-Andalus. Their position and high learning meant that the best of Africa, Europe and the Orient were to be found here. Abd al-Rahman III also ordered the construction of the magnificent palace Medina Azahara - *al-Madina az-Zahira* in Arabic, just outside Córdoba and another marvel of the Medieval Islamic world.

The famous scholar of the time Averroes was from Córdoba and is remembered for his 30 years of study of Aristotle when the Greek philosopher's work had all been but forgotten in the rest of Europe. The Cordoban worked to consolidate the conflict between philosophy and religion concluding that both were valid paths to seeking the truth. Averroes has always been held in high esteem in the West, mentioned in Dante's *Divine Comedy*, James Joyce's *Ulysses*, appearing in a fresco by Raphael. He even has an asteroid named after him '8318 Averroes'. But his work ultimately laid the foundations for later European scholars to discover Aristotles' works anew and thereby set in motion the Renaissance.

1492 and All That

"The Moors organized that wonderful kingdom of Cordova, which was the marvel of the Middle Ages, and which, when all Europe was plunged in barbaric ignorance and strife, alone held the torch of learning and civilization bright and shinning before the Western world."

After a military coup in 986 Muhammad Ibn Abi Amir, known in the West as Almanzor, took the Caliphate from al-Hakam II and the title of al-Mansor. He undertook, and won, 57 consecutive military campaigns against the northern Christian kingdoms, inflicting devastation. He had succeeded in pushing back the encroaching Christian army of the amalgamated Asturias-León kingdoms into the northern mountains by using a professional Berber army and sacking their holiest of shrines in Santiago de Compostela, though leaving the tomb of their saint St. James - *Santo Iago*, intact. Nevertheless, he took the cathedral bells with him and hung them as lamps in the mosque in Córdoba. He even permitted the destruction of the great al-Hakam II library in Córdoba in 976 losing forever some 400,000 volumes. The last great era of Córdoba came to a close with Almanzor's death in 1002. His tomb is in the town of Salem in the province of Sória.

The Moors had reached their apex and their moment of unity was becoming but a fading memory, as the rest of the Moorish kingdoms splintered into smaller holdings called *Taifas* in 1031. This happened when the Caliphate capital of Córdoba fell after bitter in-fighting thereby weakening the Moors' political position and military defences. The age old rifts between Arabs and Berbers had never been healed and still continue until this day. The strongest of these Taifas to emerge was Isbiliya. During the Abbadid dynasty, Isbiliya reached its greatest territorial extension from the Algarve in the west to Murcia in the east, also taking in Córdoba and even surpassing it as the centre of Moorish excellence in al-Andalus. The reigns of al-Mutadid (1042-1068) and his son al-Mu'tamid (1068-1091) the Poet King, were meridional moments in the history of Isbiliya. It was the most cultured of the Taifa states, as surviving by-laws conserved in the *'Treaties of Ibn Abdun'* attest to, reflecting a prosperous, progressive and colourful society. However, these very treaties open us up to an alternative view of al-Andalus as the very opposite of its illuminate and tolerant self.

The Andalusian *Maliki* jurist Ibn Abdun (d.1134) in his treaties around the year 1100 writes tellingly, "*No Jew or Christian may be allowed to wear the dress of an aristocrat, nor of a jurist, nor of a wealthy individual; on the contrary they must be detested and avoided. It is forbidden to [greet] them with the [expression],* 'Peace be upon you.' *In effect,* 'Satan has gained possession of them and caused them to forget God's warning. They are the confederates of Satan's party; Satan's confederates will surely be the losers!' (al-Qu'ran 58:19 [Modern Dawood translation]). *A distinctive sign must be imposed upon them in order that they may be recognized and this will be for them a form of disgrace.*"

Maimonides, the great Jewish philosopher and physician, the very personification of Jewish excellence flourishing under the Moors, tells in his own words a quite different reality of a Utopian treatment of the Jews by their Muslim rulers, "*…the Arabs have persecuted us severely, and passed baneful and discriminatory legislation against us… Never did a nation molest, degrade, debase, and hate us as much as they…*" One of his great works was *Iggereth HaShmad*, an essay on the legal implications of forced conversion to Islam.

The poet Abû Bakr Ibn Bakî, in response to the arrival of the non-sensual Almoravids, wrote, "*Since al-Andalus rejects me, I shall flee to Iraq, and, there, everyone will rise to greet me. The profession of the intellectual has lost all vitality since it is a life embraced only by those of low extraction and vile manners.*"

In 1066 the Jews of Granada were massacred with 4,000 being killed. Jewish communities all across Spain had prospered under the Umayyad Caliphate (755-1013). But when the Almoravid Berbers (1090-1174) arrived in the peninsular a new intolerant climate came with them. In 1107 their leader Yoseph Ibn Tashfin ordered all Moroccan Jews to convert or leave. The Jewish community quickly regrouped in Granada, only to suffer at the hands of the incoming Almoravids in 1090. Christians taken as slaves in the peninsular campaigns were deported to Morocco in 1126. Later, under the rule of the Berber Almohads (1148-1212), only Jews converted to Christianity or Islam could live in the city. The Almohads depleted both Jewish and Christian populations further. These traumatic events are chronicled by the Jews Abraham Ibn Daud and the poet Abraham Ibn Ezra. The Jews who did convert to Islam were kept in check by Muslim 'religious police', who often took their children and delivered them into the care of Muslim educators. Maimonides personally experienced the Almohad persecutions, fleeing from Córdoba in 1148, before eventually finding asylum in Fustat, Egypt.

The Jews did finally return to the city of Granada when it came under the rule of the Nasri dynasty (1232-1492). But on March 31, 1492, the final chapter of the Jews in Spain was written when Fernando and Isabel signed the edict of their expulsion. Ultimately, the Jew fared no better under the Spanish Christian than he had done under the radical Moor.

There were clear ethnic and religious distinctions in society, with Arab tribes as the masters, followed by the Berbers (never the Arab equal), then the *mullawadun* converts and last of all the *dhimmi* Christian and Jews. A *dhimma*, meaning *'being in the care of'* or *'protected people'* was a person living in a Muslim state and a member of an officially tolerated non-Islamic religion. But for this they had to pay. It was a tolerant concept by the standards of the time, however. When we refer to intolerant attitudes we are primarily concerned with the Berber dynasties of the fundamentalist Almoravids and the more radical Almohads.

"While Jewish communities in Arab and Islamic countries fared better overall than those in Christian lands in Europe, Jews were no strangers to persecution and humiliation among the Arabs and Muslim. As Princeton University historian Bernard Lewis has written: 'The Golden Age' of equal rights was a myth, and belief in it was a result, more than a cause, of Jewish sympathy for Islam."
Michael Bard

Until the arrival of the radical Berbers, the dynasties of the Umayyads and Abbadids had given the sort of tolerance that is so often highlighted when talking about Moorish Spain.

"Let there be no violence in religion"

"Fight against the unbelievers until they cease persecuting you, but if they desist, then let there be no hostility."
al-Qu'ran

In nearly 800 years of Muslim intervention in Spain only 200 had been scarred by intolerance whereas all Christian intervention during the Reconquest had been intolerant towards the Jews.

> *"...that they (the Moriscos) commended nothing so much as that liberty of conscience in all matters of religion, which the Turks, and all other Mohammedans, suffer their subjects to enjoy."*
> Archbishop of Valencia
> (Calling for the expulsion of the Moors c.1602)

The year 418 saw the first record of Jews being forced to convert or face expulsion when Severus, the Bishop of Minorca, conquered the island and claimed to have forced 540 Jews to accept Christianity. In 682 the Visigothic King Erwig passed 28 anti-Jewish laws, calling for *"utter extirpation of the pest of the Jews."* 1109, and there were Jewish massacres throughout the kingdom of Castile on the death of its king. In 1180 there was a further massacre in Toledo. 1219, and King Ferdinand III of Castile refused Pope Honorius III's demand to force Jews to wear a special badge and clothing, explaining that they would flee to the Muslim kingdom of Granada, thereby ruining royal revenues. 1230 saw attacks on various Jewish quarters in the kingdom of León on King Alfonso IX's death. In 1248 Sevilla fell to the Christians and all Muslims were vanquished from the city. The Rabbi of Barcelona, Nahmanides, in 1263 was forced out of recent retirement to debate the defence of Judaism in the presence of King Jaime I of Aragón against the apostate Pau Cristia. But the debate was halted when Nahmanides seemed to winning the argument. The Dominicans had him and his family exiled. 1341 in Sevilla, the Town Hall decreed that the Jews may only carry out business and sell their wares within the limits of their *aljamas* – from the Arab *jama* meaning 'gather' and was a Jewish or Muslim neighbourhood. In 1355 1,200 Jews were killed by Enrique Trastámara. 1361 and another Jewish massacre this time in the town of Nájera after the battle between Pedro I of Castile and his bastard brother the Pretender Enrique de Trastámara. In 1391, Valencia and Barcelona as well as other parts of Spain witnessed pogroms against the Jews with 4,000 killed in Toledo alone. 1408 saw Jews in Castile and Aragón being forced to wear distinctive markings. In 1451 Fernando and Isabel appointed inquisitors to work against the heresy amongst converted Jews. 1473 the 'New Christians' - converted Jews or

Conversos, were massacred in Córdoba. 1474 and *Conversos* were attacked in Segovia. 1480 and Isabel attempted to expel all Jews from Andalucía but the order was not enacted, probably due to the need for Jewish finances to pay for the final phase of the Reconquest of Spain from the Moors. The Monarchy received such finances from the Jews in 1490, but unwittingly the Jewish community had paid for their own demise in Spain.

Early modern times were not much better. It wasn't until 14th December, 1968 that Spain finally acknowledged the Jews of Spain as a practising religious body and revoked the edict of their expulsion of 31st May 1492. In 1986 Spain became the last Western country to recognize the State of Israel, and it was even as late as 1990 when the Spanish Jews at last received the same rights as Catholics.

The Moorish kings of Bádajoz, Granada and Sevilla grouped together in 1086 and petitioned the Almoravid Berbers, the North African powerhouse under their Emir Yusuf Ibn Tasufin. They asked for assistance against the encroaching Christian forces and ever-mounting tribute payments, *parias*, due to Alfonso VI of Castilla-León. In 1085 the Christians had taken Toldeo. Al-Mu'tamid, the poet king of Sevilla, despaired at having to choose between an alliance with the fanatical Almoravids or face Christian conquest. He exclaimed, *"Better to pasture camels than to herd swine."* The Almoravids came to their aid but turned against their paymasters in 1090 and took power. They at once made Isbiliya their capital in the South, tying al-Andalus to the Almoravid movement based in Marrakech. Al-Mu'tamid and his family, who fought on the front line to defend their city, were defeated and borne off in blackened boats down the Guadalquivir river to end their days exiled in Agmat in the Atlas Mountains. A mausoleum is dedicated to him there, which is still regularly visited by admirers. Ibn Labanna, a court poet, wrote a jeremiad on his former master of which there follows an excerpt:

> *I will never forget that morning by the river.*
> *I saw them herded onto the ships, like corpses on the decks.*
> *People gathered on both banks, sadly watching…*
> *It was time to set sail; the women wept*
> *And so did the men, calling out, "Goodbye!"*

1492 and All That

So many tears fell into the river, so much
Heartbreak sailed with those black ships.

The Almoravids – meaning 'warriors of the frontier', were the first of several waves of fundamentalists that swept into al-Andalus. They were, however, the last to unite all the segregated Taifas one last time into an imperial whole before their state also began to fragment into what has become known as 'the second period of Taifas', taking place around 1142.

In rebellion to the social and religious intolerance of the Almoravids, as well as the ever-increasing weakness of its state, various leaders turned to the new power centre emerging in the Maghreb: the Almohads, meaning 'the monotheists'. Their fundamentalist revolution began with the take over of Marrakech and then they extended their control over the rest of North Africa. They arrived in al-Andalus in 1146 and installed their capital in Isbiliya a year later under Abd al-Mumin. Once more the city took a central role in the affairs of its region. In 1172 work began on a new central mosque where the cathedral now stands. It was the Almohad dynasty under Abu Yaqub Yusuf that was responsible for the still standing gigantic minaret – *La Giralda*, started in 1184.

The Christians, meanwhile, were moving slowly but surely southwards, entering the Moors' exotic world. Toledo fell in 1085 and with the Christian victory at the battle of *Las Navas de Tolosa* in 1212 near Jaén they opened up the Guadalquivir basin and it would be only a matter of time before mass would be read in the last surviving mosque in Spain. But even at that turning point in the fate of the Moors, the Naserite dynasty of Granada – the city taking its name from the Arab *Karnatta* meaning 'pomegranate' as does the Spanish name *granada*, was confident enough of their position on the political and Spanish map that they began construction in 1237 of what is still today Spain's greatest monument and the Moor's most impressive edifice: the Alhambra – *al-Gal'a al-Hamrá* in the Arab voice, meaning 'the red fortress'.

From 1403-84 the Canaries were conquered from the Moors. The year 1479 saw the unification of Spain and its consolidation as one nation before the final and decisive push was made on the only surviving Moorish foothold in a land that had been all theirs.

The Moors had stayed 781 years in the country while both

Christian and especially Jew had flourished on and off. This came to an end when Admiral Ramón de Bonifaz crashed his boats through the defence chain spanning the river Guadalquivir in Isbiliya between the two defence towers of the still standing *La Torre del Oro* and the one in Triana, cutting the city off from its supply route. Fernando III from Castilla, 'The Saint King', as the locals call him, marched triumphantly into town on 23rd November, 1248. For Isbiliya it was all over bar the lamenting. But the Moors didn't give up without a fight and the city was besieged for 15 months before giving way. For a third time in this land the same snap shot of history repeated itself. The invading Moor had been fearless in his conquest but then soon mellowed, civilised to a high degree before falling easy prey to a more tiresome and simpler invader. From Locust to Lotus Eater and then to being finally eaten.

But now the city was to be conquered for the last time. The Phoenicians, Greeks, Vandals, Visigoths, Carthaginians, Romans, Moors and now Christian had come here and each in turn had established Sevilla as their regional capital. In the case of the Romans and Christians it became their capital on the peninsular. Fernando III, Alonso X and then Pedro I all fell for the charms of the place and founded their court here.

'Sevilla knew how to conquer her conquerors'.

Fernando let the Moors leave with their belongings and even sell their houses. But his deal for the local peasantry didn't fair so well and has marked the region until the present day. In the great land redistribution overseen by Fernando and his court the *Latifundi*, created by the Romans and maintained by the Moors, were given a new lease of life under the Christians. Great tracts of land were given to a select few creating a concentration of landed wealth and an imbalance of power in the area. In a region of agricultural dependence this had century-long consequences, which played an important part in motivating forces in the Civil War, not to mention the effects it had on the New World where the system was soon to be introduced.

Fernando III, who ended his days in Sevilla in 1252, was canonised in 1649. His epitaph in Seville cathedral reads: '...*the most loyal, truthful, the frankest, most hardworking, most handsome, most mature and distinguished, most persistent and humble who most feared God, who served him most faithfully, who confounded and destroyed his enemies and who raised and honoured all those who were loyal, who conquered Seville, capital of Spain...'* etc, etc. The 17th century also saw the canonisation of Francisco Javier, Teresa de Jesús and Felipe Neri; a time when the city became known as 'The Land of the Virgin Mary'. Sevilla and not New Orleans must be the original city of saints.

With the arrival of the Christian, the city underwent its final name change from Isbiliya to its Christianized form: *Sevilla* pronounced /se-**BEE**-ya/.

Although the Moors were ousted from al-Andalus, some were, however, two families per village were permitted to stay on. These Christianised Moors were referred to as *moriscos*. In the Berber villages of las Alpujarras, south from Granada (as Gerard Brenan reminds us), they were needed to maintain their ingenious irrigation system, which has remained intact. In 1512 these 'hangers-on' rebelled against their treatment at the hands of their new masters and were put to the sword as a result.

It must have been one of the slowest and, therefore, most determined reconquests in European history having begun its journey in Asturias at the battle of Covadonga in 722 reaching its climax nearly 800 years later at the siege of Granada on January 2nd 1492. While the defeated Emir Muhammad XI, known as Boabdil, was leaving his kingdom of Granada his mother, Aixa, is renowned to have said to him, *"Do not weep like a woman for what you did not know how to defend like a man."* Nice to have your mum around when you need her. This little episode occurred at a place tellingly called *El Suspiro del Moro* – The Moor's Sigh or *Fer Allah Akbar* as the Moors referred to it. This was where the King last set eyes upon his beloved Granada, the Damascus of the West. Their exodus left an intellectual vacuum behind them that took centuries to restore.

The lesson of history here, was that if you wanted to conquer Spain then start in the North and work your way down. The Spanish now at last had a place they could call *casa*. And what a mix they turned out to be. The Iberian melting pot had been filled to the brim with influences from north and south, spices from the east and west, religion and culture from just about everywhere. It had travelled a roller coaster ride of ever-changing, centralised and polarised hierarchies. This was enough to make anyone's head spin and now they were on the verge of discovering the

1492 and All That

New World. Wealth was about to come flooding into the country and poured into a home grown Catholic fever, headed by the Inquisition. The land hadn't stood still for a moment throughout its turbulent history.

1492 was for Spain what 1066 had been for England: a definitively clear break with the past. The Spanish had rolled back the tide of Islam and at the same time acquired an empire. However, the real discovery of Columbus' journey across the Atlantic would take a little later to dawn on them. At the outset they merely thought they had stumbled across a few islands on the way to Japan.

Some historians claim that with the expulsion of the Moors and some 400,000 Jews in the same year – thanks to the Inquisition being egged on by greedy Nobles and debt-ridden citizens, the country leapt back 600 years when the nation's intelligentsia left.

"The Moors were banished; for a while Christian Spain shone, like the moon, with a borrowed light; then came the eclipse, and in that darkness Spain has grovelled ever since. The true memorial of the Moors is seen in desolate tracts of utter barrenness, where once the Moors grew luxuriant vines and olives and yellow ears of corn; in a stupid, ignorant population where once wit and learning flourished; in the general stagnation and degradation of a people which has hopelessly fallen in the scale of nations, and has deserved its humiliation."
Stanley Lane Poole

When the Moors first invaded the land they were to call their own for nearly a millennium, they not only became its military masters but also its intellectual and cultural elite. The land they entered was found wanting and they were welcomed by the population fed up with their old rulers. The Moors gave back to the land and its peoples what only the Romans had offered. While the rest of Europe made timid steps away from the Dark Ages and toward an age of enlightenment al-Andalus made bold strides.

"Whatever makes a kingdom great, whatever tends to refinement and civilization was found in Moorish Spain."
Stanley Lane Poole

While 'cleanliness was next to godliness' for the Moors the exact opposite was true for the incoming and all-conquering Christians, who had an aversion to washing and tore down the Arab baths declaring that the Moors: *"neither themselves, their women, nor any other persons, should be permitted to wash or bathe themselves either at home or elsewhere; and that all their bathing-houses should be pulled down and destroyed."* In the city of Córdoba in the 10th century there had been 600 public baths - *hammams*, alone.

As late as the 1830's Richard Ford mentions that, *"Isabella, the favourite daughter of Phillip II …made a solemn vow never to change her shift until Ostend was taken. The siege lasted three years, three months and thirteen days. The royal garment acquired a tawny colour, which was called Isabel by the courtiers…"*

Their arrival wasn't all good news, however. The religion of Islam has never taken to the idea of the human form being represented in painting or sculpture and when they turned up in Vandalusia they promptly removed and destroyed much of the surviving Roman artwork. Roman treasure that had survived the Vandals when they had sacked the city didn't make it past the 'civilised' Moors. Although the minaret - La Giralda, is principally built of brick its base and foundations are those of stone pieced together from Roman pedestals and other constructions, as the cornerstone attends to. You can still read a bit of the Latin. The tower reads like a 3-D timeline of Andalucía's history. Founded on Roman principals and culture, extended and elaborated by the Moors and finally crowned a Christian Empire. All these elements can still be seen and felt throughout the region today. All you have to do is take note of what is going on around you.

During the intervening years from the conquest of Isbiliya in 1248 to the final christianisation of the whole of Spain, the city experienced its fair share of turmoil. Despite the occasional fracas, however, with the Moorish kingdoms that bordered the kingdom of Sevilla life took on a regular rhythm. As the frontier with Moorish lands was pushed back this steady advance of the border was marked by the towns that bear that name: Jerez de la Frontera, Arcos de la Frontera, Morón de la Frontera, Palos de la Frontera and Vejer de la Frontera among others.

Alonso X *El Sabio*, the Wise, followed his father Fernando III as King. Alfonso XI after him and then came Pedro I *'The Cruel'* or *'The Just'*, depending on your political inclination. During Pedro's reign Sevilla suffered a violent earthquake in 1365 and the architectural aspect of the city underwent a facelift in its aftermath. The king was also responsible for how we see the *Alcázar*, the fortress-cum-palace, today. The Christian king in the 1350s hired Moorish architects from Granada to rebuild the palace. There are escutcheons on the walls of the royal bedchamber featuring the coat of arms of Castilla-León – the Castle and Lion, accompanied by an Arabic script: *'Glory to our sultan Don Pedro. Allah aid and protect him'*. Following the taking of the city from the Moors, the Jewish population swelled in numbers until the tragic year of 1391 when the community was subjected to pillage and murder at the hands of the local citizens.

Pedro's turn on the throne took Sevilla up to the long awaited unifying force of Fernando II of Aragón and Isabel of Castilla. Between July 1477 and December 1478 Sevilla became their court. For their successful crusade, the only one in European history, and for the instigation of the Inquisition in their lands, they were bestowed the title of The Catholic Sovereigns – *Los Reyes Católicos*, by the Vatican. They rounded off the Reconquest in a 15-year campaign and established one religion in a land that had before been renowned for its spiritual diversity and, on occasion, tolerance. From now on to be Spanish meant that you were Catholic. Even today not believing in God, and thereby extension in the Catholic faith, implies that you are somehow not quite fully Spanish.

15th century Sevilla was marked by the feud between the city's two most prominent noble houses, namely those of Guzmán and Ponce de León. Juan Ponce de León sailed with Columbus on his second voyage in 1498 and went on to become the Governor of Puerto Rico. With the discovery of the Americas at the close of century Sevilla found itself *the* place to be for any man with ambition in the world. The Monarchy gave the monopoly on trade to the regional capital whose isolated inland port provided the perfect protection for the booty brought back from the New World where it was stock piled. In 1503 *La Casa de la Contratación* (Board of Trade) was set up in *el Alcázar*. From *El Salón del Almirante* – the Admiral's room, all business concerning the Americas was conducted, from the granting of navigation permits to the influx and outflux of trade. The city enjoyed a commercial monopoly the like of which few moments in history have ever afforded, if ever will again. The only surviving remnant of this administrative body is the sumptuous, yet modest in size, *Cuarto del Navegante* – Navigator's Chamber.

Sevilla was the New York of its age, the 'Big Orange', and many came to take what piece of the fruit they could. *"Madrid is the capital of Spain, but Seville is the capital of the world."* They used to say. Two fleets, *la flota*, sailed to Veracruz in the New World each spring, on a trip known as *la Carrera de Indias*. Wood was floated down river from the city of Jaén and, on a no-longer existent island in the Guadalquivir river, repairs and construction of the Spanish galleons were undertaken. Several immigrant communities established themselves in the city. The Genoese around *calle Genoa*, the French around *calle Francos*, the Germans around *calle Alemanes* and the Flemish were also lodged around the centre. The English more than likely took rooms at the pub. During the 15th and 16th centuries the population tripled to 120,000 people, the same as London, Naples and Paris. It even overtook Genoa and Venice as a centre of trade and commerce. While Hernán Cortés took on the Aztecs and Pizarro the Incas, Mendoza arrived in Argentina, Quesada in Colombia, De Soto took to the southern States, while Alvarado guaranteed Guatemala and El Salvador for the Spanish Crown. They sliced their way, literally, across the vast continent in a matter of months, with the word of God spreading at the same voracious speed. The gold, but principally silver, came out of the ancient Indian mines of Potosí and Valenciana, almost as quickly, packed into galleons and sent Sevilla-bound. If the Spanish fleet and 'its' gold made it past the English and French pirates, they would finally moor up on the banks of Sevilla where the precious metals were off-loaded into *La Torre del Oro*.

Sevilla was now the pivotal point between two worlds: the Old and the New. Anyone who wanted to climb the already burdened social ladder back home had to take to the high seas and seek their fortune in New Spain. Then they could return and rub shoulders with the well-to-do. Who would have guessed that all this would have happened due to some hair brain scheme to sail around a flat world? Columbus, or as the Spanish refer to him: *Cristóbal Colón*, set out in his three caravels: *La Santa María*, *La Santa Clara* (known affectionately as '*La Niña*'- the Girl) and *La Pinta* and changed the world. The native Indian population, however, still dispute whether this change was for the better. There is not one statue of Cortés anywhere to be found in South America, for example.

It was *Colón* who first found something on the other side of the world. He didn't walk off his ship onto the main continent but instead stepped onto the island of San Salvador. The wonder of setting foot ashore the American continent befell another Italian, Amerigo Vespucci, who was actually working for the Portuguese at the time when he disembarked in Brazil in 1502 and discovered the New Continent. He then changed paymasters and where Colón had fallen out of favour, Vespucci continued in his shoes. It was a long time before Colón's role in the discovery was recognised at all. He could so easily have been forgotten. (As happened to the role of the Jews on board. There was no Catholic priest on the first expedition.) This seems to be the case with the origin of the word 'America'. It could have been called Columbia. Vespucci was also the first to realize they were tredding on a new continent and not a mere archipelago.

This was the Catholic boom time with the Spanish Empire backed by the Vatican and the Inquisition tightening its grip. There was no disputing that from now on, there was going to be only one religion in Spanish territory.

In 1526 Carlos V of Germany and I of Spain chose Sevilla as the city for his marriage with Isabel of Portugal. He had new apartments built in the modern Renaissance style in the *el Alcázar* – now called *Los Reales Alcázares*, receiving the adjective Royal before it. In 1570 his son Felipe II visited the city and was said to have *"rejoiced to see the great, beautiful, rich, noble, and loyal city possessed of the best which nature, artifice and mankind could lay at the feet of a prince."* Come the end of the 16th century Cervantes, who had also spent time in the city commented that, *"...shelter of the poor and refuge of the unfortunate, in whose grandeur not only the humble can be found but the rich may be seen."*

Sevilla at this time became famous for its picaresque characters, and the picaresque novel created in Spain was later copied throughout the rest of Europe. The Wikipedia encyclopaedia has this to say, *'The picaresque novel ('picaresco', from 'pícaro', for 'rogue' or 'rascal') The term denotes a subgenre of usually satiric prose fiction and depicts in realistic, often humorous detail the adventures of a roguish hero of low social degree living by his or her wits in a corrupt society.'* Amongst the wealth of Sevilla there were plenty left out and had to get by on their wit or else perish.

1492 and All That

In 1649 the plague arrived and halved the population. The weakened city rose up in a revolt which emanated from the street *calle Feria* in 1652, reacting to the scarcity of bread.

In 1680 the monopoly of trade changed hands and passed to Cádiz, by 1717 *la Casa de la Contratación*, also known as *La Casa del Océano*, had also left. By 1778 a Royal Decree declared free trade between all Spain's ports and her colonies, thereby abolishing the old monopolistic system called *flotas y galeones*. The idea was to encourage more legal trade and reduce the alarmingly high level of contraband that was rife at the time. But Sevilla had grown used to privilege and the change of fortune was a shock to the system. Nothing lasts forever and the city began its slow and slippery economic demise accompanied by the rest of its fellow Spanish countrymen (and women) as the nation gradually lost control of her overseas dominions and world hegemony.

Sevilla had always been a middle man in Spain's Imperial dealings and now it had to return to depending on its traditional trades of agriculture and out-of-date textiles. Such a radical turn-about in fortunes hit the well-off hardest (for a change), unaccustomed as they were to the harsh reality of an agriculturally dependant economy. Sevilla went from being a world centre to a regional supplier at the stroke of a pen and what affluence had remained intact, left town.

"By the end of the seventeenth century Seville had faded. Once thronged with jostling crowds, the city streets now wound mutely past deserted buildings. The clamor of bankers and merchants on the cathedral steps had died away as fewer ships sailed into port. The famous Casa de la Contratación *no longer throbbed with the commercial enterprise at the heart of the city. Now it functioned far away in Cádiz."*
Mary Elizabeth Perry

The good times were over as a economic depression engulfed the city and a dark dawn was beginning to break over the Spanish Main. In the same century Madrid, which had become the new capital in 1561, had merely 30,000 inhabitants while Sevilla boasted 200,000 but the balance was about tip. The spoils of conquest that had been brought back, had long been squandered on flawed military offensives designed to hold together a fragile ideal of a Holy Roman Empire in Europe under Spanish stewardship. The silver barely touched the Spanish shore before it was transhipped to the bankers in Antwerp and Genoa financing the Spanish Crown's costly Netherland campaigns. In 1521 there was the *Pendón* rebellion in Sevilla against the cost of living. In 1566 the Dutch rebelled against their Spanish masters and then in 1588 Spain's 'Invincible Armada', the pride of Catholic might, failed to reach the heretical land of Protestant England.

Felipe III expelled half the total remaining *moriscos* – subject Moors, in 1609-10. 30,000 soldiers were mobilised as well as the Armada to transport 300,000 to Morocco and Tunisia. The great exodus of Muslims created a gulf in the labour force greatly affecting the regions of Valencia, Aragón and Murcia. This was coupled with the Inquisition being enforced with renewed vigour. Then in 1649 the plague that swept across Europe came to town and carried off half the population leaving behind deserted streets and empty houses. There are mass graves in various parts where thousands were laid to rest, one example is where the old *Puerta de Triana* once stood.

The War of Spanish Succession (1701-14) depleted Spain's coffers even further and pushed her into a precarious economic position. The war ended with the House of Hapsburg under Felipe V still on the throne although he had to renounce his claim to France. Britain had backed the underdog Charles VI of Austria. It was here at the Treaty of Utrecht that Britain obtained Gibraltar and Minorca, which they had captured in the ensuing conflict. Spain saw its European Empire taken out of its hands and carved up among Savoy and Austria.

The outlook in the city was bleak. Its cosmopolitan atmosphere had turned provincial as it bowed out from the international stage. Those international heydays were a distant memory. Nevertheless, the city didn't just sit back and allow melancholy to overcome it. Felipe V set up his court briefly here between 1729-33. Several administrators in the 18th century took the bull by the horns and set about revitalising its institutions and educational system. The greatest of these Civil Servants was Pablo de Olavide, whose name is still very much alive in the city's collective memory.

The hills to the north of Sevilla, *La Sierra Norte*, were a dangerous place plagued as they were by *bandoleros* – bandits. Many people had left the land migrating to the towns desperately seeking work. Don José is the most celebrated of these *bandoleros* in the opera Carmen.

The biggest upset of all though for internal affairs was the invasion by France. This intervention pushed the government into exile forming an *ad hoc* parliament – *Cortes*. The *Cortes* was forced to seek refuge in Sevilla, thereby making it the nation's capital for two years. Then when Joseph Bonaparte, Napoleon's elder brother, marched into the city under Marshal Soult the *Cortes* took flight to Cádiz where the first Spanish Constitution was drawn up in 1812, forming the First Republic. It lasted only year when Felipe VII claimed the throne for Spain and abolished the Republic.

The Spanish colonies took their moment and rebelled, though some of them on gaining their independence had it taken away from them by the Americans. This colonial loss further deepened the economic situation in mother country. The Spanish rose up against the French invader and with a little assistance from the Irish-born Duke of Wellington, the two nations, who had been enemies at the Battle of Trafalgar in 1805, were now united against a common enemy for possibly the only time in their history. The battle of Sevilla and the ensuing French defeat took place in 1815. Later that same year Napoleon met his Waterloo. The Spanish had fought seven long hard years for their independence, which the British remember as the Peninsular War but the Spanish refer to as *La Guerra de la Independencia* – the War of Independence.

Balmy days should have returned for the city and the region as a whole but the situation was worse than ever. Political interests were now fought out in the open and minor wars were being raged especially in the south between liberal and old-order conservatives. At the same time the unrest in the colonies that had began in 1808 came to a head in their total loss by 1824. At home there was a military rebellion in 1820 led from the province of Sevilla by General Rafael de Riego in support of the liberal regime. Between 1814-20 and 1823-32 reactionary absolutist regimes held government when the passions were high and the political events alarming.

Just before Fernando VII's death in 1833 the king had persuaded the *Cortes* to set aside the Salic Law of succession and allow his daughter to take the throne as opposed to his brother Don Carlos. This right was contested, however, with Don Carlos backed by the Church, Conservatives and Basques, while his daughter Isabel aged only three was supported by the Liberals and Army. The scene was set for the first Carlist War, which lasted six years until the throne finally went to Isabel

II. Sevilla was bombed in 1840 during this conflict. Come the end of the war Espartero, the most popular general of the Queen's armies, took over as Regent from Cristina, Isabel's mother.

A liberal government wreaked havoc on the ecclesiastical institutions and the old order, even confiscating all church and monastic wealth and property in 1836. So much for 'liberal'. But there was no stability in the new Queen's government with the *moderados*, Liberals and Progressives all vying for control.

After coming of age in 1839, at sweet 16, Queen Isabel II was deposed in 1868 when Liberal Army generals under General Prim effected a coup forcing her abdication. Hers had been a reign characterised by intrigue, political crises, insurrections and constitutional compromise. A republic was formed which lasted but a year until Isabel's son Alfonso XII (rumoured to be the offspring of a Captain of the guard: Enrique Puig y Moltó) regained the throne and abolished the Republic. With the great dependence of the *andaluces* on the land and the large *Latifunda* estates that had concentrated the wealth ever since Fernando III redistributed the land in 1248, it was only a matter of time before an extreme fashion of red politics began to take hold among the people of the South.

In 1860 there was more foreign war, this time with Morocco, when Spain gained Ifni. By 1884 it had consolidated its possessions of Spanish West Africa. There was further struggle on the home front in 1868 and the liberal 'Glorious Revolution' – *La Gloriosa*. In Córdoba, in 1872 the first Anarchist Congress was held. The Anarchists were later to play a key role in the Spanish Civil War of the 20th century. (The Anarchist Party CNT was later formed in 1911 and won most support in Andalucía.) 1873, and a Republican government was formed, but only lasted 2 years before the monarchy was restored once more. These continual upheavals in the administration were frequently implemented by force of arms and continued until the Civil War broke out in 1936. In 1888 the Socialist Workers' Party Trade Union, the UGT, was founded. The 19th century closed its doors in Spain with peasant worker unrest in 1892, followed in 1898 by war with the U.S. when Cuba revolted against its Spanish superiors. The resulting defeat for Spain plunged the Motherland into deep financial strife.

As surely as anthropologists saw the plague coming to Europe through the hindsight of the frailty of medieval bones due to poor diet, so historians are able to look back at the inevitability of the Spanish Civil War.

In 1923 General Primo de Rivera led a military coup and became Spain's first dictator. Disillusionment with the parliamentary system combined with the fears of private business interests, ensured support for the illegal take over by his Falangist party. His time in power lasted until 1929. Two years later the victory of anti-monarchist parties in the municipal elections forced the abdication of the king and the Second Republic was declared.

The Wall Street Crash stopped a frail economic revival in Sevilla dead in its tracks. It had been spearheaded by an Ibero-American Expo, that now failed to achieve its goals and kick-start the economy. Political agitation continued its, by now, natural course of extremism.

"Things rarely happen by halves in Spain."
John Hooper

The Republic could no longer control, or worse still was seen as not trying to control, extremist groups attacking the right, the church and the established order of business. The violence and anarchy generated by the Communists and, at the time the aptly-named Anarchists, was finally answered by the army under General Franco who rose up in the Spanish Colony of Ceuta in Morocco. So began the first war to use industrial techniques of mass destruction. The Basque town of Guernica /ger-**NI**-ca/ or *Gernika* in Basque, was bombed by the Germans to aid Franco and at the same time put into practise their Blitzkrieg strategy. They also wiped out the population of Durango. Franco wanted to teach the separatist Basques a lesson by destroying their most sacred site. Their hallowed tree which marks their meeting place survived and so did the Basque identity. But the right-wing rebellion hadn't been an overnight success as the army had predicted. Not all generals supported the revolt and many sided with the legitimate and democratically elected Republican government.

Both the Republican and the Nationalist rebels carried out violent reprisals on each other. While the Republicans shot priests and landowners outright, Nationalists inflicted massacres on the civilian populations of the towns they captured. Sevilla was a centre for the Republicans and an important stage for the central conflict between the landed class and the working majority. In the end the city fell to the rebels when, in a celebrated episode, General Francisco Queipo de Llano announced over local radio that they had surrounded the city and were entering through all its major roads. Then with a handful of men and a few trucks the General drove them round and made an entrance, one after the other, along the principal routes of entry into the city in order to deceive the citizens. They believed their eyes, which defeats the old adage that seeing is believing. Once they had laid down their arms it was too late to pick them up again. When the war had come to a head in 1939 executions were frequent and easily carried out in retaliation by the winning Fascist faction. The prisoners were not particularly well treated either, and many were sent to labour camps. One such camp was near Sevilla and around 2,000,000 were kept in concentration centres around Spain until order had been fully established.

The proceeding years saw Franco establish a church-state modelled on that of the 16th century King Felipe II under his sole ruling *Falange* party. The legitimate democratic government had been replaced by a dictatorship. Franco was escorted everywhere by a mounted Moroccan guard in full regalia. The Moroccans had helped his campaign enormously by terrorising the enemy as much as fighting them. The economy ground to a halt until the tourism trade began to open up and the economic 'miracle' occurred that saved Spain falling any further down the financial ladder. It was maintained by foreign investment and economic know-how. The country gradually and welcomingly became dependant on tourism. They eventually gained international respectability when Eisenhower was limousined into town and around the sights. The Americans needed land to stage bases for the Cold War effort in 1953 and Franco needed foreign funds. For that he also needed a new image. The 1960's saw blessed times for the economy as foreign investment came flooding in. Spain was second only to Japan in its financial growth largely due to tourism and remittances from immigrant Spanish workers principally located in Germany, France and Argentina.

Against all Franco's best efforts to bring up King Juan Carlos as his heir and establish an absolute monarchy the young king, urged on by his Greek wife Sophia, started to mix in different company. And after Franco's death in 1975 the nation at last made timid steps toward democracy. In 1977 the first general elections were held and in 1982

Spain's first freely elected President took the reigns of power. His name was Felipe González, a lawyer from Sevilla. Between 1979-83, 17 regions in Spain, including Andalucía gained their status as autonomous communities.

Andalucía is the second largest region in the country at 87,278 km² – occupying 17.2% of Spain's territory with a population of around 8,000,000, the largest in the country. In Sevilla province there are 104 *pueblos* – towns, and in the capital city live 704,000 people, a million if you take into account the surrounding area and satellite towns. It's the nation's fourth largest concentration of population. Today Sevilla is recognized by one organization as the poorest province in Spain and the last figures at the time of writing showed 85,000 unemployed. The city offers work predominantly in public services.

In a sentence then, and so that we finally have a clear idea of the city that has brought us to this point, we could say that Sevilla has:

'a secular body, an ecclesiastical soul and spiritual mind.'

A little like the three strata of their tower La Giralda: Roman, Moor & Christian. It's all in their blood and culture here.

- DOS -
LANDMARKS & LEGENDS

"Quien no ha visto Sevilla no ha visto una maravilla."
(Moorish expression)
'Who has not seen Seville, has not a wonder seen'

Sevilla, the blood and soul of the South and the inspiration of a nation, is the founding city of Andalusian aspiration, priding itself on its reputation for spontaneity, intensity and artistic expression. In one form or another you will encounter it, whether it be in the streets, bars or on a more fantastic scale at one of its many *fiestas* staged throughout the year. As the backdrop to Carmen, Figaro, a certain barber and also home to Don Juan, the city can still bring to life an age-old legacy of passion and romance handed down from its distinguished past. Once you have spent time in this city you will find it hard to turn your back, or more importantly your imagination, on her.

As alive as Sevilla's traditions are, the city has a modern perspective too, most recently demonstrated in its hosting of EXPO '92.

All is not milk and honey though; there are the harsh realities of an area hit by high unemployment. The resulting homelessness and begging is evident on the streets. Petty crime, such as bag snatching and theft from cars, is commonplace. This is not to say, however, that it is a dangerous city. On the contrary, the exact opposite is true. The streets are very safe and well lit at night, often populated with revellers, street cleaners and people returning home. It is a welcoming environment and anything but a threatening one.

Let's go for a stroll down Sevilla's memory lanes then and take a closer look at what buildings her history has hidden around each corner and what culture we can bring to light, for there is much to see and marvel at.

Sevilla is located in the southwestern corner of Spain in the west of the region of Andalucía near Portugal. It is situated in the lower Guadalquivir valley straddling the *Río Guadalquivir*, which splits the city in two. The airport is situated someway out to the north, the Santa Justa train station within city limits to the east. The two major bus stations; *El Prado* and *Plaza de Armas* are well placed in relation to the centre. Trying to get your bearings on a city can be disorientating though as what should be

North is in fact East and what should be East is South. What's going on here? Artistic licence is the answer. It simply fits better on the page to shift it 45° to the left and anyway… it looks bigger! Any city map then will place the eastern tip at the top of the page and north will be to your left. The metropolis covers about 140km² in an almost oval shape.

A vast area of the centre is populated by traditional Spanish town housing huddled together with their cast iron balconies in their pinched streets. The suburbs, however, tell another story. They are vast areas of characterless high-rise buildings stuck on the end. Needless to say what pulls in the punters is in the old centre.

The city is very straightforward to get around by bus but a one-way nightmare if you are driving. There are no hills so biking it round would be a breeze if it weren't for the unpredictability of Spanish driving.

'¡La lluvia en Sevilla es una maravilla!'

Sang Rex Harrison in his Castilian dubbed version of My Fair *'Señora'*. The rain is a 'marvel' because there isn't any. That was until Seville ended a four-year drought in style by giving its rendition of a Northern European, rather than Andalusian, climate. And don't go trying to explain that that is not the original version of the song to the people round here or you'll soon see just how quickly you can get nowhere.

Set at 6m above sea level its annual temperatures are around 19°C, with infrequent rainfall averaging 20". And the all-important stat that everyone wants to hear: an average of 2,878 hours of sunshine a year. Las Palmas in Gran Canarias has 2,998 hours. But because Sevilla gets so hot in July and August, 113°F, you won't be going out much to enjoy it. Instead, you will have to hideaway indoors preferring to come out at night when the sun has finally given up the ghost and stopped scorching the earth.

The typical description given by the local people of their climate is the following:

'Nueve meses de invierno y tres de infierno.'
- Nine months of winter and three of hell -

This is met in the other direction by the British climate:

Landmarks & Legends

The English winter - ending in July,
To recommence in August.
Byron, Don Juan

Though the climate has been somewhat erratic of late the famous heat of Southern Spain's summer arrives each year as surely do the dual celebrations of *Semana Santa* and *La Feria*.

The summer starts around April and burns on until October when within 24 hours things can change completely and it's time to don an overcoat once more. The only time when rain is predictable is in April.

Yes, *Andalucía* does have a winter. Mild though it is by Northern European standards, jackets and jumpers are required.

The climate is Mediterranean and those who come in search of clear blue skies, late nights spent drinking on *terrazas* and basically the classic Southern Mediterranean lifestyle then Sevilla shan't disappoint.

Sevilla like all Spanish cities and big towns has a beautiful and picturesque old core encased in a modern area looming over it in stark contrast. Its old centre is enormous at 4.7km², even by Spanish standards, and is said to be the biggest in Europe accounting for 9% of the total area of the city. However, if you have seen Rome or Venice then this boast on behalf of Sevilla may be nothing but that. Bologna also makes the same claim. But don't let this put you off wandering its charming Andalusian labyrinth – it is big.

When you have monuments in your city that verge on icons, when it possesses a place in history and played a role in the intellectual and artistic make up of the nation then you have something to brag about. But none of this will have any meaning or significance in the here and now if the place cannot manifest a tangible presence to its citizens and visitors.

Through elaborate and popular outpourings of civic festivity the city keeps its identity and culture alive, as well as up-to-date. The nature and knowledge of the city's achievements and past glories (in the pacifistic not military sense) are given new life in the people. They feel part of something. The shelves in the local bookshops are crammed with in-depth titles about local customs, culture and creations.

So, a family here that may appear 'trapped' in their box-like apartment, know that they can participate in collective celebrations throughout the year that bring the city's people together and in so doing reaffirm their cultural identity and beliefs. Their fiestas reassure them and give them self-belief, which translates into confidence. They know that at the back of their minds they have something to lean against. They have a strong feeling of who they are. Where they have come from, where they are going and where this journey might lead, are not issues for them. They have already answered these questions. And answering rightly or wrongly here, of course, makes no matter because the important thing is that the doubts have been silenced. They know that next year will follow the same seasons and fiestas as the last. In between there will be some work and exams to do and then it's off to the beach for the long summer. So there's nothing to fret about really, it's all planned out. There will always be something to look forward to.

If you can leave your modest flat regularly and stroll the streets aimlessly with your family, eat and drink well without having to take out a second mortgage, participate annually in the greater scheme of things in the fiestas of your city and your own culture then what are the effects of that on the average citizen? Well, the following expression goes someway to answering that:

'En Sevilla 'Soledad' es nombre de mujer.'
- In Seville, Soledad (Loneliness) is the name of a woman -

The name *Soledad*, abbreviated to *Sole*, pronounced /*solay*/ with a short 'o' and short 'e' sounds, is indeed a name given to a woman, but her anguish of loneliness is not one that people here believe finds a feeding ground in their city. They always feel part of something and something worthwhile at that. For that reason they do not give in to feelings of despondency so easily.

Civic pride is alive and very well in Spain but nowhere does it seem to have a cleaner bill of health than in Sevilla.

"Hercules built me; Caesar surrounded me with walls and towers; and the King Saint took me."

This brief summary of Sevilla's history, which was inscribed on the no-longer standing gate that lead to Jerez in *La Puerta de Jerez*, shows that the city has had many influences passing through it over the centuries, some of which have left a lasting impression.

Within the limits of the old city one will find a wealth of architecture in its rambling streets lined by sixteenth and seventeenth century Spanish town houses, strewn with *plazas* and an almost biblical amount of churches. As you make your way round you will discover, from a distance, beautiful *patios* open to the street. Alas they are private and not open to the public. But this architectural 'peep show' is all part of the sightseeing in old Seville, which can start from almost anywhere.

You will find an explosion of colours, columns, styles and scale that will leave your eyes and thoughts done for the day. Ancient Africa at its height and Mediaeval Europe at hers, unite to give light to this architectural treasure trove whose buildings bridge two continents while giving the present new meaning for those that behold them.

This plethora of buildings has something for everyone and each corner its own unique history connected to the city, to Spain, Europe or the New World.

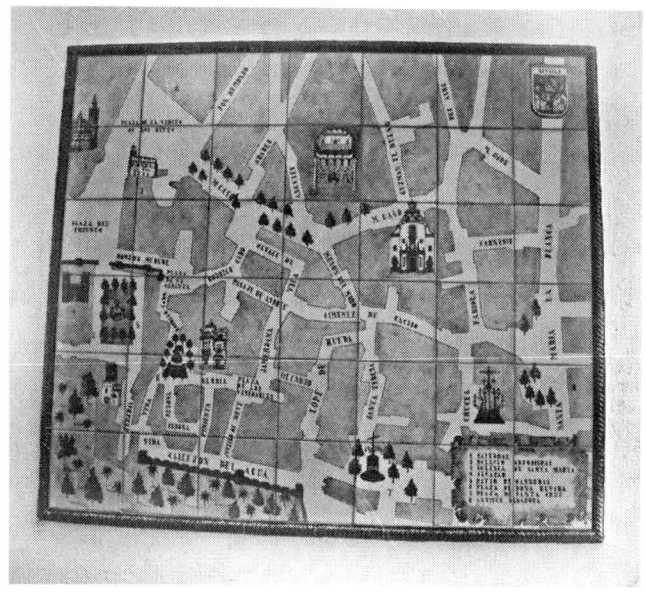

Any walk through Sevilla, any visit and any discussion should always start in Barrio Santa Cruz, where Sevilla's monumental concentration of historical building pays tribute to the city's history throughout the ages. It would be difficult to find another place that holds so much in such a tight confine. So many styles: Moorish to Renaissance; periods: the 9th to the 19th century; types: minaret and church to castle and cathedral; colours: bare stone to painted façade; religions: Islamic, Christian, Jewish and there are palaces and gardens alongside town houses with adjoining *plazas*. Discovery of Sevilla's architectural, along with cultural and urban heritage, definitely starts here.

The city's focal point is La Giralda /hee-**RAL**-da/, and therefore its emblem. It is an early medieval minaret dominating the skyline, towering 98m/312ft above the largest gothic cathedral in the whole of Christendom, *Santa María de la Sede*. Dating from the late 12th century it was preserved by the Christians on their retaking of Sevilla and it now holds sway to the cathedral's bells. La Giralda was undertaken at the behest of the ruling caliph Abu Yacub Yusuf of the second Almohad dynasty from Morocco, who took Sevilla as their capital in al-Andalus. It was started in 1184, 12 years after the no-longer standing mosque was finished. There are 35 ramps leading up to a landing at each section, which carry the visitor to the top. The muezzin could ride up and call the faithful to prayer and thus save his legs. The tower was also used for astrology. The base is made from free standing stone, all Roman in its 20m deep foundations, while the rest is Moorish brick work called *pisé*, which is basically thin layers of dried clay compacted together. The decorative interwoven brickwork above the windows is referred to as s*ebka*.

Sitting atop it all was once a massive golden dome surmounted by a further three spheres and a small half-crescent moon, later toppled by the 1365 earthquake.

When Fernando III took the city, the disconsolate caliph Axataf asked the Christian King's permission if he would be allowed to dismantle the minaret, symbol of Moorish Imperial might, piece by piece and take it back with him to Africa. Fernando replied that he would behead one Moor for every brick that fell. La Giralda along with the Hassan tower in Rabat and the Kutubiyya tower in Marrakesh make up a group of medieval Moorish towers built at the same time and in the same style that collectively are known as 'the three sisters'.

"Florence has its ancient palaces, Pisa its Campo Santo, Naples has Herculanum and Pompeii, Granada the Alhambra, Cordoba its Mosque and Seville La Giralda."
Alexandre Dumas

In the same rush of building fever the Moors also extended the city's boundaries to include some 740 acres, fortifying the barrios of Triana and La Macarena. They also erected the recently restored Buhaira palace then just outside the city walls. The Almohad dynasty saw a period of prosperity for its citizens.

When a solution for the fallen spheres was finally realised in the 16th century, Christian Spain topped their victory over the Moor by symbolically crowning their architectural pinnacle of achievement with a predominantly Christian motif: a belfry. Now the song of the muezzin was replaced by the proud ringing of a different tune. The architect that stepped in to change the face of the minaret was Hernán Ruíz the Younger. The project was carried out between 1558-1568. The very distinct *andaluz* Renaissance style known as *Regional* was used with its play of strong ceramic strips over stone facing. Perched precariously above the belfry, floating in the bright blue Andalusian sky, broods a bronze figure of Faith. The sculpture was cast by Bartolomé Morel and sculpted by Juan Bautista Vázquez. The figure acts as a weather vane, which in Spanish is *giralda*, the actual weathercock itself is affectionately known as *giraldillo* – 'small weathercock'. The original statue underwent a four year restoration and the best part of €600,000 was spent.

Not all agree that the work improved the overall symmetry of the building. Pure it is not, but beauty is in the eye of the beholder. It must have been the first skyscraper in Christendom and just to appreciate the achievement it stands at 97.5m while the world famous St. Stephen's Tower built 1836 and 800 years later reaches two centremetres less. St. Stephen's Tower today, we all know as Big Ben, after the portly Master of Works at Westminster Palace Sir Benjamin Hall.

La Giralda was the tallest tower of its day and a marvel of the Muslim world. It has also been the tallest building in the city since the time it was built – 842 years. No taller building was allowed to be erected. That was about to change with the proposed construction of a 150m tower – *la Torre Triana*, in the science park across the Guadalquivir river but the *Junta* changed its mind as it would affect visibility. So, La Giralda will still continue to be the protagonist on the Sevillian skyline for the visible future.

There used to be a replica in Madison Square Garden and there still stands one in Kansas City, the town twinned with Sevilla. Badajoz has a smaller example as a shop front, there's one in the Spanish town of l'Arboç, the Hotel Biltmore in Miami and one can clearly see the strong inspiration in the twin towers of the huge El San Remo building in New York.

El Patio de Los Naranjos – the Orange Tree Patio, is the only surviving part of the original mosque, which once stood at the feet of La Giralda, along with a piece of the doorway leading into it. The door panels and knockers made of brass are also Almohad originals and are decorated with 880 Kufic inscriptions. The door is known as *La Puerta del Perdón* – The Gate of Forgiveness. Unfortunately, you'll be passing out from it and not in, so maybe it won't work for you. This was where the ablutions were traditionally performed. The fountain and basin that stand in the centre are of Roman origin.

The great mosque, started in 1172, was known as *Dhema Mukyarrim*, renamed by Fernando III *La Iglesia de Santa María la Mayor* when he retook the city in 1248. But the church that was constructed here was a poor relation to its previous Moorish mosque, torn down to make way for the present occupiers to try their hand at knocking up something more to their liking.

> "Let us erect such a grand temple that
> we shall go down to posterity, if only as madmen."

So exclaimed the canons of the chapter, when they decided upon the construction of their Gothic cathedral in 1402. They got round to the finishing touches a hundred and seven years later! In fact, they had stuff to finish on an off and finalised the project in 1880 when the architect Casanova rounded off the dome, which had collapsed on two previous occasions. The architect commented on seeing the final piece in place, *"it should hold up now."* The area they filled was almost equivalent to that covered by the original mosque: 126m x 80m. They were possibly motivated by the present grandeur of the Islamic building to build beyond it. Standing at 30m tall the cathedral's nave sits on 60 pillars.

There are some treasures to marvel at here, such as the final resting place of Christopher Columbus, or *Cristóbal Colón* as we should now be calling him. But debate poured doubt as to where he was really buried. Some believed it was his brother in the cathedral and *Colón* was in his brother's grave on the other side of the pond. Their bodies were exhumed and the DNA studied. The remains of Fernando III are also kept here in the Council Chamber – *La Sala de Juntas*, and the public can take a peek inside the tomb and gaze upon the 'uncorrupted remains' of the Saintly King every 30th May, naturally the day of Saint Ferdinand.

There is some Italian sculpture, some of the finest stained glass windows in Europe as well as the cathedral's central masterpieces of the *retablo* by Zurbarán and in the Saint Anthony Chapter House – *La Capilla de San Antonio*, is Murillo's *La Visión de San Antonio*. The other chapels are also highly decorated. The elaborate Choir, or *coro*, has 117 stalls carved from different exotic woods. Felipe II in the 16th century said that the cathedral of Sevilla had a better Sacristy than he had Royal Chapel in El Real de Escorial near Madrid – Spain's biggest building.

The cathedral may be seen more as a storage space for treasure than a place of serious worship but it is one of the busiest cathedrals you are ever likely to pass through. In the *Biblioteca Capitular y Colombina* – Chapel Library and Columbiana, are stored the cathedral's illuminated manuscripts and collection of books that Hernán Colón, the brother of *Cristóbal*, brought back from his travels. He amassed 20,000 volumes in all and bequeathed them to the city of Sevilla. The manuscripts are deemed priceless. There is also a sculpture of Christ on the Cross claimed to be the best example of Spanish Baroque found anywhere. Six feet in total, it was sculpted by the greatest of them all Juan Martínez Montañéz known to his contemporaries as 'the God of Wood' - *El Dios de la Madera*. *La Custodia* is also to be found here: a 13 foot casket weighing 990 lbs of solid American silver finished in 1587, a year before *la Armada* set sail, and is brought out to parade the streets as the centrepiece during the *Corpus Christi* celebrations each year.

There is also the curious '*Lagarto*' meaning 'Lizard', actually once a crocodile full of life, a gift to Alfonso X, The Wise from the Sultan of Egypt but the one hanging in the cathedral today is a replica of the original. Why a crocodile? you ask. And why did they call it a lizard when it obviously isn't? They had probably never seen a reptile this big before. It must have been like being given an alien to place over the mantelpiece. It now hangs from the ceiling in the *La Puerta del Lagarto*, which must have been a fashion of the time because there are other churches in Europe that also have a hanging lizard-crocodile. In the Sacristies and Chapterhouse there are fine examples of the Renaissance style. In the *Sala Capitular* – Chapterhouse, the elliptical dome reminiscent of St. Peter's Rome, was decorated by Murillo and would surely feature in any 7 Wonders of 16th century Europe.

The cathedral has impressive gold work, gates that defy belief in their form and scale as well as columns that disappear into the heavens. The baptistery is by far the most intricate and interesting part of its exterior.

Virginia Wolf described the place as *"Elephantine"* and the writer Rainer Maria Milke *"...there is something hazy and imponderable about this high-blown overweening dome, an out-trumping spirit that seeks to out-trump God himself..."* Comments like these will only encourage visitors to pass through its doors. It has earned the nickname among Spanish of *'La Montaña Hueca'* - The Empty Mountain.

Evelyn on the other hand found the following: *"The cathedral is magnificent, one of the most beautiful in Europe. A great spacious Gothic church full of superb sculpture hidden in dark corners and behind iron grilles."* Ultimately the decision is yours, you are the beholder.

As you leave the cathedral via the main entrance, that leads onto the main road *La Avenida de La Constitución*, take the time to look up and you will see iron cast vases filled with lilies, this is the symbol of the Cathedral. Then look down at your feet and you will notice that on the curb are painted some yellow arrows. Believe it or not this is to point pilgrims in the right direction to the town of Santiago de Compostela in the north of Spain in the region of Galicia. The original route is actually across the north of the country from France but this one from Sevilla is probably the longest which people make, on foot, each year. A handful of enthusiasts maintain the path. How they go about this though is anyone's guess. We're talking here about 1,030km and only a small group of people to take care of it. Walkers follow *La Vía de la Plata* - the old Silver Route, which the Romans trampled when they brought silver down from the mines in Asturias and Galicia to then load it onto boats and carry it back to the heart of their empire.

The trinity of buildings that comprise the Cathedral, Giralda and baptistery backs onto the bright and lively *Plaza de La Virgen de Los Reyes*, which was once occupied by buildings belonging to the mosque and later cathedral, but were eventually demolished in 1790 to give greater space and light. Off to one side of this *plaza* is the imposing façade of *El Palacio Arzobispal* home to the Archbishop of Sevilla, completed in 1705. Opposite it stands a whitewashed convent, *El Convento de la Encarnación*. The street that leads northwards directly away from La Giralda is *calle Mateos Gago* and was the prime street of the Roman *urbs* – town. It leads up to Sevilla's highest point, which is only 50ft above sea level.

Los Reales Alcázares, from the Arab word *al-qasr*, meaning 'fortress', is reason enough for visiting Sevilla. It stands off the *plaza* flanking the cathedral, *La Plaza del Triunfo*, 'triumphant' as the name suggests because the monuments were saved from an earthquake on 1st November, 1775 that devastated Lisbon and even parts of Morocco. It was also the greatest natural disaster to ever affect Sevilla. A contemporary source relates that, *"all of Seville's streets became one vast theatre upon which scenes of bitterness and desperation were played."* The tremors, emanating from the epicentre in the Atlantic beyond Lisbon, were strong enough to make the bells of the Giralda peal. Innumerable buildings and monuments were left in a state of disrepair.

Of all the *Alcázares* to be found scattered around *Andalucía*, Sevilla's is the only one that carries the title of *Real* – Royal. The Moors made greater use of its fortifications while the Christians gave greater emphasis to its palace. The site was, however, founded by the Visigoths. Behind its impressive complex of Moorish walls and turrets are contained some of the finest rooms decked out in the *Mudéjar* style, as well as its beguiling gardens. *Mudéjar* refers to the Moors that were allowed to stay and they developed a new Arab style fused with the incoming Renaissance influence that conformed to Christian taste. *Mudéjar* is derived from the Spanish word *dejar* which means 'to let/allow'. The present appearance of the palace, though, was nearly all undertaken by the Christians directing arab hands. The walls running north from the entrance and its impressive towers are original dating from 913 and were raised by the Caliph of Córdoba Abd el-Rahman III. They look good for at least another thousand years. His reason for their construction was to protect against further Norman attack.

The Spanish King Pedro I, also known more accurately as Pedro 'the Cruel' or 'the Just', depending on whether you owed him any money, had the place comprehensively extended and decorated. All the work was necessary to make way for his harem supplied every 5 years by the donation of 100 concubines. It is to him that the Alcázar owes its present day splendour. In the main entrance to Pedro's newly-built apartments in *el Patio de la Montería*, where the Royal hunt used to gather, he had inscribed: *'The highest, noblest, most powerful all-conquering king, Pedro I, king, by grace of God, of Castilla and León ordered these gardens, palaces and gates to be built, which were done in the year of our Lord fourteen hundred and two.'* Despite all the colourful adjectives and the flood of coats-of-arms bearing *Castilla* and *León* there can still be seen in Kufic script on the palaces walls: *'There is no one God but Allah.'*

Part of the gardens was recently discovered in a dig and the pollen from the original flowers that had once adorned the Moorish palace was unearthed and identified. The pollen had lain dormant for centuries. Planting then restored the greenery to its former glory with its original combination of flowers. The gardens are the most exotic in the city with its labyrinth, grotto, soaring cypresses and dizzying palms. It is hard to decide which is more sumptuous: the palace or its gardens.

History and legend abound within these majestic walls. It is like no fortress you are used to and its history is equally surprising. Two stories that are worth a mention both involve Pedro. During Pedro's reign the Moors were still entrenched in their kingdoms around Granada. The 'Red King', the Emir of Granada Abu Said, and entourage came to stay in Sevilla in the *Alcázar* at the invitation of Pedro I. But once there, Pedro's intentions of playing clean were soon brushed aside when his eyes fell upon the opulence of the Moor's jewel collection. One gem in particular, which has since been described as a *'fair ruby, great as a racket ball'*, caught his attention in particular. During their stay, which seems to be the model of the time for such intrigue, the Moors were murdered in one of the passageways as they made their way to bed. The gem now belonged to Pedro, but not for long as he sadly had to relinquish it in payment for services rendered by England's Black Prince. Pedro gave the stone to the Black Prince's wife in return for help against Enrique Trastámara, Pedro's bastard brother. Once in Britain the balas-ruby, known as the Black Prince's ruby, found its way into the Imperial State Crown and there it has rested ever since, second in importance to the Cullian II Diamond set just below it. But... it's not a ruby, it's a red spinel. Still valuable mind, but then €15,000 isn't €150,000. Spinels were often used to substitute real rubies if the gem was on public display, similar to cubic zirconia replacing diamonds. No one is quite sure though, as to whether the spinel in the crown was once a real ruby or was swiped by a daring jeweller when it was sent to be cleaned, as has often happened throughout history.

Pedro I fell in love with Doña María Fernández Coronel, who to avert his attentions disfigured her face by throwing burning oil over it in the tower of *el Convento de Santa Clara* where she had taken refuge from the king in hot pursuit. María preferred to remain ugly the rest of her life rather than have to bear the proximity of the king. Her 'uncorrupted' body is displayed every year in the convent on 11th. December. Doña María was not the reason why Pedro received his nickname 'the Cruel' though. That he earned by killing his own brother don Fadrique Alfonso, supposedly in *el Patio de las Doncellas* in *los Reales Alcázares*. His brother awoke to hear Pedro making the order to *"finish him off once and for all… kill that damn, wretched dog."* Don Fadrique managed to get as far as the patio when the soldiers caught up with him and cut him down. Pedro dealt the final blow himself. Don Pedro had never loved his wife Doña Blanca de Borbón, but that didn't stop him from having his brother, the Grand Master of the Order of Santiago, murdered for committing adultery with her.

Pedro certainly gave the city its money's worth as far as legends went. Another tells of a night in the streets in the Alfalfa area and the murder of a nobleman witnessed by an old woman from her balcony. She heard the clicking of the knee joint of the murderer as he made his escape. Don Pedro was known for such a defect after a riding accident had left him lame. The dead noble's family petitioned the King for vengeance. Don Pedro gave his word that he would find the culprit and display their head in the street where the man had fallen. The old woman not before long presented herself at court and when asked to identify herself she answered that she knew who the murderer was. When Pedro summoned her he spoke to her aside and when he asked her to tell him who the guilty man was she simply pointed at a mirror, so the others would not see. Pedro could only see his reflection. The woman was paid her reward and ushered out of the palace. The next day a crowd had gathered in anticipation as the city's bailiff announced that the guilty party had been discovered and their head would be placed in the street near the scene of the crime. To everyone's disappointment he produced a box apparently containing the head and then mounted it in a niche in the wall. Then it was locked behind a metal grille and left under armed guard. Years later Pedro was killed in a civil war against his bastard brother Enrique Trastámara and the first chance the citizens had to break the box open they took. Inside they found a terracotta bust of the King. Today the street has been renamed *calle de la Cabeza del rey don Pedro* and in a niche sits a stone reproduction.

Later the Catholic Sovereigns, *Fernando V de Castilla, II de Aragón* and *Isabel I de Castilla,* took their turn in the Royal residence and added to the apartments, as did Carlos V Holy Roman Emperor when he stayed here for his wedding. Under Carlos V of Germany and I of Spain, the nation reached its apex of European and world ambition and the Alcázares was given its final royal renovation. Carlos V hung up some of the best tapestries of the time depicting his Tunis campaign. One in particular is of historical note for its timely reminder that nothing is set in stone and everything is about interpretation. The weaving depicts a map with Spain in the South and Africa in the North.

If you never have the time to visit the Alhambra in Granada and are keen to know what all the fuss is about, what inspired Washington Irving to pick up a pen and his famous *'Tales of the Alhambra'*, then *los Reales Alcázares* is a good introduction to Spain's Arab architectural wonder of the High Middle Ages.

On leaving the *Reales Alcázares* you will spill out onto *La Plaza de Banderas*, meaning 'flags' after the troops that used to be inspected here. (Now you're thinking: Tony Flags?) Today it is open to the public and contains apartments running around the beautiful orange-tree filled *plaza*.

Superstition holds that those who jump over the chains around the fountain will never marry. If you trip over them it only means one thing: you just made yourself look like an idiot. Immediately right from the exit of the *Alcázares* or in the far left-hand end of the plaza looking at it from the cathedral is a small passageway that leads into the Jewish Quarter – *La Judería* also called *Barrio de Santa Cruz*, which follows the old palace walls and the charming *callejón Agua*. It is the most charismatic stroll the old city has to offer. At the end of this alleyway is the *Plaza de Alfaro* one of the settings for Rossini's Figaro.

Next to the *Alcázar* in *La Plaza del Triunfo* stands the *Archivo de Indias* – The Indies Archives. The building was originally constructed as an exchange, *La Casa Lonja*, finished between 1583-1646 and designed by the Royal architect Juan de Herrera of *El Escorial* fame. Today it houses a unique and voluminous array of historical information documenting the discovery and colonisation of South America at the hand of *Colón* and *los Conquistadores*, from the moment the explorer stepped ashore San Salvador to the 19th century.

Its sober Castilian style stands in contrast to the exotic and vibrant buildings of Moorish and Gothic Sevilla but its interior, and especially its library, where exhibits are changed regularly, are especially refined. The reason for the Exchange was in response to the complaints of the church that had to deal with the hundreds of merchants who congregated on the cathedral steps and at times when it rained even spilled into the cathedral itself – on horseback! To think that the Wall Street of the time was in fact just some church steps. The large posts surrounding the cathedral were chained together to stop mounted merchants from trotting into the cathedral during a downpour. The chains are still in place.

The sixteenth century saw Sevilla fill with immigrants arriving to seek their fortune. And with this great wealth came not only privilege but also poverty, in equal measure. There was easily enough to go around, of course, but prosperity always leads to hoarding. The city became known for its hawkers, *pícaros*, crooks, churchmen, beggars, merchants, orphans, the ill, the hungry and its *'lost women'* as they were referred to at the time. Street names stand as testament to their earlier place in the city's history and the various guilds – *gremios*, which they housed. *Calle Curtidores* – Tanners; *calle Refinadores* (Refiners); *calle Lineros* (Linen makers) and *calle Alfareros* – Potters.

After the decline of Sevilla's position as the monopoly holder of trade with the Americas, the *Lonja* lost its entrepreneurial patrons and fell into disuse. In 1660 until 1674 it was the centre for an Arts Academy founded by Estéban Murillo but by the end of the century it was providing housing for people of the area.

It was in the second half of the 18th century that the building found a new and quite unexpected lease of life as a records office for all that could be found on the Americas, Indies and the Spanish involvement therein. This was the initiative of the King of the time Carlos III. Spain's actions in their colonies came under strong attack from the Scotsman William Roberts and the Frenchman Abbé Raynal, an extension of the Black Legend – *la Leyenda Negra*, put about by England and France to undermine Spain's monopoly on her new overseas possessions. A propaganda turn about was needed to head off the historians' claims against the Spanish Crown and they decided the first thing they had to do was gather together all the necessary information and then start up the intellectual fisty-cuffs.

The manuscripts started arriving in 1785 and today the collection houses some ninety million pages of text kept in forty-three thousand files taking up 5½ miles of shelving. Today the squat, square yet well-mannered archive building offers guided tours to let the curious gaze upon America's first memory.

Opposite and to the left along the *Avenida de La Constitución* is a beautiful *Mudéjar* palace, now a bank and behind it is the 16th century old Royal Mint – *La Casa de la Moneda*, reborn as apartments. The hidden courtyard that it surrounds has a very Castilian feel to it like *La Lonja*, making it a unique and reserved corner in a city otherwise playful in style.

By the river next to the functional *El Puente de San Telmo* stands *La Torre del Oro, Burj al-Dhahab* in Arab, and for many the symbol of Sevilla as opposed to the much-famed Giralda. 'The Tower of the Gold', or as some translate it 'The Golden Tower', was once part of a series of towers that extended along a wall emanating from *los Reales Alcázares* constructed at the beginning of the 13th century by the Almohads, Sevilla's last Moorish rulers. The original tower, which only had two levels, was started in 1220 and only took a year to complete. The present pinnacle, the third level, gold in colour, was added by Sebastian Vander Borcht in 1760. There is even the tale that Perdo I locked a golden-haired damsel in the tower taking advantage of her husband being away at war. The survivor today was principally a river defence with a chain stretched across the water from the tower to a similar construction in Triana in *calle Fortaleza* thereby denying access to ships. *La Torre del Oro* gained its name possibly from the gold brilliance with which it shone when it was originally covered with *azulejos* tiles, but many believe its name is derived from the time when it was used to store the incoming shipments of gold and treasure from the New World. It is called *'del Oro'*, which means 'of the Gold' as opposed to *'Dorado'*, which means Golden. The dodecagonal tower is purer in Moorish form than the Giralda, which many believe was defaced by the Christian belfry. The peaceful looking tower certainly has a strong, faultless almost classic feel to it and now houses a maritime museum and luxury apartments for the ministry of defence with ceilings six metres high.

Outside the walls of the Alcázar run a warren of streets that comprise the old Jewish quarter of *Barrio Santa Cruz*, which used to sit outside the city walls but are now contained within its own perimeter. The fact that it is populated by tourists during the day who are then joined by local carousers at night, speaks volumes for the popularity and charm of this part of the city. You should pass through it at least once but you are guaranteed to make a return visit. Here *patios* and greenery combine among tapered passageways to intoxicate the stranger with a suffocating dose of romantic Andalucía. Fountains sprout water, balconies cascade geraniums and cobbles carpet the maze of streets. Restaurants, *tabernas* and brusque buskers imbibe those in need of wine, song and time to take in the surroundings at a more leisurely pace. It is the most emblematic district of Sevilla and one of the most picturesque neighbourhoods in all of Spain. History presses in on you as your heels clack along legendary lanes where hooves and heavy boots once passed. Architecture and seigniorial houses from the 16th century abound in this culturally rich district. A town house named *Los Seises* after the ceremony of the same name celebrated in the cathedral was the domain of Bishop Deza the first Bishop of the Inquisition (1498-1507). Cervantes lived in the area and it was also the haunt of Don Juan. It is where the *corazón* - heart, of ancient and exotic Sevilla still resides. On many of the doors you will notice a knocker in the form of a hand or a hand holding a fruit. The hand is supposed to represent Fátima the daughter of the prophet Mohammed while others believe the hand in reality embodies the five pillars of Islam: alms, creed, fasting, prayer and the pilgrimage to Mecca.

The beautiful *barrio* is one more testament to their community's contribution in creating the townscape and cultural outlook of this country. But the history that these alleyways belie is well hidden under its restoration and time faded memory. The first record of their presence in the city dates from the 4th century when the Christian Visigoths were here. Their situation changed more than likely in tune with their economic fortune, which seems to be the historical pattern. When the Moors arrived they were welcomed by the Jewish community who were about ready for a tolerant ruler. But fortunes took an unexpected turn for them and they were forced to leave first by the Almoravids and later by the Almohads. Into the Christian kingdoms they went until they were even forced to leave there. What is it about the subsequent religions of Christianity and Islam that refuse to accept their founding father: Judaism?

So, in the 13th century they returned to Sevilla where they were welcomed by Fernando III and the successive Christian rulers Alfonso X and Pedro I. They were allocated an area of some 40 acres by the Alcázar encompassing the neighbourhoods of *San Bartolomé, Santa Cruz* and *Santa María la Blanca*. But in the 14th century things turned sour again and human nature once more proved it is never far removed from its basic instincts. The Jews were the subject of persecution and rioting broke out in 1391 after the Archdeacon of Écija don Fernando Martínez, resident in Sevilla, went round the city to whip up anti-Semitism and he succeeded in sparking the tinder box.

The Jews had become very successful financiers, especially for don Pedro I, and with them out the way there would be no debts to pay and one or two nice houses back on the market. In March the first attack occurred with the civilian population looting their shops and attacking the Jews. The Sheriff – *el Alguacil Mayor*, put down the riot. But this didn't stop the Archdeacon from banging on the drum even harder and on 6th June the crowd crashed through the gates of the *Judería* with cries of *"Death to the Jews!"* Barrio Santa Cruz only had two gateways, one in the street *Mateos*

Gago and the other in *La Puerta de la Carne* that lead into the countryside. The bloodlust rioters entered from both ends at the same time and put men, women and children to the knife. The murder lasted a whole day and by the end of it the toll was 4,000 dead. Some managed to escape and begged protection from the King. But Enrique III was only 11 years old and his Regency was unable to offer guarantees in a land split by factions vying for power. When Enrique came of age though, one of the first things he did was have the Archdeacon arrested. He fined the people and *Ayuntamiento* – Town Hall, so much that it could not be paid in cash up front and took them 10 years to remit. The Jews saw one of their synagogues destroyed which stood in the space of *la Plaza de Santa Cruz* and the other two were expropriated and converted into churches: the temple of *San Bartolomé* and the parish church *Santa María la Blanca*. Only a few dozen families remained in the city.

In 1483 all Jews that refused baptism in Andalucía were expelled from the territory. Nine years later the process was complete when the remaining Jews were thrown out from Spain in 1492 as Spain chose to start a European un-enlightenment. But neither edict greatly affected Sevilla, as elsewhere, because there were so few Jews left to banish.

The *Santa Cruz* district possesses more *Flamenco Tablaos* today than it does churches. The famous *Plaza de Refinadores* holds a statue of the mythical Don Juan immortalised by writers, and as Sherlock Holmes has his 221b Baker Street so Don Juan has a real place for some of his fictitious actions in this *plaza*. *La Plaza de las Cruces* was also another literary haunt of his. It was also in this area that the writer (full name following) Miguel de Mañara y Vicéntelo de Leca (1627-79), who many believe to be the inspiration for Don Juan, lived. He later dedicated his life to the church after seeing his own funeral procession returning home late one night through the labyrinthine streets of *Santa Cruz*, a famous scene, which appears in Don Juan.

Fortunately though, in this picturesque corner of the world the area has retained the proportions and street plan given to it by its Jewish creators. This beautiful spot of *Andalucía* is peppered with *azoteas* – rooftop gardens overflowing with hanging flowers. Geranium, mint, carnation, jasmine, spikenard, bougainvillea, hibiscus, oleander make up the garland that crowns Sevilla's most decorative *barrio*.

Staying on the same side of the river, one of Sevilla's key shopping areas is to be found off *Plaza Nueva*, centred round the streets of *Velázquez*, *Tetúan*, *Sierpes* and *San Eloy*. Just off *calle Sierpes* is a plaque commemorating the site of the city's Royal prison, where Cervantes was temporarily installed in 1592 for non-payment of taxes and it is said where he first began Don Quixote, pronounced /don kee-**HO**-té/. His death in 1616 coincided on exactly the same day, and same year, as that of Shakespeare's on St. George's day, 23rd April and for that reason the date has been chosen by UNESCO to celebrate World Book Day, an idea first started in Catalonia in 1929.

At the end of *calle Sierpes* is *La Campana* an area reputed to be the original centre of Sevilla. (The geographic centre of the municipality is in *calle José Gestoso* where a marble shell set into the wall of a house marks the point from where all distances for legal and administrative matters were measured out in steps, leagues and miles.) The name *La Campana*, literally meaning 'bell', was given to that area as it wasonce the site a fire station and a bell would be rung the moment an engine was about to issue forth.

These streets display the tapestry of Sevillian society as the masses go bargain hunting. Among the modern establishments there are still one or two traditional shop keepers still plying their trade. The lively streets take on a market feel from springtime onwards when they are covered by tarpaulin to protect against the unreasonable sunlight. They are also a magnet for pick-pockets and those setting up gambling tables, which are illegal. Unfortunately, there is nothing that attracts them more than you, the visitor.

At the end of *Plaza Nueva*, near the cathedral, is the Town Hall – *Ayuntamiento*, sandwiched between *Plaza Nueva* and *Plaza San de Francisco*. The building is in two sections connected to appear as one. The original segment is toward the Cathedral and makes up a third of the present-day structure. It was decorated in the *Plateresque* style, after the silver *plateresque* manner of adornment popular in Europe at the time along Baroque lines. It wasn't until the second half of the 19th century when the other two thirds of the hall were added in a neo-classical style. The original council chambers were built in response to the city hosting the royal wedding of Carlos V of Germany and I of Spain and his wife to be, Isabel Queen of Portugal. The initial building, *el Corral de los Olmos*, situated by the Archbishop's Palace was chaotic and deemed insufficient for such an occasion. The city gentry decided it was time to move out of their chamber by the Cathedral and have a permanent residence worthy for civic business. The wedding took place in 1526, but construction of the Town Hall was not completed until 1572. It was paid for by a local noble whose funds ran out thus leaving the construction incomplete. You can see this by finding the rough bulks of stone still awaiting a sculptor's hand to finish them. It has been suggested that the job be completed but that idea hasn't caught the citizens' imagination. Much of its charm comes from its appearance as a work still in progress and something which adds to its unusual asymmetry.

Its main balcony looks out over *la Plaza de San Francisco* where much of the city's history has passed before it. Here the Inquisition held their first tribunals and burnings before they struck on the great idea of first trying their victims in the *plaza* and then parading them to a field now the formal gardens of *El Prado* - meaning prairie, and setting light to them there. At least it got the local population out of the city for the day. Bullfights were even held here in the *plaza* before the permanent *Plaza de Toros* was eventually set in place. In *Semana Santa* – Holy Week, part of the official route of religious processions goes by here when the *plaza* is packed with chairs and onlookers seated on either side of a barricaded walkway. In the *Corpus Christi* celebrations another large and centuries-old procession is also acted out here before finally returning to the cathedral. The Town Hall is one of the most beautiful *ayuntamientos* in all of Spain, which is no small thing in a country that has a fair collection of historic civic buildings.

You may have noticed around Sevilla on the buses, official posters, manhole covers and on the *Ayuntamiento* itself the curious symbol NO8DO.

The '8' here should be a skein of wool – *una madeja*, in Spanish. During the 13th century King Alfonso X, the Wise, for all his astuteness ran into financial difficulties and his son Prince Sancho, with the aid of his mother doña Violante, rose up in arms and gathered in the support of most of the other kingdoms to depose Alfonso. Only the Town Hall, Clergy and most importantly here, the people of Sevilla, where don Alfonso X had wisely taken refuge, stood by him. Even the nobles had ridden out to join Sancho. The citizens swore they would die by their King. Luckily as it happened, Alfonso passed away before such drastic measures were required. Before he went the way of the Dodo he bestowed on the city its now familiar and unique symbol NODO. The emblem contains the clever message encapsulated in the two syllables 'NO' and 'DO' with the skein of wool also playing a fundamental part in deciphering the Alfonso code. The combination of the three elements comes out as: '*NO madeja DO*', playing on the Andalusian phonetic pronunciation of '*No me ha dejado*': You haven't left me.

In *Plaza Pilatos* stands *La Casa de Pilatos*, a house in mixed Renaissance, Roman and *Mudéjar* style apparently modelled on Pontius Pilate's house in Jerusalem when its noble occupant, don Fadrique, went to the Holy Land. This sumptuous palace has some of the finest *patios* and some good examples of its combined styles that embrace what is referred to as the *Regional* Style. Sculpture from Rome, Greece and the Renaissance are in evidence. Lush gardens fill exuberant courtyards with refreshing fountains and colonnaded galleries overlooked by coffered ceilings. *'Fountains give from the land what the skies refuse to yield '*. *Mudéjar* style breathes colour and sumptuous geometrical carving into a complex of four quads and two gardens. Statues, columns, carving, 4th century art treasures and a Roman forum house plan with terracotta roof tiling are complemented by the exotic Arab influences that one can find everywhere in Andalucía. The visit may be short but town-houses round here do not come any better, especially after its recent retrieval from a ruinous state.

Nearby in *calle Santiago* is *el Corral del Duque*, the most impressive *corral* in the city. The communal building with its three-tiered wooden balconies set around a beautiful cobbled quad with fountain and lofty palm trees, is the only one of its kind left standing. Erected in the 17th century it is now a listed building. From outside its imposing walls one can only imagine the haven hidden inside, as the doors as kept firmly shut tight. The *corral* continues to provide private housing, albeit upgraded. Visiting dignitaries and Hollywood superstars from its golden era, like Douglas Fairbanks, were ushered in to have their picture taken amid this characteristic setting. A four-star hotel also enjoys the peaceful seclusion.

By 1st century BC the city was surrounded by walls, which were further extended by the Almohads to take in a total of 740 acres. In its most complete state there were 15 gates leading travellers to and fro the city. Today, in contrast, there survive just two *La Puerta de La Macarena*, which was much restored in the 19th century. It was through here that visiting Monarchs entered when they came to the city. The other is the minor gateway of *El Postigo* in the Arenal area near the cathedral. The names of the former gates, now names of areas in the city, still retain their original titles telling us today in which direction the inhabitants were headed: *La Puerta de Jerez, La Puerta de Carmona, La Puerta de Córdoba* etc. Or which part of the city the gate connected to the centre: *La Puerta de Triana, La Puerta del Arenal* and *La Puerta de Macarena*.

The city walls did well to last as far in time as they did, but with the redirecting of the Guadalquivir River the once heavy flooding that the city had endured throughout its history, ceased to plague it. So, the city walls that had been left in place as a primary defence against the floodwaters, were now no longer needed. With the threat removed and the poor state of much of the stonework as well as its impediment to commerce and communications, they were torn down. In 1861 the city lost its picturesque Moorish crenellations and with their disappearance also went some 600 hundred years of history and a beautiful remnant of her Moorish past.

Today some forlorn fragments have remained scattered about the city especially the impressive stretch along *calle Resolana Andueza* in La Macarena district, 450m in length with one principal polygonal tower and seven smaller square turrets. These two sections of the city's once far-reaching walls stand surprisingly well-preserved.

Opposite this last stretch of Moorish defences is the Andalusian Parliament building, originally planned as a hospital and formerly known as *El Hospital de las Cinco Llagas* – the Hospital of the Five Wounds. It was started in 1545 and halted before completion in the 17th century. It is almost 186 yards square in shape. Funds ran out and it has been endearingly left incomplete like the Town Hall in *Plaza Nueva*. It is an impressive two-storey building like the *Palacio de San Telmo* with a long, stretching Sevillian Baroque façade, colourful domes on its corner towers and a characteristically high-decorated entrance.

Moving back to the other side of town in *calle San Fernando* is the splendid Baroque University of Sevilla, which was once the tobacco factory and whose most famous employee was the smouldering Carmen. It has three Royal Academies: Medicine, Arts and Fine Arts. The faculties of Science, Veterinary and Law were added later. It is the second biggest building in the whole peninsular after *El Real de Escorial* near Madrid. Sevilla saw the very first potato, tomato and tobacco arrive from the New World. It was here that Europe was first supplied with tobacco. Initially snuff was produced until the fashion changed to smoking. The factory here was expanded to meet the demand and as it was prolific so was the structure they threw up to accommodate the growth in business. The Sevillian doctor Nicolás Monardes was the first to introduce the plant into Europe in the 16th century defending its curative qualities. We take the word 'nicotine' from his name. Since then his theory has gone up in smoke.

You would be forgiven for thinking that this had once been a palace and not a factory; it is a far cry from the wool mills of industrial England. It is 200 yards by 160 in size and it even has its own chapel and prison, which was used for keeping captured smugglers. The moat with its turrets, which once protected and still surround great part of the edifice, is now empty.

The factory, made of a soft-yellowed stone that glows mildly in the daylight, was erected in 1620 the same year as the Pilgrim Fathers sailed from Plymouth to the New World, a time when the imperial balance of power in Europe was about to tip in England's favour. Its entrances are triumphal affairs and its interior is that of long barrel vaults. The cathedral nave-like ceilings lead between bright *patios* where fountains play their familiar tune for the studious passers-by. There is one large colonnaded *patio* in its southwest corner. In its centre there is a smaller, though, nonetheless impressive courtyard with another dozen *patios* scattered around it.

If you fancy a look see then just go right on in, but make sure you don't burst into a crowded lecture hall while in search of a loo because here Spanish lecture halls are packed!

Just off at an angle on the other side of *La Puerta de Jerez* in the direction of the cathedral is a small chapel, *la Capilla de la Puerta Jerez*, that once served Sevilla's original university *El Colegio de Santa María*, founded in 1506 by Maese Rodrigo de Santaella. The chapel is all that remains. At the time Sevilla had in fact three universities. Now it has two. The second is out of town north-eastwards, named after Pablo de Olavide, the 18th century *Asistente de Sevilla* (1767-78), who did much to organise the city and bring it up to date in what were poor economic times for the area and the region's capital. He was also responsible for installing German and Swiss immigrants in the depopulated Sierra Norte - the hills in the Sierra Morena mountain range that run to the north of the capital.

If you are in need of refreshment on leaving the old Tobacco Factory then across the street in *calle San Fernando* there are several establishments that serve ice-cream, sandwiches, beer and the like and at least two of them have garden *patios* that give out onto the Moorish walls of *los Reales Alcázares*.

Behind the faculty and centred around the avenue of *La Avenida de Perú* are the consulates of Peru, Honduras, Uruguay, the USA and Chile. The decorated buildings were constructed as part of the Iberian-American Expo of 1929, a showcase of American and Iberian business and technology of the era, which due to the Great Depression of the '30s never fulfilled their primary purpose. The Peru Pavilion in a neo-Inca interpretation, if such a thing can be imagined, is arguably the most impressive of the consulates. The other American consulates were put up in Hispanic colonial style. Next to them stands *El Teatro de Lope Vega*, named after the great local playwright, who turned out his works daily! The theatre is the city's première venue for dance and drama leaving the bigger, newer and more central theatre of La Maestranza by the river to entertain illusions of grandeur with its classical music concerts and operatic season. The theatre also incorporated *El Pabellón de Sevilla*, as well as *el Casino de la Exposición*, which is a fine example of Neo-Baroque architecture in the city. Opposite and set into *El Prado* park is what is left of the exotic looking *Pabellón de Portugal*. By the river we find the grand *El Pabellón de Argentina* and the less spectacular *Pabellón de Guatemala*. If you walk further up along *El Paseo de las Delicias* there are some gardens here by the Argentine Pavilion and on the other side of it are the remaining pavilions of Mexico looking very Aztec, Colombia looking very Native Indian and oddly enough *El Pabellón de Marruecos* - Morocco, which was a Spanish colony at the time and whose pavilion features hand carvings by artisans from the Maghreb.

The busiest of the '29 Expo buildings, however, was not constructed as a pavilion but as a hotel and today it still serves this purpose. The Hotel Alfonso XIII, pronounced /**TRE**-sei/ from *trece* meaning thirteen not thirteenth, after the name of the last King of Spain before the Second Republic was established in 1931. The grand *Mudéjar* cube stands coyishly yet reassuringly behind a few palm trees and ornate iron grilles keeping it at a safe distant back from *calle San Fernando*, next to the old university building. It is one of Spain's best hotels if not in actual fact the nation's flagship of hospitality and luxury. An Arab prince came to stay and decided that he would have the rooms completely renovated in his suite to accommodate his entourage. You will not have to go to such extremes to enjoy the Alfonso XIII, a drink in its hallway encircling the inner *patio* is a must if you desire a quiet moment in elegant surroundings. The exterior is as luxuriant as its interior with *azulejos* ceramics decorating the façade. There are four *mirador* – vantage point towers, reminiscent of an Andalusian farmstead – *hacienda*, where the owner would climb up to survey his land and... workers. The interior is sumptuous and thought fittingly enough to house the heads of state at one of the European Summits held in Sevilla. However, despite all this not even the Alfonso XIII can claim to be the '29 Expo's architectural centrepiece.

Vast construction was undertaken from 1909-1929, which also left Sevilla with its elegant botanical park *El Parque Maria Luisa* across from the consulates; well worth a stroll especially in the morning when the police off-load and promenade their pure bred Spanish steeds through its leafy avenues. The park was originally part of the gardens of the *Palacio de San Telmo* and contained one of Sevilla's first ever *Neo-Mudéjar* buildings: the Queen's Sewing Room - *Costurero de La Reina* built in 1890, which now stands outside the grounds and opposite the park. The Neo-Mudéjar became widely used across the city and many examples still exist. The city would be lacking without them among its collection.

But the explosion of building that lifted Sevilla into the 20th century had at its centre a *tour de force* in the gigantic semi-circular *Plaza de España*. It took 14 years to complete (1914-28) and needed around 1,000 people to do it. A total of 50,000m^2 of which 19,000m^2 was construction and the rest left as open space. It flanks the east side of the park and this monument by Aníbal González, the chief of works for the 1929 Expo, and finished by Vicente Traver is possibly the world's most spectacular edifice in red-brick! It tells the story of the *Reconquista de España* from the hands of the Moors. The decoration is in polychrome tiles, carved bricks, and white marble. The style is playful at times with ceramic balustrades leaping in high arches over the 525m canal that curves round the *plaza*. The style is a mix of *sevillano*, more locally known as *Regional*, and the classic from the 16th, 17th and 20th centuries. The large court is centred by a fountain, which often attracts flamenco troupes to gather for their group photographs. The building is justly emblematic of Sevilla. There is a main pavilion, *El Pabellón de España*, in the centre of the colourful red brick semi-circular monument. Now it is the *Capitanía General Militar* and contains sumptuous interiors, *patios* and a 600-seater theatre, arguably the most beautiful in Sevilla, with a glorious stained glass dome built by a North American company of the time. Fanning out on either side run colonnaded walkways with coffered ceilings that link up two smaller pavilions and then continue to their journey's end by connecting with two highly impressive towers. Twinned and ornate they stand at 80m tall at opposing points of the semi-circular structure, ever present on the city's skyline. They are an architectural delight and such a structure would probably look out of place, but not here in Sevilla. It is now occupied by government offices, one of which is the immigration office and the other is owned by the M.o.D and *Junta de Andalucía*. Try and avoid the coach loads of tourists arriving before lunch and be careful here at night if you decide to catch a glimpse of the sight when floodlit. Part of this temple to ceramic art is now under restoration. The two principal bridges will take 18 months of work to restore to their former glory and the best part of half a million euros. Soon it should be as resplendent as it was during those 6 months of grandeur in 1929 when it was briefly the stage for the *Ibero-Americano* Expo.

At the entrance to the Expo stands the statue of El Cid the knight warrior who spear headed much of the campaign against the Moors. Now it stands a little isolated amid traffic. A copy also exists in New York opposite the Hispanic Society.

The *Parque de María Luisa* was donated to the city by its owner the dowager Duchess of Montpensier, María Luisa Fernanda de Borbón. The park was originally part of the gardens of her palace, the enormous and decorative *El Palacio de San Telmo*, which was initially started in 1682 and completed in 1796. It was built to train naval officers and took as its name Saint Thomas, the protector of seafarers. It is one of the biggest buildings in the city and has the grandest Baroque entrance verging on the Rococo. Its north side is surmounted by twelve intricate statues of illustrious *sevillanos*. It is a veritable rooftop museum of sculpture. The palace was then occupied in 1849 by Antoin d'Orleans, Duke of Montpensier the son of the King of France who married the Spanish princess María Luisa, *La Infanta*, sister of Queen Isabel II. María Luisa donated it in 1893 to the people of Sevilla. The building is presently the official residence of the Andalusian presidency.

In 1849 María Luisa had brought in a Frenchman to design the palace garden. With her donation it was annexed to the exhibition site and another Frenchman, this time garden-designer Jean-Claude Nicolás Forestier, was hired to maintain the original style and pave the way for the rest of the 346 acre Expo area. The park he left behind incorporated history and people, botany and beauty, architecture and folly, *plazas* and small spaces, water and grotto. *Glorietas* were designed and dedicated to people in history while folly buildings peer out from behind trees and across water. The formal mixed with the informal. The vegetation was brought from around the globe and not only served to decorate but also to inform with most of the planting having its own plaque to identify it. Here you can, *"read, be inspired, draw, paint, write, love, hear trills and silence..."* And if you do all that and are not too careful you can even have your bag stolen.

One sculpture of special note is found near the entrance to the park on the west side near the north tower of *La Plaza de España*. It features a bust and a bench of marble that encircles the base of a century-old cypress tree. Seated under the hanging branches are three *señoritas* representing the three facets of Love: Love Deceived, Love Fulfilled, and Love Lost. All this was in homage to the great *andaluz* poet Gustavo Adolfo Bécquer and it certainly has the desired effect of making you stop and take note of your thoughts. The park is a maze of discovery and a Pandora's box of delights. It was after all, carved from previous gardens called *'Las Delicias.'* It is filled with strawberry trees, alamos, acacias, eucalyptus, banana plants, chestnut, myrtles, roses, bougainvillea, passion flowers, rose-bays and geraniums.

"The Parque de María Luisa was transformed into an extraordinary blend of bustling European Avenues, peaceful oriental courtyards and romantic landscaped gardens, deserving of every kind of praise…"

And that is how we find the park today.

To the far end of the park is the pretty *Plaza de América*. Also part of the '20s Expo with some stunning architecture enfolding the square on three sides. Again there are examples of the Neo-*Mudéjar* and Neo-Classical. The *Pabellón Mudéjar* was also built by Aníbal González and its influence from the *Alcázar* in Sevilla is clear. Opposite, in this delightful corner of Sevilla, is the intricate yet formidable looking Plateresque *Pabellón* in Renaissance style. Today it is the *Museo Arqueológico*, which contains many of Sevilla's ancient remains including many Tartessian and Roman objects of interest from the ancient sites of *El Carambolo* and *Itálica* respectively. It is one of Spain's most important archaeological treasure houses with its Phoenician, Greek and Carthaginian remains and the most important in the land when it comes to Roman sculpture.

The third building in the *plaza*, in the Gothic style this time, was once the Royal Pavilion built for the Monarchy and today is occupied by *La Junta*. All three were built for the '29 Expo and the divergent styles blend harmoniously because they all tend toward beauty and grandeur. This a truly beautiful spot and often missed by the independent traveller but sadly not by the package tour.

"Don't forget that the soul of a city is its colour. Colour; all our life it's that: colour."
Alfonso Grosso.

There is also a daily spectacle given by its resident white dove population, no doubt descendants from their '29 and '92 Expo ancestors realised at the opening of the fairs, in its adjoining *Plaza de Paloma* - Dove Square. Here they descend like a vast spiralling cloud and are fed by the local bird lovers. If you've never been to Trafalgar Square then you could always get your photo taken here. After all, every *sevillano* has in their home a snapshot of their child feeding the doves in the *plaza*.

When the final Expo '29 stone was in place 117 buildings had been constructed, many of which still survive today. It is surprising just how many were put up at that time across Sevilla and how strong the Neo-*Mudéjar* influence was. As a counterpoint to Sevilla, Barcelona held a World Fair during the same year, which saw the unveiling of Mies van der Rohe's Barcelona Pavillion; as far removed from any regionalist influences as the the traditional imagination could travel at that time. While Sevilla was looking to her past Barcelona was looking to the future. The minimalist marble, steel and glass structure was rebuilt after it fell into disuse and stands alongside the *Palau Nacional* – National Palace, reflecting its timeless lines in its adjacent mirror pool.

The Expo never realised its full potential and its Master of Works Aníbal González passed away just four days before it opened with its gardener Jean-Claude Nicolás Forstier dying a year after the exhibition. One could believe that the scheme had been cursed but its park and buildings have left a legacy behind them in step with the extensive cultural heritage already given by the previous passing emperors and monarchs. It is quite likely that the architects that went to work on Sevilla's Expo of '29 rest happy that they in their time seized their day and did it for the greater glory of their city.

"In 500 years time the descendants of those that visit this exposition will see with their own eyes these same buildings, mellowed by the passing of the centuries, but with the same magnificence of today in their lines and solid construction."
[Expo pamphlet of the time]

Leading from the main transport artery, sandwiched between the park María Luisa and the river Guadalquivir, stretches Sevilla's grandest avenue, which surprisingly many guide books ignore and most tourists miss. *La Avenida de la Palmera* - the Bel Air of Sevilla is an impressive palm-tree lined avenue as its name suggests. What the name doesn't tell you is that behind the swaying palms are many of the biggest palaces and private houses in the city. It is the most exclusive city centre address and contains the remainder of the grand buildings of the 1929 Expo. Standing shoulder to shoulder with them are more modern examples, as well as one huge convent and church. If it is not too hot and you haven't got a car, then a stroll down the avenue reaps rewards.

Before we take to the other side of the river though, we should first visit another museum in Sevilla: *El Museo de Bellas Artes* – the Museum of Fine Arts. Sevilla has a fair collection that any city would be proud to boast. The Fine Arts Museum is reputed to be Spain's most important after El Prado for religious paintings and that is exactly what it contains. If you haven't been satisfied for images of the Virgin and crucified Christ then this is the place for you.

The building on the other hand is a different matter. It is worth entering just for the interior alone. It was once the convent of the Merced and still has silent *patios*, colonnades and impressive rooms. The architect Juan de Oviedo, who worked on this grand edifice, also created part of *La Casa de Pilatos*. It contains three *patios*, an imperial staircase said to have been copied by ensuing architects and the quite unbelievable *Claustro Grande* – Great Cloister, where the art on display takes second place. It was completed by Leandro de Figueroa with the impressive neo-classical façade was added in the 19th century. The construction and consequent redevelopment of its space to accommodate the art collection did no favours for promoting *sevillano* efficiency for getting things done. Not only did the roof continually cave in throughout the 19th century, but things were not finally finished until 1985 and even then rooms were often closed to the public.

The museum's art collection covers religious subjects from local artists. Once you have been round you'll find it hard to accept it as a provincial museum. Spanish medieval, Sevillian medieval, Renaissance, *retablos*, Mannerism and Baroque vie for your attention and they may well win it. Unfortunately, the really great works that should be hanging here are pulling in the crowds in Madrid, in El Prado.

If you find the place a little depleted then you would be right. It is not that the building is too big for its own purpose. The French marched through in 1810 when Napoleon put his brother on the Spanish throne, which didn't go down too well with the non-French speaking population. The French army arrived in the city and Marshal Soult decided to permanently borrow 999 pieces from the museum. Most of these have never been returned. The French army also did one or two other things in the town that didn't go down a treat either but that was nothing compared their *pièce de resistance* in the Alhambra palace in Granada, which they damaged severely.

The circumstances under which the museum came by its collection were far from conventional. In 1836 the government in all its wisdom expropriated all church, monastic and convent property. The requisitioned works of art in Sevilla were put under one roof in the now ex-convent, which had first been granted to the monks of *La Merced* way back in the 13th century.

Zurbarán, Murillo, Valdés Leal, the outsider Goya and the foreigner El Greco are in evidence. However, ironically, local-born artist Velázquez is exiled up north in El Prado. But canvas painting is not all that are on display, one can also find examples of embroidery, decorative arts, furniture, gold work, pottery and sculpture.

The *plaza* that spends its lazy days in front of the museum offers the visitor a place for positive contemplation and on Sunday it is a browser's art market.

Crossing the river and into the neighbourhood of Triana you arrive in the '*Alma*' – soul, of Sevilla. This once predominantly gypsy area, the most interesting part by the river, stages some of the most famous *pasos* during *Semana Santa*, the biggest pilgrimage train to *El Rocío* and features strongly in many of the songs of old Seville. The primary nightlife is to be found around the street *calle Betis* by the river. The *barrio* also hosts a lot of flamenco and fiestas around May, all of which are posted in the cultural guide *Giraldillo*. The area is no *tour de force* of monuments but a highly pleasant part of the city where a very neighbourly atmosphere still prevails. Of all the churches in Sevilla the oldest is to be found in Triana, *La Iglesia de Santa Ana* in the quiet *Plaza Sacra Familla*. Santa Ana was founded by Alfonso X, the Wise in the 13th century and there are stories of a tunnel that connect it with the cathedral on the other side of the river. Just next to this church is the delightful bar *'Bodega Siglo XVIII'*, cosy with part of an old church's cloister as an awe-inspiring backdrop for an evening's drinking.

The *barrio* is the prime producer of ceramics in the city especially in the ancient art of *azulejos*, brightly coloured tiling in Arab or *Mudéjar* designs. It was an art form handed down to them from the Moors and Sevilla sprouts *azulejos* from all angles. You will feel their presence everywhere. The Moor left many tangible things in Sevilla but it is said that they left in its people a special sensitivity for the aesthetic. The chief ceramic workshops are in *calle Alfarería*. Over the centuries there have been influxes of Italians, Flemish, Germans and French who have all played their part in the development of ceramic art in the city. The 20th century saw a renaissance in the textile, which still remains popular to this day.

To the north of Triana and beyond is *La Cartuja* – meaning 'Charterhouse', an immense area of some 198 acres, which was used for the Expo '92. Sevilla. Ever since 1717 when the city's economy went under with it relinquishing its monopoly trade with the New World, Sevilla has forever been seeking a way to kick start its economy and begin the long walk back to their long lost position in National and World affairs. In every *sevillano* there is a sense that their city has been forgotten and it is their duty and destiny to make the world sit up and take note once more. To understand this will bring us closer to understanding why the locals possess an almost tangible pride and where great part of their self-belief stems from. Of course they do also enjoy some beautiful monuments, good food and lively fiestas on a regular basis. If they achieve the centre-stage recognition they so dearly yearn for then they will be the first city to have been culturally dominant in their history.

Faculties of the university have taken up residence on this modern Expo site as well as an increasing the number of bars. A number of tourist attractions and a theatre are also situated here among the remnants of the Expo pavillions. *La Cartuja*, so named for the Carthusian monastery founded on the site in 1400, enjoyed comparable seclusion from the old town and held the remains of *Cristóbal Colón* for 30 years. All that has changed now and the only agricultural land left of the original area has been sandwiched between the Alamillo Park and the Science Park.

When the government repossessed ecclesiastical property in 1836 and subsequently exercised a cultural exorcism not seen since the time of the Expulsion of the Moors and Jews in 1492. For *La Cartuja* this meant that the monastery was sold on by the Mendizábal administration in Sevilla, and more than 400 years of history was exchanged for hard cash. The fortunate buyer was an Englishman, Charles Pickman from Liverpool, who made wholesale changes to the place and set up a ceramics factory in 1841, *Pickman Sociedad Anónima La Cartuja de Sevilla*, which remained in service until as recently as 1982. He was later made a Marquis: *Marqués de Pickman*. The chimney stacks are now as much a part of the monastery's skyline as are its domes. It has all moulded into one to such an extent that if anyone were to tamper with the industrialised part of the monastery the locals would surely complain of the 'heretical' damage. It is astounding what one can grow accustomed to over time.

The 1992 Expo in Sevilla was held the same year Madrid became European Capital of Culture and Barcelona staged their memorable Olympics. Only the cultural capital was a flop. The other two events exported Spain's name and fame around the globe. For the first time in its modern historical life the nation felt as if it had finally got back on its feet.

It may have ended well but things couldn't have started worse for the Expo when a specially commissioned replica of the first vessel to circumnavigate the globe sank as it left the slipway. Then the ship that was retracing Columbus' journey across the Atlantic suffered a mutiny. Next up, the centrepiece pavilion disappeared in flames only a week before the event was supposed to open. And to round things off, on the very eve of the event police apparently opened fire on demonstrators with live ammunition. The public, however, turned up in their droves and the word of mouth was that it was everything it was cracked up to be and more. Even the mortal heat that sweeps through these plains every July and August didn't keep the foreign visitors away, even though the whole area had been heavily supplied with free water and medical services, just in case.

To this very day the people here still talk fondly about the event, as if it had only happened yesterday. When they celebrated the tenth anniversary of the Expo they held an exhibition entitled: *'Those 6 months.'* It has had much to do with the making of the present state of mind of the citizens if only to give them some self-confidence for a modern future in a very traditional city.

There were 110 countries and 22 international organisations present. By all accounts the modern British pavilion had played its part by offering the visitors something new, which was the spirit of the occasion. Its architecture was cutting edge with its façade a cascade of water and it housed modern exhibits. Fortunately, it a reproduction Georgian town house hadn't been put up. However, the British were a bit tight fisted in not leaving it behind as a gift to Sevilla and instead took it with them. Most nations by contrast left their structures standing and they have lived on as a permanent advert to each country. Interestingly, the Mexican Pavilion was built in the shape of an 'X' as a message to the Spanish to tell them that their country is spelt with an 'X' and not a 'J' in *Méjico*.

The investment was enormous and left Sevilla with much needed infrastructural changes. A circular motorway was built plus a huge four-lane bridge crossing. A controversial high-speed train link with Madrid at extreme cost was put in place. The capital was linked to the south instead of with the nation's leading industrial city Barcelona to the east. The city was greatly blessed with government funds and this some circles say was because Sevilla was the hometown of Felipe González, the President at the time. It has left the city with excellent communications, the beautiful Alamillo Park and a river path that any metropolis would be keen to have.

The most important aspect of Sevilla throughout its history has been its river. No river, no Sevilla. The city is unique in Spain because it is an inland port and they don't come much more inland than this, 65km from the coast, the same as London. The mouth of the river is located by the town of Sanlúcar de Barrameda. Sevilla's river at high tide is saline from the seawater and at low tide it is 'sweeter' as the concentration works the other way favouring the river that flows downstream. The Romans called the river *Baetis* after the southern region that they named *Baetica*, supposedly after the mythological King Beto of the Tubal dynasty. It is the longest river in Andalucía at 657km and the fifth biggest in Spain. The river flows from its source high up in the crags of Cazorla far off in the eastern province of Jaén. It flooded Sevilla regularly and that was why the Romans preferred their town of Itálica on a plateau, away from the river's flood plains. Those that lived in the Guadalquivir depression in the other lesser Roman town of Hispalis had their houses built on stilts. The Moorish walls helped act as a defence against the flooding but it wasn't until the 19th century that work on the river's point of entry into the city was tapped and diverted away from the city centre. But the engineering work wasn't enough to stop flooding altogether. Records show the first big flood was 1626, then 1796, 1892, 1947 and the last flood was 1961 but this time from another river the Tamarguillo. Now they have it under control and the heavy body of the river winds its way behind Triana out of harm's way. What actually flows through Sevilla is a canal and not the river itself. The canal passes by the city and eventually rejoins the main body of water and continues out to the Atlantic. There was a time when the northern part of the canal was dried out as a solution to the flooding. But with the advent of the '92 Expo a complete overhaul meant that water would be channelled through its historic course again.

The Welsh writer Jan Morris, who knows a thing or two about Spain, believes that the Spanish have an ability when it comes to building bridges. If you were to come to Sevilla then you would be inclined to agree with her. The fact that the citizens survived for centuries with just the one bridge and then frantically built the rest in 75 years is odd to say the least. But Sevilla made up for lost time and now has a handsome collection. So, after the Triana bridge was given the industrialist treatment and erected in iron in 1845 no other bridge was undertaken until the 1929 Expo. The second was *el Puente de San Telmo.* In 1968 another was finished. It looked as if bridge building was fashionable all of a sudden. Next in Los Remedios it was *el Puente del Generalísimo* named after Franco.

Then four new bridges were constructed across the river for the '92

Expo and they have given the city an avant-garde edge, which has done for Sevilla what Gaudí did for Barcelona and what the Guggenheim has achieved for Bilbao. The most impressive of these last four is el Alamillo bridge by the controversial Valencian architect Calatrava. It stands as tall as an Egyptian pyramid at 150 metres inclined at an angle of 58° with 13 struts holding the main structure in check, reminiscent of strings, giving an unmistakeable impression of a harp. The locals call the bridge '*el Puente de la Buena salud*' – the bridge of good health, due to its over erect stance.

At the end of the tow-path towards San Jerónimo Park there is... an egg, from Russia looking more fibreglass than Fabergé. It was constructed by a Georgian artist, Zurab K. Tsereteli (d.1995) to mark the Discovery of the New World and to symbolise Russia's gratitude to the USA for helping with their transition to democracy. Inside this 15m tall 'egg' is an image of *Cristóbal Colón* called 'Birth of a New Man'.

The connection between the egg and Columbus occurs in the anecdote of Columbus meeting with the Spanish crown when he tried to get funding for his voyage. They insisted it was futile because the world was flat. To prove that nothing was impossible he asked them to stand an egg on its end. They laughed saying that too was impossible, until Columbus took the egg and lightly hit it on the table leaving it standing upright.

The Georgian sculpture is not liked greatly by the locals who take their appreciation of art seriously, albeit traditionally, but at least it is something that marks man's presence and livens up an otherwise dead corner of the city. A replica stands in front of the UNESCO building in Paris. The egg was planned to be part of a two-piece work with the second sculpture standing in Puerto Rico, but the 120m tall *'Birth of a New World'* was not well-received and the burden of undertaking its construction fell to the town of Cataño. The metal was left rusting by the sea.

It is hard to pass along the river on a popular afternoon after the *siesta* and not recall the impressionist image of Seurat's *'Bathers'* that hangs in the National Gallery. The skateboarders, cyclists, anglers, walkers, dog owners comparing, rowers pulling their boats out, scooters, water passing through the reeds, lovers' hands passing through their hair, the occasional car, a police car, the late night tourist boats, carousers in paddle boats. All this makes up the *paseo* - stroll.

The locals are very much shaped by their Moorish, Spanish Baroque and Roman influenced houses and especially their river, which has marked the passing of time. The *alegria*, dignity, beauty and proportion of the buildings in the old centre has imprinted its character on the people.

> *'We shape our buildings: thereafter they shape us.'*
> Sir Winston Churchill.

The scale of a typical Andalusian street with its serpentine curves or elongated lines rarely allows you see to the end. Whitewashed walls, inhumanly clean at times stand along the road side and façades decorated by aesthetic iron grilles protect their contents. The attraction of these town houses comes not from what they show but from what they hide. Andalusian house design is the great flirt of European architecture; she keeps you at a safe distance and shows you just enough to pique your interest and desire, out of reach behind her slender and deceiving bars. She is the tease of the party: her front door is open and you can go to the porch gate but that is as far as you will ever get. You came so close, yet never arrived: that's why the image stays with you. Would the eyes have been pleased beyond that door or disappointed? You will never know.

The narrow streets that wind between the town houses serve as thoroughfares rarely as a vantage point for viewing anything. The house fronts are on top of you in these walled-up passageways. Even from the opposite pavement it is difficult to appreciate a Sevillian town house properly. The best you can do when photographing anything is stand at one end of the street and look down it like the barrel of a gun. This is how most people end up taking their photos. One street is apparently the same as another and yet no two façades are alike. But the diverse buildings bob with life like regal flagships decked out with bunting in overcrowded moorings. The *rejas* – ornate characteristic window grilles, have become an art form in a city susceptible to adornment. For the most part they date from the 19th century.

It's a fact, well-known by those who have spent any time amongst the *sevillanos*, that they are difficult, though far from impossible, people to infiltrate. The *rejas* reflect their citizens in this respect: they have a welcoming and attractive aspect but are not as open in nature as they may appear. The locals are more accessible than their houses though and the grilles pose greater problems for the fire brigade.

Streets in spring are filled with the smell of orange blossom and jasmine. Doorsteps are scrubbed and water splashed onto the pavement in front of buildings to clean it and take the sting out of the summer heat. Yellow powder is in evidence on almost every street, spread around doorways and the nooks between walls and pavements. This has been put down to deter dogs from marking their territory.

Sevilla also possesses that rare phenomenon of an optical illusion and strangely enough involves the emblem of the city: the Giralda. You can see the Giralda from *calle Trabajo* in Triana, at least 700 metres in the distance. If you walk down the street toward it and the river after about 400m you will come out in calle Betis, from where you'll see that it's further away than when you started – and not a lot of people know that about the city.

It is claimed that all Sevilla is a garden and yet gardens are not a preoccupation in Spain. There may be a greater need for greenery in a land deprived of rain but many of the 'supposed' gardens here are in actual fact private. There are some parks but still the city is lacking. Sevilla may appear greener than Madrid but, as in the capital, supply does not meet demand even though the list seems a long one: 17 gardens and parks of varying size and condition are to be found in Sevilla.

Participating in the Counter-Reformation, Sevilla became what could easily be called a 'monastic city'. In 1671 it housed 45 monasteries and 28 convents. The Augustinians, Dominicans, Franciscans and Jesuits were the principal orders. The open road for Catholicism that Fernando and Isabel had created was quickly jammed by religious traffic and transformed Spain into the most popular country for monastic orders. Ironically, the monastery was a system developed by the North Africans, the very people they had just thrown out.

Today there stands some 136 churches and other religious buildings including 7 convents and 8 monasteries. If church hopping is your thing then there will be much to delight you. Colour, casting, shrines, images, silver and centuries-old interiors are easy to come by. Here are a handful of notables:

San Luis by Leonardo de Figueroa started in 1699 an impressive façade with two octagonal towers and a mix of strong colours. This Baroque church is one of the biggest in the city and one of the best-hidden in *calle San Luis*. In its interior are paintings by Lucas Valdés. The building is audacious, bright and Sevillian Baroque at its boldest.

San Marco is in the same street and at a beautiful crossroads of neighbourly activity and architecture. The tower is the reason for coming and you would be forgiven for thinking that it was once a Moorish minaret like the Giralda. It is in fact much later *Mudéjar* dating from the 14th century but it is purer in form than the Giralda. It gives an idea of what the big guy could have looked like had it not been revamped by the Christians.

El Divino Salvador is on the erstwhile site of a Roman Basilica, Visigothic cathedral and in 830, the city's first mosque by Ibn Abaddas. The Moors used the area for silk trading. An inscription in Arabic dating from the 10th century still remains in the church and tells of the reforms made when the mosque was built. The *Patio de Naranjos* – orange tree courtyard, contains the original Moorish walls now sunk into the foundations as well as the base of the minaret. Your knees touch the top of the Arab arches.

The prime districts of the old centre are *Santa Cruz, El Arenal,* the extensive *El Centro* and *La Macarena*. All this is enclosed by the modern areas of *La Paz, León XIII, Vista Hermosa, Retiro Obrero, La Barzola, El Fontanal, La Calzada, San Bernardo* and *El Porvernir*. Opposite on the other side of the canal or 'river' are the two areas of Triana and Los Remedios. We have taken a look at the main centres of interest but still there is more to see in this city. It is worth to briefly tour and note one or two curiosities that are scattered about.

We start from Sevilla's present day epicentre: *La Plaza de La Virgen de los Reyes* at the foot of La Giralda. Near here is *calle Marmóles* where we can find tucked away in this forgotten corner the remaining three columns from the Roman Temple of Hercules and Mars. These columns are said to be the ones that Hercules himself drove into the ground when he founded the city. Four of these columns stand proudly at either end of the boulevard in the *Alameda de Hércules*, which have been restored to its former glory. The columns were placed here in the 16th century along with the statues of Caesar and Hercules.

In *calle Susona* is the skull of a Jewish woman who, for the love of her Christian knight, revealed her family's plot to do away with him and then looked on as she saw them executed for it. She was later consumed by remorse for her actions and according to her wishes her skull is displayed here to warn others against committing such an act.

The area also hides its churches well, which were once synagogues. But we all now know the tragic chapter of the Jew in this corner of Andalucía: dispossessed not once but thrice.

La Plaza de San Leandro is where don Juan Tenorio, the 17th century nobleman in Tirso de Molino's story *El Burlador de Sevilla y Convidado de Piedra* – The Rogue of Seville and the Stone Guest (Don Juan to most non-Spanish speakers, published in 1615), is supposed to have lived. *El Pila de Pato* – the Duck's Basin, was moved here from the Alameda area. It is also the *plaza* where the painter Diego de Velázquez was born. Today a statue in his honour stands in *Plaza de los Refinadores*.

Saint Teresa of Ávila believed that any mortal that could resist the temptations of Seville would be received unto heaven. And it is the city, not the *Burlador*, that seduces the thousands of visitors each year. Little do they know of the sin they are committing.

The area behind the church of *El Divino Salvador* hosts the city's oldest mercantile district, once the sight of the Roman Forum and the first great mosque of Moorish *Isbiliya*, it is Sevilla's ground zero. The shops today are stowed away in nooks and crannies. Watchmakers, lace makers and jewellers all huddle together. The *Plaza de Salvador* in front of the pink-faced Salvador church was the original meeting place of the old city.

Calle Cuna leads off from the *plaza* and at the end is *El Palacio de Lebrija*, a palace built in the 15th century but later heavily redecorated by doña Regla Manjón, who 'lifted' whole mosaics from the nearby Roman city of Itálica. The entire first level is covered with these mosaics. There are also architectural remains and works of art from other palaces on display. The walls are covered in yellow Triana *azulejos*. Elsewhere in the building floors are tiled in a typically Spanish geometrical style known as *opus scetile*, which include some of the finest examples of the art form. Today it is open to the public for a modest fee.

Moving across the street we arrive in an area that eventually runs through to the Macarena district and near the Andalusian Parliament. It has three convents to its name, and ten churches of note. The *Convento de Santa Paula* is so rich in artistic treasure that it has been classified as a historic monument. In *calle Sol* is the oldest house in the city: *La Casa del Rey Moro*, noted for its beautiful colonnaded patio where each column is different in style.

Nearby in *calle Dueñas* is *El Palacio de las Dueñas* a huge private residence. It is surprising to find such a palace here due to the tight confines of the neighbourhood. It belongs to Europe's most aristocratic titled family. The owner was the late Duquesa de Alba. The Duchess possessed the most aristocratic titles and according to etiquette Queen Elizabeth II should bow to her and not the other way round. Apparently visits can be arranged.

Calle de la Feria is one of Sevilla's longest and liveliest streets, which has been doing a roaring trade from the 13th century and celebrating its street market every Thursday since. It was in this very place that two rebellions were ignited, in the mid 15th and 16th centuries. The first involved a power struggle between two 'noble' families and as mercenaries were two-a-peseta in the area, the families went shopping and started a fight. The second involved the people for their own sakes against the authorities over rising food prices, abuse and municipal corruption. An argument between a baker and customer started it off! (Wasn't that how a fire got started and destroyed a city?) So, be warned; next time you tell someone in Spain not to jump the queue, who knows where it may lead?

In the church of Omnium Sanctorum is *el Pendón Verde* - the green banner (green being the colour of Islam), which the Christians captured from the Moors on taking the city in 1248.

Parallel and to the south of *calle de la Feria* is *La Alameda de Hércules* - *alameda* meaning promenade. The area used to be filled by the river *Baetis*, which flowed through until the Visigoths changed its course. Thereafter, the area would just flood until it was eventually drained by the Moors. But it wasn't until the 15th century that anything permanent was built on the site along with the planting of some 2,000 trees. In the 18th century further draining was carried out turning it into a fashionable area for the city's gentry to stretch their legs and trot their horses. In the 19th century it took on its present dimensions and appearance. That was until more recently the prostitutes, crime and late night carousers stumbled in. The well-healed took to their heels and moved out to more politer areas. The present authorities are keen to clean the place up and they have already revamped the *plaza's* most impressive French Renaissance residence and have also undertaken the construction of a subterranean car park. It is still a pleasant place to stroll around Sunday mornings with a flea market and people stopping for an early breakfast or the occasional tapa.

Moving towards the river you will pass the two founding convents in the city. They were established by Fernando III when he displaced the Moors. The convent of San Clemente occupies the site of the summer Residence of the Abbadid monarch El-Mu'tamid. It was then converted into a Cistercian monastery. The other convent is Santa Clara in the street of the same name. Today people visit its small but charming garden within its walls. The tower of don Fadrique is the oldest remnant of the convent dating from 1252 and reads like a vertical book of styles, telling the transition from the Romanesque to the Gothic. It now houses a modest archaeological museum. It was built on the previous site of the palace of the monarch's illegitimate son *el Infante*, don Fadrique and is one more interesting architectural gem that the city has concealed within its streets. The tower has no defensive design as it has always been well inside the city's walls and was built instead so that don Fadrique's mother-in-law, his lover, could catch doves without catching cold, or so the fable goes.

The end of the street falls into the sleepy *Plaza de San Lorenzo*. In one corner of this tree-shaded *plaza* is the church of the same name famous for housing one of the most revered images of Christ used in the *Semana Santa* processions: *Jesús del Gran Poder*. The statue by Juan de Mesa is considered the height of Sevillian Baroque sentiment in wood and therefore receives its just attention from the faithful and the small church is much visited. From here it is an agreeable walk through the *barrio* of San Lorenzo meandering down toward the *Museo de Bellas Artes*. The fine, quiet streets are home to what was once an aristocratic district and while today's inhabitants are less presumptuous, their buildings are not. *Patios* flourish and it is the perfect Sunday urban stroll.

There is the Convent of Santa Ana, c.1606, which gives its name to the street. In *calle Cardenal Spínola* there is *el Convento Santa Rosalia* from 18th century.

Once past the *Museo de Bellas Artes* we have come nearly full circle and find ourselves by Triana Bridge and close to the centre. If we walk up *calle Reyes Católicos* toward the shopping centre we will meet Sevilla's last great Baroque church: *La Iglesia de la Magdalena* by Figueroa. Not only is it a surprise to find such a big bulk of masonry among such slender surroundings but it also contains a richly worked interior by Lucas Valdés with paintings by Zurbáran and Valdés Leal. An interesting detail is found stuck to the side of the church in its *plaza*: a huge marble cartouche by the architect, defying gravity. Of course the site also has its own piece of invisible history. It was once the location of the Dominican *Convento de San Pablo*, which was a key centre for study at the time and housed a famous library along with valuable works of art. It was a base for Bartolomé de las Casas, monk and personal friend of Columbus – or *Colón* as we have now come to know him, who wrote his famous book *Historia General de las Indias* based on his friend's personal notes. He was also the first to defend the rights of the indigenous Indians and debated the status of indigenous people subjugated by an imposing power. This took place in the famous meeting in Valladolid in 1550 when he confronted the establishment's brightest Humanist Juan Gines de Sepúlveda in the intellectual fight for the freedom of the Indians and at a time when Carlos V was contemplating the complete withdrawal of Spain from the Americas.

Of the old centre there remains only one segment to discover: *El Arenal*. *Arena* means 'sand' and refers to the fact the whole area had once been covered by the stuff when it acted as the old port district. Now it is a densely populated area with more bars than most small towns can muster, as well some of Sevilla's finest tapas bars and restaurants. The architecture is among the most attractive and at the same time most archaic. There is a sense of *barrio* among its inhabitants and an aura of Sevillian history enshrined in its lanes. The bullring is here, the cathedral is just behind and the river in front of it. In such a cross-fire position, it doesn't take a great deal of imagination for the visitor to realise that much of Sevilla's history must have been played out in this quarter. Gold arrived in this port area from the Indies, the Christian invaders breached the city's defences here, while merchants, clerics and bullfighters would have been everywhere. There is no logical plan to the area, you never know what to expect or where you may come out as you wander around aimlessly taking it all in. Although *Barrio Santa Cruz* is lovelier, mystifying and ancient it can feel claustrophobic and empty of people at times. *El Arenal* is anything but, and the residents outnumber the tourists. Nightlife and daylife are both prolific in the neighbourhood. Traffic squeezes through it while the people continue their lives in the side-streets oblivious of the outside hustle and bustle.

Calle Arfe Seises is home to some of the most traditional grocers with their windows as carefully organised as any Roman mosaic. At the end of the street is the area's most original building *El Postigo del Aceite* now selling ceramics, not oil as the name suggests. *El Positgo* meaning 'wicket gate', still exists behind *el Postigo del Aceite* and is one of only two survivors from the original city wall. It has a Moorish core but its shell was much altered in the 18th century to give it its present appearance. To the left of *El Postigo* building is reputedly Sevilla's finest seafood restaurant *'La Isla Cristina'* (remember to look at the prices first!).

El Arenal extends down to the river where it meets *El Paseo de Colón*, a mainfare of car drivers and *paseo* walkers. Along the *paseo* standing in pride of place and demanding attention are the *Plaza de Toros de la Maestranza* bullring and *El Teatro de la Maestranza* theatre. The theatre was built for the '92 Expo and is surmounted by an eye-catching ceramic dome. It hosts sellout classical music and operatic seasons and is as interesting inside as out. Behind the theatre is the Baroque *Hospital de los Venerables*, which is connected to another very Spanish looking building; the old Artillery Depot, which is still in military hands. The hospital cared for the poor and sick, buried criminals and gave alms. It also contains a chapel – *capilla*, which is worth visiting with work by Valdés, Leal and Murillo. The tomb of Miguel Mañara finds its resting place here. More about him later.

The bullring – *la plaza de toros*, was constructed in what was once the *El Baratillo* meaning 'bric-à-brac'. It was built in stages over 119 years and completed in 1880. The bullring was squashed in amid the town houses that still stand in the area, which explains its oval as opposed to perfectly rounded shape. *Calle Adriano* which runs behind the ring is full come the day of the *Corrida* - bullfight, and the tree-lined avenue. Its whitewashed buildings with ochre frames and red painted doors are typical in Sevilla and very much connected to *La Corrida*. The red and white colours of the Maestranza bullring are flown on a flag similar to that of Austria. When the flag is raised the bulls are 'running'. Inside the long, brightly-colonnaded gallery that flows round the yellow oval of sand, the roof of the cathedral and the Giralda belfry can be seen peering curiously down into the ring. It is just another unique view that Sevilla offers those willing to discover her delights.

Opposite stands one last reminder of the city's history, personality and fame: Carmen. The statue marks the place where she is supposed to have met her end. And where we meet ours.

One should not forget that inside Sevilla's many scattered markets you will find as good a place as any to see the heart of the city beating and take the pulse of its people rising in the lively and abundant atmosphere. Some markets include Triana market by its bridge. The Arenal market in *calle Pastor y Landero* as well as the one in the middle of the long *calle de la Feria*.

So what has taken your fancy among the city's architectural heritage left to it in brick and mortar? Was it the great mass of the Gothic cathedral with its sculpture and goldwork? Or the Moorish legacy in the shape of the *Giralda* or the purer *Torre del Oro*? Perhaps the Moorish and Christian mix which left behind the *Mudéjar Reales Alcázares* was lovelier? Or were the charming streets of *Barrio Santa Cruz* your favourite? Maybe the unique splendour of the 1929 pavilions with *El Parque María Luisa* and the unimaginable *Plaza de España* set alight your imagination? Some prefer the more futuristic *Cartuja*, while others are taken by the more traditional such as *El Palacio de San Telmo* or the resplendent *Hotel Alfonso XIII*. Did you go for the *Antigua Fábrica de Tabacos* or was it the *Ayuntamiento* - Town Hall? Or something like the Bullring perhaps or maybe one of the impressive bridges was more to your liking? For many it is simply the pleasure of walking the pinched streets and coming across the delight of a door left ajar revealing a flower adorned *patio* with gleaming *azulejos* tiles and an elegant first floor balcony gazing from above.

If you have had time to do everything, which would be impressive, then a good guess is your favourite was all of the above.

View of the city of Seville (Alonso Sánchez Coello)

- TRES -
¡AY, TRIANA!

- Triana es mucho Triana -
(Local Expression)

The tourists come to Triana, not in their droves but in their isolated groups to wander the streets and soak up the atmosphere of a real *barrio andaluz* going about its daily business. Carriages often echo over the constricted cobbles, the hooves reverberating as the visitors take a more traditional mode of transport around the area. A favourite street here is *Rodrigo de Triana*. From beginning to end it has all of Triana's characteristics. It is quiet in parts and noisy in others. Full of bars and banter and yet void of it at times. It leads you to the *plaza* and the church of Santa Ana. You pass a *casa de vecinos* – literally a 'neighbours' house', which is a distinctive communal '*corral*' dwelling with a central courtyard. The area is littered with them tucked away in its cramped streets. There is the dance academy of Manolo Marín that attracts people from all around the world to come and stamp rather than tap their feet. There is a scattering of restaurants as well as a handful of shops with daily supplies of gossip and, of course, more raillery. The *coros rocieros* – Rocío choirs, can be heard through the grilles of the wrought-iron *rejas* of people's homes on a late Friday afternoon. Friends gather to sing *rumbas* and *sevillanas* and clap over *tapas* and a glass of *fino* to keep the spirits up, the glasses empty and the street filled with *alegria*.

¡Ay, Triana!

Triana is adored by the city's populace, who see her as a social institution and wish to keep her just the way she is.

If you ask a Londoner where he's from he'll say London before he says England. A New Yorker will also be proud of his city and country but probably say he's from The Big Apple and then the U.S. And those from Triana while abroad would like to say they are from Triana but they know that on the international stage they won't get far, so they say they are from Sevilla. However, when in Spain if another Spaniard should ask them where they are from then Triana speaks volumes and could well be their first choice of answer. Even if you have only been a short-stay visitor to the city you too may well have heard mention of this *barrio*. The place is immortalized in Spanish history, fable and song. Spanish folklore would be lacking if Triana had not played her part in the nation's cultural orchestra.

The first sight anyone catches of the neighbourhood is one of the lasting images the city casts. As you approach the river, chances have it that you will walk out to the *La Torre de Oro* or *La Plaza de Toros* and then the magnetic effect that any river has, will draw you to its banks. On the other side of the river, laid back behind a flank of three-storey-high town houses and shouldering each other out the way for space, is Triana. Its river façade is to one side of the perfectly proportioned Triana Bridge. Behind this mottled front, life in Sevilla takes on a rhythm of its own and one that seems to have changed little despite the traffic and fashions.

Triana takes its name from 'tri' three, where three rivers once converged namely *El Guadalquivir*, *La Taguera* and *Tamarguillo*. The centre of Sevilla was formed around La Alfalfa and Plaza Salvador and later spread to its neighbouring areas until it eventually crossed the river and Triana was born.

Saints Justa and Rufina, b.268 and 270 AD respectively, were sisters from Triana. The two women were arrested by the Roman authorities at their shop in *La Puerta de Triana* after they had decled to pay a contribution toward the Roman God Venus, being carried shoulder high through the town. After they had refused to yield to a pagan image, which they said was nothing more than clay, they were accused of being Christians (heretics at the time) and the locals threw stones breaking their ceramics. The sisters responded with similar projectiles breaking the image of Venus. Before they were torn limb from limb the authorities arrived, arrested them and condemned them to death. Justa perished during the night and Rufina was carried to the amphitheatre to be throne to the lions. She walked out and when the lion drew near, instead of tearing her to pieces he licked her feet. This only angered the crowd further who demanded that she be beheaded, and that was how Rufina ended her rebellion. The two sisters thus became the city's first martyrs as well as the first recorded Christians in the city. Justa is remembered in the name of the new train station, which connects Sevilla with Madrid: *Santa Justa*. And they are also reputed to have saved the Giralda from the earthquake in 1755, which completely levelled Lisbon and affected much of Sevilla.

In the 9th century the Muslims extended their fortifications to include the area of Triana thereby making it a permanent settlement. The fortified wall and moat once stretched the length of what is now *calle Pagés del Corro*. The fortifications were put up in response to a massacre in 891 from the Yemeni and Bedouin tribes of mercenaries that were encamped in San Juan del Aznalfarache, an area to the south of the city, on the high ground overlooking it. According to accounts of the time some 20,000 were killed and others sold to slavery in Morocco, which does sound hard to imagine but these were rough times.

¡Ay, Triana!

Later in its history Triana found itself in a privileged position to reap the rewards of the galleons arriving from and leaving for the New World, which moored alongside its riverbank, now *calle Betis*.

Later it became linked to the Inquisition in the 16th century when the religious institution decided to set up their HQ in the San Jorge castle overlooking Triana Bridge. The castle was originally built by the Moors before it was taken over by the Christians and later requisitioned by the Inquisition. Eventually it was knocked down in the 19th century, the same time that the Inquisition disappeared. Today it is the home of the good-humoured Triana market, where a glass viewing area peers down onto the castle's original foundations. Next to the market in *calle Castilla* you can find the small alleyway of the *Callejón de la Inquisición*, where the unlucky heretic of the day was marched down to the river to see if they would sink or float. Sink (tails down): you were innocent, and probably died from drowning, and float (tails down): you were guilty. And with medieval logic like that it wouldn't be surprising if they had all been keen on learning apnoea. It was here in the castle that the first tribunals, called A*utos-da-fě* - a Portuguese phrase meaning 'act of faith', were carried out in 1481. The Inquisition was 'officially' abolished in the 1820! But apparently kept on going in the field of censorship until the 1960's.

During the centuries of booming trade with the Americas, Triana housed sailors recruited for the yearly fleets that travelled there, as well as those who attended to the boats. The street *Pagés del Corro* used to be called *La Cava de los Gitanos*. From Los Remedios its extension was known as *La Cava de los Civiles*. So, the Gypsies principally occupied the south of Triana.

There were *gitanerías* – gypsy slums, in Sevilla where they would congregate. Although they were at first forced to live outside the city walls in ghettos there was no actual law stating that they could not mix. There were *payos* - non-gypsies, living amongst them in the *corrales de vecinos* – communal housing with its by now familiar courtyard. By 1783 half of all the Gypsies in Sevilla lived in Triana.

¡Ay, Triana!

The English writer and painter Richard Ford was in the city for its no-longer existing carnival in 1833 with his wife where they saw Gypsies dancing and wrote: *"The scene of dancing is generally in the neighbourhood of Triana, which has become the Trastevere of this city and the cave of bullfighters, smugglers, rogues and gypsies, whose women are the première dancers on these occasions."*

With the gentle and subtle gentrification of Triana in the fifties many of the Gypsy families left the *barrio* and moved elsewhere in the city, unable as they were to pay the growing rents. They left their mark, however, on the area and it still beats to the rhythm of clapping hands and stamping heels. The area has never been rich, but for what it lacks in cash it makes up for in character. Flamenco fills the district at night when it throbs to the *compás* of Gypsy music imbued with its oriental and Jewish overtones in its *tablaos* – Flamenco bars. Its most famous and popular *tablao* is *Anselma* in the street *Pagés del Corro*. Inside the building's ceramic decorated exterior is a small nondescript bar to one side behind which a keen eye will make out a small plaque: the only reference to its name. Outside there is nothing to advertise it except the music that comes pouring out. The place is always packed and the crowd frequently spills out of the entrance and onto the street. Amidst the onlookers you will find a group of guitarists and singers sat in a circle while a couple dance in the centre with their arms raised. Most join in the singing and the dancers change as a new pair dare to step forward. Everyone joins in the clapping whether they have tanned skin or not. It doesn't take long to pick up the basic rhythm. The lighter variant of Flamenco, called *flamenquito*, is found in the bars facing the river in *calle Betis* and keep the night-owls up until dawn.

The *barrio*'s most famous son has probably been Juan Belmonte, arguably Spain's greatest ever bullfighter, (some say 'Manolete' holds the title) who appeared on the front cover of Time magazine in 1925. He saw off 109 bulls in 1909, a figure not matched before or since. His life wasn't taken by a bull in the *plaza* like the famous Manolete. Belmonte had been friends with Hemingway and when he learned of the writer's suicide he commented, *"Well done!"* And did the same thing himself five months later. A sculpture to the local 'hero' stands in *La Plaza del Altozano*. There is hole in the sculpture's torso and by looking through it you will see the Giralda of Sevilla where his heart is supposed to be. More recently Triana's favourite

¡Ay, Triana!

son is the Flamenco dancer – *el bailaor*, Antonio Canales. Haven't heard of him? Well, he has danced in the White House, so he can't be doing too badly.

It was also a man 'adopted' by Triana, Rodrigo de Triana, who first spotted land on Columbus' venture to the New World shouting "*¡Tierra!*" from the caravel *La Pinta* at around 2am, 12th October 1492, which allowed Chris the chance to step ashore San Salvador. Rodrigo had spotted an island of the *Lucayas* archipelago, modern day Bahamas, whose native Indian name was *Guanahaní*. *Colón* changed the name to give thanks to his 'Saviour'. As Rodders was the first to sight land he won himself 10,000 *maravedís*. Unfortunately, when he got back to Spanish *terra firma* Chris said that *he* had been the one to sight land first and so the reward was never given out. Juan Rodríguez Bermejo (Rodrigo de Triana) was really from Lepe, a small town in the province of Huelva, but we don't want to upset the locals or change the street named in his honour in Triana. He had also been a Muslim made to convert to Christianity - a so-called *morisco*. A statue to him stands at the south end of *calle Pagés del Corro*, who ended his days in North Africa. So, what an unfortunate character he was: almost starved to death on the voyage, certainly no hotel accommodation waiting for him when he arrived in the New World, returned to find himself out of pocket having been up half the night trying to spot land and to top it off had his name wrongly recorded for posterity. In short: should have stayed at home.

It was from the riverbanks here in *calle Betis* that Magellan set sail with the backing of the Spanish Crown in his bid to navigate the globe in

1517. He died on the island of Mactan in the Philippines in 1521 and his second-in-command, a Basque, Juan Sebastian Elcano brought the surviving eighteen man crew limping in to dock, where they had started out five years previously.

Another of Triana's claims to fame is Figaro's barbershop '*Los Pajaritos*', also in *calle Betis*. Carmen is also supposed to have lived here but obviously no address can be given. Don Juan played it safe though and kept to the noble area of Santa Cruz, perhaps it was a bit too wild for him this side of the river.

Triana is not only linked to the international stage through world history and high opera it also has a place in the literary global village as well, in the pages of *Rinconete y Cortadillo* by Cervantes. In *calle Troya* a large ceramic plaque announces to the curious that this was the spot that formed the vagabonds' meeting place: the Court of Monipodio.

Today the *barrio* is the home of two of the biggest *Cofradias* – fraternities of *Semana Santa*. *La Estrella* is based in the chapel *Virgen de la Estrella* in *calle San Jacinto* and *La Esperanza* is found in the Mariners' Chapel - *Capilla de los Marineros*, in *calle Pureza*. In *calle Castilla* is the oddly named church *Iglesia de la 'O'* owing to Maria's sound of surprise, apparently, when the angel visited her to give her the good tidings that she was to be the mother of the son of God. We have no idea what Jospeh's thoughts were on the subject but one doubts they were *"O, right you are then."*

Further along the same street is the chapel *Capilla Patrocinio*, which houses the statue of *El Cristo de la Expiración*, showing Christ's last mortal breath and popularly known as *El Cachorro* – 'the puppy'. The story behind how an image of Christ on the cross became to be known by the name of something fluffy and full of life is interesting and more than just a local legend but historical fact... so visitors are told. In the 17th century Triana used to be divided into two areas *La Vega Civil* and *La Vega Gitanos*. A sculptor from *La Vega Gitanos*, Ruíz Gijón, had spent time searching the hospitals for inspiration for an image of Christ but to no avail. A local gypsy from *La Vega Gitanos*, going by the nickname of *El Cachorro*, was a popular man with the ladies and had a good time of it by all accounts. That was until one unfortunate night when he was caught in a fight over a woman and knives were drawn. In the fury of the moment El Cachorro was stabbed right through the heart. This moment, and his subsequent death, was witnessed first hand by Ruíz Gijón. He at once went to work struck by what he had seen and when the final work was displayed people were amazed to see the expression of the dying Gypsy in the face of Christ. El Cachorro, evidently means 'puppy'.

Triana also hosts one of the city's most traditional festivals: *La Velá de Santiago y de Nuestra Señá Santa Ana* in the high heat of the Sevillian summer. Its famous *calle Betis*, one of the busiest arteries and popular with tourist and native citizen alike, brims with life, as it does very night.

To one end of the street colourful marquees serving beer and food are put up by Triana bridge. Further down river there are fairground rides for the children and all the while there is an unending stream of people trying to stroll the overflowing river esplanade, which offers the city's most beautiful view and one of the most singular of any European city.

. During the day there is more food and music but the principal attraction of this summer fiesta is out on the water. Everyone comes to see the *Cucaña*. Floating in the river exactly half-way between the two bridges bobs a blue and white boat painted with the colours of the sponsoring bank. Protruding from its bow is a green, greased pole. On the boat are the young hopefuls waiting in turn to try their luck at snatching the red flag positioned at the end of the pole. All you have to do in this leap of faith is come away with the flag in your hand as you fall waterward, while cameras whirr and the spectators shout you *'on'* in encouragement or *'off'* in good humour.

Triana maintains a proud distance and individual character apart from the main city centre and likes to taunt those that find themselves living on the opposite side of the river with good natured comments such as, '*Triana que comparte su río con Sevilla*' – 'Triana who shares its river with Sevilla'. T-shirts also display slogans such as '*Triana, República Independiente*' and advertise '*Unversidad de Triana, Facultad de Arte*' – 'Triana University, Art

Faculty', because to have *arte* here is a quintessential part of being *andaluz*, especially *sevillano* and Triana is deemed to be at the centre of this artistic and spiritual expression.

Sevilla's oldest church is here, Santa Ana – referred to as the 'cathedral' of Triana. It was founded in the 13th century by Alfonso X, the Wise, the son of Fernando III, the Saint who freed the city from Moorish dominion. Alfonso founded the church in thanks for being 'miraculously' cured of an eye disorder. It is the oldest church that has survived Sevilla's turbulent history but not the first that was built. The church is a magnet for the faithful in the city. It is here every year, on a Wednesday, that Triana takes its embroidered image of the virgin – *El Simpecao*, dialect for 'without original sin', out from safe keeping and transports it to a silver gilded wagon, *carreta de plata*, while the throng congregates in the *plaza* outside. It is then accompanied by people on foot and horseback on Andalusia's greatest pilgrimage trail to the hamlet of *El Rocío* in Huelva, situated on the edge of the Doñana National Park. The whole ceremony starts early and the image of the virgin leaving the church is signalled by rockets booming across the entire neighbourhood as horses and wagons clip along the cobbled streets. The same scene is also repeated across the city with other groups leaving from La Macarena, El Divino Salvador as well as from the cities of Huelva, Jerez, Cádiz and the towns and villages surrounding El Rocío. There are even brotherhoods that come down from as far afield as Barcelona, Madrid, Valencia, Córdoba and even Brussels, wherever the *andaluz* immigrants have scattered to.

The bridge, one of the symbols of the city, is the barrio's greatest possession and very dear to the hearts and historical memory of the *sevillanos* and *trianeros* alike. The first stable bridge in the city, *El Puente de Barcas*, spanned the river in 1171. It was made of wood and floated on a flotilla of mastless boats that rode at anchor thereby adjusting to the changing current. Several times the boat bridge was smashed through or swept away and had to be rebuilt. The wooden structure was the preferred type due to its cheap maintenance until at long last the city had an update and a permanent non-floating structure was put in place in 1852, the year after the Great Exhibition in London's Crystal Palace. The present bridge was constructed from iron between 1845-52, taken from the Roman mines of *Cerro del Hierro* in Sevilla's *Sierra Norte*. The joint architects were Fernando Bernadet and Gustavo Steinacher. It was a copy of the no-longer standing

Pont de Carrousel in Paris. But it actually looks like a more polished version of the bridge at Coalbrookdale (1777-79), the world's first cast-iron bridge. Even though the design was a mere copy, and not an original, didn't bother the officials that held the design competition and they were more than happy with their choice. As the bridge was a mixture of iron and stone the city of Sevilla has never known an entirely stone bridge in its three millennia of history. It took the direct route from wood to iron. Its symmetrical three arches with sturdy stone bases support an aesthetic bridge noted for its iron rings and crowned by delicate lanterns of the era. The Structural Expressionist style is *'an open and light framework'*. It is incredible to know that the city managed for so long with only one bridge. London had its first stone bridge in 1176 which took 30 years to build and 158 workmen died in the process.

Crossing this causeway each day is one of the glories that living in this city, and above all this *barrio*, can afford.

The bridge is one of several pieces of decorative industrial architecture built at the time in the vicinity. Next to it on the other side of the riverbank is the former *Mercado del Barranco* (c.1883) now used for exhibitions. Further along from this intricate iron structure along *calle Arjona* is the must-see old Córdoba station (c.1901), a small relative of the Eiffel-built Atocha station in Madrid that links high-speed trains with Sevilla. Built in traditional brick, iron and glass the motifs are in fact neo-*Mudéjar* and used as the Sevilla pavilion for the 1929 Ibero-American Expo.

Triana is, and has always been, famous for her ceramics. Since Roman times the area has been working with clay and excavations in ancient Rome have unearthed earthenware from here. With the arrival of the Moors they introduced the art of tiles, or *azulejos*, which has become a stamp of regional, if not national, identity. No house, bar or official building is replete without its *azulejos*. They are to be seen at every turn in Andalucía and even beyond. *Calle Alfarería* is still home to this timeless profession of potters.

The description of colourful characters of Spanish folklore were the mainstay of the romantic writers when they opened Europe's eyes to the forgotten and forlorn Spanish south in the 18th century. Through their writings many travellers were soon to follow and the effect still hasn't worn off. There are many moments in the social and festive calendar when the famous folklore, traditional dress, music and culture will find their way back into modern city life and into everyone's imagination.

You may even see a man dressed in top hat and tails walking around the area. He works for a business whose black and white cars are parked up around the area in the *avenida* that separate the *barrio* of Triana from Los Remedios. The man, known as *El Cobrador del Frac*, is a debt collector. He won't break down your door and take your kids away until the money turns up. No, this guy will just plague you with his presence until you pay him to go away. Have a debt outstanding and the client refuses to pay up? Why not enlist the help of *El Cobrador del Frac*? He goes out and hounds the person down. When your debtor comes out from the safety of their home *el cobrador* is waiting for them. On their way to the office right up to the door he is with them. In the restaurant they are outside or at the table next to them. Out on the town with friends? Not a problem, they will have a new friend until the bill is paid in full. This guy will have his tail coat on their tail and, of course, everyone will know that they don't pay their debts, which could be a dilemma if they wanted to do business with someone and this guy in top hat and tails, sitting next to them.

There are several ceramic workshops next to the *Andalucista* political party office in *calle Fabie*, which is near a Flamenco dance studio. And more elsewhere in the neighbourhood. The small toiletries shop offers the older men a chance to talk about football, while the corner store lets the older women congregate, complain about the slow service and their fickle health. The harmonica player jaunts down the street vying for airspace as another musician hits the ebony keys of a piano in his flat. From another open window strums a Flamenco guitar. Opposite an electric guitar is played on a Sony CD. Men with long hair carry Spanish guitars over one shoulder while women with hair tied tightly back carry themselves smartly to various dance studios. A gathering of a *coro* – choir, commences and the voices raise Triana in her spirits and people stop outside to listen. It is moving and rousing at the same time. Margarita in her wheel chair is ever present in the street selling lottery tickets wherever she can and often taking Rafa's children on her knee and babysitting them for a while. José, the Major type with clipped moustache, is fond of conversation and stops everyone as they pass. He just wants to know how they are doing.

At the other end of *calle Fabie* another ageing gent takes up his position where two roads meet on the corner of a fried fish shop and the shop opposite. He directs the traffic for those that need it, points pedestrians in the right direction and keeps up a steady rhythm of banter. His humour makes the people smile and local workmen salute him each morning. Everyday he comes out wearing a raincoat if it's raining or lighter clothes if it is warm. He lights his cigarette, dons his simple looking baseball cap and is all set for the day's repartee. The children greet passersbys and they return the polite words. The fish shops – *freidurías*, open and the queues start to form slowly. At around ten the places are buzzing. The bars that have seen a steady trade all day now see even more as the cold beer and coffee drinkers turn to whisky for the evening. Tourists mingle in conspicuously and the odd horse and carriage strains by with four plump looking *forasteros* – outsiders, pointing around them. Balconies are hung heavy with clothes drying as sounds are shouted from them while local police casually stroll their least stressful beat. Another person arrives at the bus stop and everyone greets the newcomer, "*Buenos días,*" says one.

"*Hola. Buenos días,*" reply the others.

There is life in the street because there is life in the people.

¡Viva Triana!

- CUATRO -
TUNA NIGHT

Between two worlds life hovers like a star,
'Twixt night and morn, upon the horizon's verge.
Byron

La Noche de la Inmaculada : The night of the Immaculate Conception, on the 8th December, produces one of Sevilla's most emotive nights. A night where its name for artistry, legend and romance comes to life in the voice of its citizens and its medieval tradition. Cloaks sway and mandolins play while the people gather to awaken the soul of their city walls with poetic voice.

In the old centre just behind *La Avenida de La Constitución* is *La Plaza del Triunfo*, contained within the millennium-old Moorish walls of the *Alcázares* and enclosed by the rigid Castillian-influenced Royal Exchange and cathedral baptistery. The setting only lacks people to bring all the architecture to life and that is exactly what they do on the night of *La Inmaculada*.

As the weather finally turns, Sevilla leaves autumn behind her and embraces winter. The duvet cover is now no longer sufficient to fend off the chill and the extra blanket has worked its way out of the cupboard and onto the bed. The heels clacking over the cobblestone streets now resound with more urgency as people hurry from one place to another. The climate has closed in and the people have zipped up. Necks are thickened by wrapped scarves and bare legs are now encased in leather boots. Long coats have replaced long dresses and the few that don't smoke now also exhaled white wisps as they breathe the brisk air. The autumnal light traces sharp lines around monuments better suited to the Andalusian sun.

On the night in question the bells peal overhead marking the commencement of festivities. The moment they stop, the singing begins. The *plaza* is brimming with several thousand people gathered to witness the spectacle, if not more. A low, makeshift stage has been placed in front of the white column bearing the statue of *La Virgen de la Inmaculada* in the centre of the *plaza*. It is twelve o'clock and things are just about to start. One should take up a position by time-worn walls of the Moorish fortress, and push your way through everyone, and their cousin, onto high ground to get the best view possible.

A group of about twelve men in their twenties wearing medieval garb process up onto the platform. They are already playing their guitars and mandolins with capes and flags flying while one of them, holding a tambourine, is dancing in circles. It is something out of Black Adder almost, but with everyone in key. Their black cloaks are decorated with badges and long multicoloured ribbons hang from them. Doting girls look on, with some of them also wearing ribboned cloaks. They are living proof that music is mightier than muscle when it comes to drawing the attention of the ladies.

They slow up and form a semi-circle facing the statue of the Virgin and start to strum slowly. The troupe leader shouts out the name of the song: *Clavelitos*, the one they apparently always start with and within moments the crowd begin to build voice. Once they reach the chorus the whole *plaza* resounds with song as the citizens gentley rock to the rhythm of the music. You don't have to be able sing to save your soul, let alone in Spanish, but as soon as you join the swaying to and fro it won't be long before you attempt a bit of singing as well.

The musicians are called *Tunas*, with each member known as a *Tuno*. They are essentially university students that practise in their free time and then play in the local streets for the night owls and tourists as well as at private *fiestas*. Some even travel around Europe paying their way by busking their medieval tunes.

One *Tuna* troupe went all the way to Germany to play in the street for the girlfriend of one of the player's. It was her birthday and she listened from her balcony. It is typical for them to be hired to sing to girls in their balconies here. Although, they have the voice of an angel they have the reputation of a fallen one. The Italians do the same to ask for a girl's hand in marriage and then invite all the neighbours to join their impromptu street party. It is the least they can do for waking them up.

Their tone of voice once heard is not easily forgotten or easily imitated. It seems peculiar to Spain. Nearly every university faculty has their own *Tuna*. The oldest one in the University of Sevilla is that of the Biology faculty and as tradition dictates, it is their privilege to start the proceedings on the 8th December. This means that they get to carry the crowd with them year-in year-out by playing the most popular songs. By the time the others get their 7 minutes of fame everyone has been sung out and the best songs already played. So, if you plan going along you have to get there early otherwise it'll be all over bar the singing of the now unaccompanied *Las Tunas*.

Troupes from all over Spain and Portugal attend the evening's events and the queue of players tails off into the distance. There is need for crowd control, but barricades keep the walkway to the stage clear. They may start late but they go on even later. Once their turn has been and gone the players then take off into the dark confines of the old Jewish quarter to twang the night away in front of their faithful followers. So as soon as one has had their fill their next plan is to go off into the labyrinth of streets of *Barrio Santa Cruz* and find the individual groups for themselves.

There is no need to hurry things, though, and one should stay on to savour this unique night. Voices of the old and young can be heard and few hold back as the *Tunas* lead everyone in song. The mystery of Sevilla has a perfect setting in this *plaza* as it is filled by ardent voices lending its past passions fresh vigour. What makes the moment so poignant though is to be amongst people that appreciate their music and are capable of producing it when the occasion is called. It is something that one can only admire and something the Spanish are renowned for.

The crowd begins to thin out as their opportunities to sing along dwindle with the passing of the groups. The time then comes to turn attentions elsewhere and head into *la Judería* to see it in a very special light.

Walking into the slender Jewish streets one finds the *plazas* occupied by different troupes entertaining all those willing to give them the time of night. No neighbours come out to complain and many are out on their balconies listening to the non-stop revelry. People *plaza* hop and listen to all the various ensembles and the even more numerous *aficionados* following them. There is banter, soloists, exhibitionists and always improvisation. It is a unique time to be in this picturesque corner of old Europe.

A cross roads empties into a small *plaza*, which is filled by bars, *al fresco* tables and chairs. One bar, taking up a corner of a building, has its windows and doors open to the streets. From inside issues bellowing voices and patrons spill out from the seams. Everyone is hypnotised by the show taking shape in the bar. The *Tunas* are under-the-table and playing on top of the bar. The troubadour barflies sway from side to side while they bend their elbow to the bottle and simultaneously pluck their instruments. Beer flows onto the floor as heat, music and voice blast out from what is a furnace of medieval carousing. The players hold their instruments to their chests - no straps needed - strumming their strings home without missing a note. Their legs work miracles to keep them on the bar instead of on their heads. Rarely can one come across such musical spontaneity mixed with such drunkenness, open feeling and mass participation. It is all done on a local level and in magnificent surroundings.

When you finally make it back to *la Plaza del Triunfo*, you will probably find *las Tunas* still queuing up and filing onto the stage to sing their turn. It will be 5:30 in the morning and the celebration still has more legs than a millipede. It is time to leave them to it and hum your way over the river and into Triana. It is the perfect run up to Christmas.

- CINCO -
THREE 'MAGIC' KINGS

'A good conscience is a continual Christmas'
Benjamin Franklin

In the build up to Christmas a trip to *El Corte Inglés*, Spain's only national department store chain, sees its aisles filled with trolleys burgeoning with Christmas delicacies. Entire legs of *jamón serrano*, Spain's *crème de la crème* culinary product, stick out conspicuously from trolleys. Full crates of champagne, along with bottles of Scotch whisky and beer, are crammed in alongside the ham. Whole cheese truckles, salmons and kilos of prawns are added to the hoard. And of course no festive season in Spain would be complete without the grapes for New Year's Eve. The totals at the check-outs ring off small family fortunes. It is not so much the quantity but the quality of the produce that causes the sizeable dent in the family budget. To say the Spanish like to eat would be an understatement. They need no excuse and no encouraging. It is their *razón de ser* when taking their summer holidays. So you can imagine them going to town at Christmas, which is a month's holiday dedicated to just that: eating. Only, it's condensed into ten days. They are the true Hobbits of the Shire eating and drinking their time away while preparing for local *fiestas*.

The setting of the southern Christmas scene begins with the *Belén* - the Nativity. This is for the Spaniard what the Christmas tree is for the North American. In *Plaza Nueva* a large book fair is erected and on the other side of the Town Hall in *Plaza San Francisco* is a fair dedicated solely to the sale of figurines for the re-creation of the Nativity scene at home. There are objects and *objet d'art* for all pockets. Some are authentic works of art. It is worth a walk round just to soak up Christmas if you have never seen it before. All churches erect a *Belén* and some are so good they even charge a queuing public. In Triana, in *Plaza del Altozano* a lonely guy stands watch over a life-size *Belén* with only a brazier to accompany him through the night.

In every main street, amidst a sea of illuminations, is the Spanish symbol of *Navidad* - Christmas, the Northern Star replete with trailing tail. Whether the family has a Christmas tree or *Belén* at home the star will always be there.

Three 'Magic' Kings

In the shops there are festive products to bring the flavour of the moment to life. From the town of Estepa come the famous *polvorones*, which are soft flour based biscuits made of *mantecado* - shortcake dough, in various flavours from chocolate and lemon to cinnamon and almond. In just three months the small rural town does its business for the entire year, taking in around €45,000,000. But the centrepiece of any food shop window will be *los roscos de reyes*, - Epiphany cakes, which are large, doughnut looking, filled with cream and topped with *glacé* fruits. From big to small and from cheap to costly, they are all over town and Spain. Then the nuns from the convents open their doors and bring out their specially baked goods for the occasion.

Before 6th January has arrived, the traffic is brought to a standstill as elephants from the American or Italian circuses parade through the centre of town. Whatever you might think of the circus, to see an elephant walking around Sevilla is enough to make any child's imagination work over time.

But the great event for many in the run up to Christmas Eve is *'El Gordo'* - The Fat One, the national Christmas lottery. For many it is *the* event of Christmas, especially if you win. It is one more moment when Spain attracts the attention of the world. It is officially the biggest lottery in the world in terms of money paid out and money paid in. The top prize reaches several hundred million euros with hundreds of other substantial prizes also up for grabs. The process is far from simple and extremely Spanish. One ticket costs several hundred euros if you want to buy a complete number, but everybody opts for a share in one. So, ticket number #1 is divided into a hundred parts and you buy a share: a hundredth or even a tenth if you're feeling lucky and well off. If ticket number #1 wins then you'll receive in kind a tenth or hundredth of the total prize. What is the benefit of this system? Apart from landing the government a wad, it also ensures that such a great pot of honey gets distributed a little more evenly than just going to one queen bee. The workers get a fairer share for once.

The effect on society in bringing people together is obvious as factories, neighbourhoods, companies, groups of friends and even whole village communities buy and share out the fractions in the purchase of one ticket between them. And if they win? Then everyone is in the *fiesta* drinking for the same reason because 'everyone's a winner baby!' Even if you're not into lotteries you may be taken by the idea that it's difficult for the biggest prize to go to just one person and the fact that there are enough secondary prizes to make most winners' lives very comfortable indeed.

Three 'Magic' Kings

By the 22nd December, the previous three months of ticket selling comes to a head and bars and living-rooms are packed as the country is hushed into a silence that only the Spanish National Team taking penalties in a World Cup can command. TV sets are switched on in every corner while the National Grid strains to meet the demand. Spain's autonomous regions maybe divided at times but the 'Fat One' always brings them together. As two large brass spheres spin round, churning out numbers and combinations left, right and centre, the numbered balls that issue forth are held up by uniformed children from an orphanage in Madrid who chant out each number in their all-too-familiar monotone. Time stands still and then for the fortunate few their lives are changed forever.

For those who have not had their fill there is an opportunity for another bite of the cherry on January 6th. *El Niño* - The Boy, may not be a heavyweight like *El Gordo* but has enough puppy fat on his bones to keep the chill off anyone's bank account should they win.

The greatest advantage of this time of year when living abroad in Spain, is you get two Christmases. The 25th you can celebrate back home and then once you're in Spain you can get ready for 6th January. On the 25th the Spanish dress to the nines for a quiet dinner at home of prawns and roast meat. There will be wine, beer, champagne and when all is cleared, long drinks consisting of whisky or rum on ice with cola. Parents, who don't mind the northern invasion on their customs, also entertain their children by giving them presents from St. Nicholas - *Papa Noël*. But the true Spanish day for present giving is Epiphany when the Three Wise Men, known here as *Los Reyes Magos* - The Magic Kings, ride into town. Their names: *Melchor*, *Gaspar* and *Baltasar* are as well-known as those of the Simpsons.

The night before, 5th January, is the big moment for many towns and cities in the south when their love of public gatherings and festivity brings out families in their droves. In Sevilla the movement starts around 17:30 in *El Excelentísimo Ateneo de Sevilla* in *calle Orfila* and gradually moves around the city. Everyone is well wrapped up and the children expectant in the street. Many carry umbrellas even though everyone knows there is no chance of rain. The preparations have taken months and many people have been involved. Although it is one of Sevilla's most modest celebrations, the city has been mobilized and such a celebration in any neighbouring country could easily qualify as its principal *fiesta*, but not here. This one is low key and done just to give the kids a few minutes out with the parents on the street. It's nothing to get really worked up about.

Three 'Magic' Kings

With Melchor, Gaspar and Baltasar mounted on their thrones and the tractor engines cranked the *Cabalgata* heads out on its non-stop parade of the city. Starting early in the evening they won't touch base until the small hours, normally coming to a stand-still around 1 or 2 in the morning. The TV cameras start rolling, the police wave the Magic Kings off and the long-winding procession fronted by a marching drum band takes to the streets.

Children wave from the huge floats as the crowded spectators wave back and everyone cries out for more. The air is suddenly filled with shining, flying sparks of silver paper raining down as heads bow and bodies bend to collect the sweets being thrown skyward by the Three Kings and their young helpers. Thousands upon thousands of sweets are showered over the waiting spectators. Now the umbrellas make sense. Adults upturn brollies to increase their cache. The five *carrozas* - floats, all artistically decorated, throw out five tons of sweets in their tour about town.

Petardos - firecrackers, another tradition, jump around people's feet accompanied by laughter and near heart attacks. Once again when you think all has been said and done and everyone has had their fill they all get up early the next day and do it all over. This time they attend their neighbourhood *cabalgatas* when floats, marching bands, flying sweets and music parade their local areas. Not only do they throw sweets to the crowd but even toys and array of other presents.

The unloading of sweets from all angles is constant and the contentment on the children in fancy dress in the floats evident. The crowds are so great that only the front row can get any of the goodies. The candy and floats are sponsored and themes for the floats include the kids' favourites from films and books to animals and sport. The three Magic Kings are often footballers from the local first division teams of Sevilla and Betis. The tractors are all supplied brand new. The streets are hung with line upon line of festive lighting while the trees have their branches and trunks covered with fairy lights. No emblematic comer of the city is left untouched. The Town Hall and other buildings are given the full monty as far as the lighting is concerned with all window frames and entrances decorated by strip lights. The civic drapes are brought out for the occasion and proudly hung from balconies, giving a regal touch to the proceedings. There is no escaping the lighting. The city is positively bright by night.

Although Andalucía is known for its sun and *fiesta* and not as a primary destination for Christmas it is only a matter of time before people associate it with its yuletide season. After all, what better place to be for the festivities than a land world famous for its ability to celebrate? The noise from the drums and cheering through the night is exactly how I would imagine Andalucía celebrating Christmas: in its own inimitable style.

- SEIS -
A FLEMISH FLAMINGO

Sorrow is knowledge: they who know the most
Must mourn the deepest o'er the fatal truth,
The Tree of Knowledge is not that of life.
Byron

There are many aspects of life, culture and a sense of place which epitomise Andalucía for Spanish and foreign visitors to the region. It may be her people, the language, a local dish, the *tapas*, her *fiestas* or painters. However, for those who really know and love this unique corner of Europe there are probably four icons of its flamboyant culture that stand head and shoulders above the rest: the bullfight, *Semana Santa, las ferias* and of course Flamenco. Each can be experienced in other parts of Spain and even around the world but it will always lack a vital ingredient: the essence of Andalucía. This land is the birthplace of the Flamenco art form and nowhere else can the full force of a performance be properly seen, heard - or more importantly – felt, than here.

If Flamenco conjures up for you an image of loud clacking and agonised clucking and feel it all too painful to bare then perhaps reading this you may be convinced that there is much more to it than meets the ear. The singer Manuel Molino, a wealthy butcher, went deaf as a result of his powerful singing of *siguiriyas*, so you could be right about it being too loud. However, you might have been misled and a pleasant surprise in store on your next visit to Spain. This is of course presuming aforehand that you like dance, culture, music of the highest and most direct calibre as well as raw human feelings brought out in public for all to share.

A bit of background will help us get to the roots of the music, its influences and legacy. Only then will we really understand what lies behind the singer, dancer and guitarist. So, what's in a word? What does *Flamenco* mean? "Flamingo!" You say. A possibility. "Flemish, then?" An alternative. *Flamenco* in Spanish does also mean 'Flemish'. But then what on earth could the cold northern Flemish have to do with the fiery southerners? The answer is a hypothesis. In fact, there are about seven theories to the origin of the word altogether.

When Carlos V the Holy Roman Emperor, who was also Carlos I of

Spain, brought the Flemish influence to bear in his Spanish court, their interference and privileged standing was not well received. 'Flemish' or *Flamenco* was soon used to brandish anything seen as undesirable and foreign. At around the same time the Gypsies were being persecuted and their gatherings in café bars, where Flamenco filled the air, often ended in trouble. Like the Flemish, they were also an unwanted presence and so their song and dance was also condemned as 'Flemish'.

Another on the 'Flemish' theme, but going the other way this time, is a thesis from the Catalan musicologist Carlos Almendros, which has been gaining weight of late and goes something to the following tune: the Flemish, long known for their quality of their choir voice, were drawn to Spain and her court during the time of Spanish Imperial supremacy in the search for patronage. Therefore, anyone noted for possessing a good singing voice was known as 'Flemish', which is to say *Flamenco*.

Another interpretation is when the Flemish arrived they fell so completely in love with Spain that they were converted to the cause wholeheartedly, becoming more Papist than the Pope and more gypsy than the Gypsies, until they became one in the same. There are none more fanatical than the recently converted.

The Gypsies arriving in the peninsular were natives from Bohemia where they were called *Flamencos*.

And then there is another about a jack-knife or *navaja* also called a '*Flamenco*', which was commonly used to settle disputes the permanent way. Flamenco is derived from two Arab words *felahmengu* meaning, when joined together, meaning something along the lines of 'humble people' or 'peasant without land' - *campesino sin tierra*. And the Arab influence in this music is of central importance.

Another theory accepted by some *Flamencólogos,* those that study the subject, is that the dancers and singers of these new Gypsy arrivals wore suits that made them appear like flamingos.

The true origin of the word eludes us and the origin of the Gypsy people is equally as obscure. Thought to have started their exodus when a group of its people, under persecution, fled the northern territory of the Punjab around the 8th and 9th centuries, they eventually found their way into Egypt. 'Gypsy' comes from 'Egyptian'. In Spanish the word is: *gitano*, with a guttural 'g' sound /hee-**TA**-no/. From northern Africa they took the long road round and finally made it into their chosen land of Spain in the early part of the 15th century. The first ever recorded evidence of their presence was in 1425 where a document shows Alfonso V of Aragon allowing one *'Don Johan de Egipte Menor'* to settle in his kingdom having arrived from France. Before this time there is no written record of their existence in the peninsular. But since then there has been no doubting that Spain, for this dispossessed Gypsy people, has been their land as much as anyone else's. And the south of Spain without them would be like England without Shakespeare. So deep are their roots in this region and their identification with it now that the one cannot be separated from the other. Today more than half of all their people found in Europe are located in Spain and eighty percent of all Spanish Gypsies reside here in Andalucía.

They arrived in a land undergoing great changes as the culmination of almost eight hundred years of Moorish occupation was about to be rolled back forever and with it the expulsion of the Jews.

The impact on the Gypsies first arriving in Andalucía, possibly attracted by the fertile land, must have contrasted strongly after the arid flatlands of Castilla-La Mancha. The Polish traveller Sobieski, a hundred years later describes his impression on entering the South:

> *"...in every part the view rests on wide expanses, such as forests, lemon trees, olive trees, cypresses, date-palm trees and rich vineyards... After the desert that we have crossed... it seemed I had found myself in a paradise."*

The Gypsies hung on but the Jews never returned in anything like their former numbers. The Gypsies fused with the *Moriscos* - Moors converted to Christianity, just at the time that the *Santo Oficio* - Inquisition, was persecuting them. From the frying pan into the Holy Fire.

After having wandered from India, through Egypt and travelling through Europe from East to West, their Gypsy roots went into the Spanish cultural melting pot. Arab, Jewish and Christian: a mixture of cultures spanning 7th to the 15th centuries found their way into the gypsy bloodstream, merging to produce their distinctive sounds and today they form a central part of the country's national heritage. The three religions combine their despair: from the Hebrew they have taken the religious; from the Arab the philosophical and from their Christian self they have retained its social expression. There are even touches of Greek and Byzantine liturgy in the music.

The Gypsies came into contact with the songs of Moorish Spain: the *Zambras, Zejeles, Moaxajas* and *Jarchas*. They also brought with them an abundant measure of music and dance of ancient Hindu origin. The arm movements in Flamenco draw evident comparisons. Their Romany language also reveals their geographic starting point. But Flamenco in its basic nature is primarily the fusion of Gypsy and Andalusian folklore.

Its sorrowful overtones and preoccupation with personal suffering and loss are well known by even those that have never been near a *tablao* – bar, where Flamenco is performed. The traditional bars have now turned highly polished business acts where people perform their art. What is less well known is Flamenco's equally motive inspiration founded on political and social derision. A people who have been at the rough end of social stigma will beyond doubt express much of that feeling of rejection in their music. Especially when that persecution has followed them all the way across three continents: from Asia, Africa and finally into Europe. The themes of anarchy, socialism and capitalism are also dear to their heart. This is as much a song of protest as it is one of mourning and *alegría* - joy.

The Catholic Sovereigns in the 15th century ordered that the Gypsies should take work and settle, if not the following punishments would be applied:

"that each be given 100 lashes for the first time, that their ears be cut and they spend 70 days in chains, and they should return to exile, as it is called; and for the third time that they be made captive by those who will take them for all their life..."

[Edict of the Catholic Sovereigns, proclaimed in Medina del Campo, in 1499; taken from petitions from *Las Cortes* in 1525, 1528 and 1534.]

Los Reyes Católicos - The Catholic Sovereigns, threw out the Moor, and the Jew along with them for good measure. Then they turned their attentions to the Gypsy. Maybe when you have focused your political policies around flushing out an enemy it is a little difficult to stop the wave of persecution. Ferdie and Lizzie threatened to throw them out with the rest of the undesirables if they didn't work or find fixed abodes and abandon once and for all their nomadic way of life. It was the Gyspys' resistance to authority, their inbred instinct to roam and not tow the official line, that brought them such grief.

Then it was the turn of the Emperor Carlos V, who further enforced previous laws concerning the Gypsies and increased the penalties for any transgressor. Felipe II, another devout Christian of the time, prohibited them from travelling and working from fair to fair if they didn't possess the necessary documents. Documents which were made extremely difficult and cumbersome to obtain. The result of such relentless treatment lead to armed uprisings.

In 1611 a gang of Gypsy *bandoleros* - bandits, attacked but failed to take the town of Logroño. In 1633 villages were overrun by *bandoleros*, which provoked Felipe IV rightly or wrongly to force Gypsies to work only in the countryside and have no contact with nails or iron. Carlos II followed this up in 1695 by stating that they could only live in 41 named towns and should more than three Gypsies be found together and armed then they could face... the death penalty. Felipe V only made matters worse for them, if such a thing were possible, by reducing further their possibilities of work. The evident result of this was to exaggerate their isolated social position and drive them further into despair. But there was still more to come when in 1748 Fernando IV tried to round up 9,000 Gypsies and send them off to Africa as slaves. This, however, never took hold due to the complicated logistics of the exercise! We must not forget their persecution in Germany or England where things were little better for them.

"It seems that the Gypsy men and women are only born into this world to become thieves: born from thieves, bred with thieves, study to be thieves and, finally, turn out to be common-or-garden thieves in every way and they earn it by stealing and the thieving is in them like inseparable accidents, that cannot be removed and only death can cure."
[*La gitanilla* - Miguel de Cervantes Saavedra]

Things finally started to turn the other way in 1783 with the arrival of Carlos III who pulled back the inhibiting laws discriminating against the Gypsies and restored them their full rights enabling them to live and work where they so desired. Finally, in Spain, their historical turmoil came to an end, at least in the official sense.

It is during the 18th century that Flamenco comes off age and becomes the strutting, stomping, polka dot fancy that we have come to imagine. When the Gypsies at long last settled, stopped possibly from furthering their exodus by the Atlantic Ocean, their dance and music fused permanently with the local influences that surrounded them.

The birth of Flamenco coincides with the forming of the *gitanerías* - Gyspy slums in *Andalucía*. Triana in Sevilla, Santiago and San Miguel in Jerez and La Viña in Cádiz, which still produce prodigious artists today, centuries later. They are the cradles of the majority of the most interesting songs and dances. The appearance of the first totally Flamenco style occurs in the neighbourhood of Triana.

Flamenco also took root at a moment when the rest of Europe was taking a great interest in the Spain and her, until then, forgotten heritage. The Romantics arrived to drool over the peninsula and their impression is still the one we have with us today. Principally the English and the French but there were also Italians, Germans, Scandinavians and Poles that came to see for themselves. The writings of George Borrow and Mérimée, the prints by Doré, the sketches and oil-paintings of John L. Sergeant and the musical impressions of the Russians Glinka and Rimsky Korsakov.

Now we begin to see some of the deep-rooted influences behind their music and especially their singing. The deepest and saddest of which is known as *Cante Jondo*. crudely translated as 'deep song'. (Pronounced /**KAN**-té **ON**-do/ The 'ay' is a short sound and the 'J' in *jondo* is silent.)

En gitana soleá
Voy yo cantando mis ducas
Tantas, que no caben más

In a Gypsy mourning
I sing my griefs
So many, that there is no room for more

All of this went into the social aspect the Gypsies imbued their songs with. At the start of the song you clearly hear the Arab muezzin and in the musical style *Seguirillas* one hears the music of the synagogue. They will always start with a signature '*¡Ay-EEE!*' in an almost identical style of the mosque leader calling the faithful to prayer, as was once the tradition for more than three quarters of a millennium in Moorish *al-Andalus*. The call of the muezzin was transformed by the Gypsies to call upon their innermost feelings to come to life in their music, taking form in their voice and shape in their movement. This *¡Ay-eee!* in Spanish is called a *Quejío* /ke-**HEE**-o/.

Through the Moors' empire in Spain music not only arrived from

North Africa but also did the sounds of Persia and Iraq. In addition there is the Hindu influence the Gypsies brought with them. The Flamenco word *debla* meaning 'grave song', and alludes to the name and chorus of the song in *debilla barí,* is reference to an overseeing goddess or mother figure common in Indo-Asiatic religion. Flamenco is therefore not the work of any one particular people but rather a fusion of peoples and their cultures in this intangible art form left to the guardianship of the Gypsies of Andalucía.

Flamenco has become, not only for the Gypsies, but also more importantly for Andalucía, a living historical document. It is not an easy music to digest for some who feel as if the singer is trying to exorcise demons. It is, though, a music dripping in soulful longing, whose atavistic sentiments are its essence.

There is no doubt that it is a human experience that touches three of our central artistic nerves, namely: song, music and dance. In all three, Flamenco excels and in all three it shines uniquely, having moulded from its past something that seems completely disconnected from anything seen before in Europe. It is indeed a rich culture.

Roots - *raíces*, as we are discovering are the starting point for any artistic undertaking in Spain. They are now, more than ever before, of paramount importance as we enter Gypsy territory. Here it is *the* most important word. That and not forgetting *duende*. Without *duende*, Flamenco and a large part of Spanish culture loses a sizeable piece of its soul and *all* of its mysticism. *Duende* exists but it is intangible, it resides in some people but not all of us. It may be displayed in a particular moment but not all the time. It manifests itself when a series of factors are in place and people are open to it. It is that sublime moment when you are able to escape yourself and surroundings and put the daily complications behind you with all of their illogical implications. It could be likened to an out-of-body experience. It is certainly spiritual and comes to the fore where our world touches what we believe our spiritual one should be. It is something you feel but never investigate to its conclusion, as you know it feels right. You know that a part of you resides there and the Flamenco artist performing for you has put you in contact with this emotion... known as *duende*. It is a Flamenco word, but is no means exclusive to it. It expresses that rare, sought after moment of high artistic expression which finds a place in any performing art. Bullfighting is also closely linked to *duende*. There is no reason, however, why such virtuoso moments of magic cannot be felt in other non-Spanish art forms such as Jazz for example. These performers have *duende* and you are grateful for it.

To understand the lyrics while the singer draws you into their realm of the senses, even for the native, is at times nigh on impossible. To understand the lyrics will naturally stir the blood more vigorously and make the mind wander further but only if the lyric is of any value. But more often than not with singing, on discovering the true written meaning it only leaves you feeling disappointed and wishing you hadn't taken the trouble to find out in the first place. You do not need words to feel another's sorrow or pain. That is easily transmitted through the tone of voice and physical expression. Not knowing exactly what Pavarotti sings in *Nessun Dorma* does not affect in the slightest, its evident power.

It is the expressive and emotional capacity rather than the perfect voice that counts as a good song in Flamenco. What is prized is its sheer force of the emotion and the direct line it takes from within the performer to the public. It forces you to experience what the singer, guitarist and dancer are feeling and expressing at that moment. This sensation of entrapment is what for many caught in an auditorium for the first time find disconcerting, it is a sense of emotional claustrophobia. And it is this that brings the faithful back to challenge and call upon their more melancholic or *alegre* self. Picasso referred to Flamenco as: *"the joy of sadness"*, which is a characteristic of melancholy.

For some strange reason there seems to be greater honesty with one another and with one's self when touched by melancholy. It holds an honesty that is rarely, if ever, achieved through any other human emotion. Anger makes man extreme, greed calculating, lust selfish, vanity insane and love irrational. Only melancholy can finally make a person accept their rational self and confront the truth of their own reality.

"Melancholy is at the bottom of everything, just as at the end of all rivers is the sea. Can it be otherwise in a world where nothing lasts, where all that we have loved or shall love must die? Is death, then, the secret of life? The gloom of an eternal mourning enwraps, more or less closely, every serious and thoughtful soul, as night enwraps the universe. "
Henri-Frédéric Amiel (1821-81) Swiss philosopher, poet.

But it was with the birth of the guitar that Flamenco gained a new lease of life and paying public. Possibly no other musical instrument suits Flamenco better, even though more and more instruments are being introduced into the art form. The guitar accompanies, marks the rhythm for the singer to follow as well as allows a rest for the singer but not for the listener.

It was in the 14th century that the guitar replaced the Moorish lute in *al-Andalus* - Moorish Spain, and from its introduction there was no turning back. The first five-stringed variant appeared in the 16th century at the hand of the Andalusian poet and musician Vicente Martínez Espiel born in Ronda in the province of Málaga in 1550. Then we had a wait on our hands, some two centuries, for the eventual emergence of the six-stringed instrument. In 1760 friar Miguel García, known as father Basilio, produced his innovation and was the first to write music in modem notation. However, it wasn't until the arrival of Francisco Tárrega (1854-1909) born in Castellón, that anyone really used the instrument to its full potential. His compositions moved many of the great composers of the day to write music for the guitar. And it was the knowledge that Tárrega brought to the fore that the great master of our time Andrés Segovia (18931987), born in Linares in Jaén, followed and improved upon. Andrés Segovia took the Spanish guitar into all the great musical conservatories of the world.

However, there often seems to be more than one history in existence at any given time and this is especially true when dealing with icons of national identity. The guitar is no exception and there are histories claiming the Germans invented the six-stringed instrument in the 18th century.

To make the instrument truly come to life it must be played without a plectrum. It is a hand-played instrument and the notes must be extracted and moulded from it. Flamenco had now found its musical accompaniment, which was portable, beautiful, human and above all something that was difficult to master and necessary to tame. In short, it was perfect for Flamenco. And the guitar only accentuated the singing and enriched the culture further still.

They say that comedians are, at heart, the most serious of people. John Cleese went into politics, Tom Hanks went to 'Philadelphia' and Robin Williams taught the poetry of Walt Whitman at Welton College for a time. This split personality, or the need of one great emotion to counter act a propensity for another, is also strongly reflected in Flamenco. The depth of their emotion is world-renowned but this has also been to their detriment covering their other great emotion, which is *alegría* – joy. If you have had

had such a bad time of it then you had better make the good times count when they come because they won't be around for very long. This philosophy shows the Gypsies taking the bull by the horns. Not a moment for exteriorising their happiness is wasted when the time comes. Today though, to catch this spontaneous act is less and less frequent as the Flamenco stage act becomes more and more commercially tamed. But this is one of the principal roles of dance in Flamenco: the Flamenco *fiesta* would just not be possible if there was no outpouring of joy. The dance is where all may participate and feel a part. Only in the new coming world of the 'professional' is there no room for the layman and laywoman to get up and display their *arte*.

Everyone here in Spain, but especially Andalucía, has *arte*, to a lesser or greater degree, of course, but it is something that everyone has and is encouraged to display. "*¡Qué arte tienes!*" This exclamation is common currency in Andalucía, meaning that you have a way with words, or with music or anything where individual flare may be appreciated. Even in humour you may have *arte*. In Flamenco the connotations are almost tangible.

As early as Roman times the women of Cádiz, known then as the city of *Gades*, were brought to Rome to dance. Such was their fame, *'the girls from Gades'* - in Latin *puellae gaditanae*, that eventually Emperor Theodosius banned them on moral grounds and the advice of San Juan Cristóstomo. Julius Caesar had visited the city on at least four occasions and one of the dancers enjoyed such success that her name of Telethusa is recorded in the Roman chronicles of the time.

With the eventual fusion of dance with the world of Flamenco the art form finally had what it had been missing: movement. The voice of the singer and the guitar found a physical expression and with dance becoming an almost separate culture it created its own accompaniment and traditions of elegant hand movements, rhythmic footwork and captivating choreography. Whatever the singer and guitarist could do the dancer could do just as well.

Flamenco has its three distinct components, each with a heritage of its own but without the others would cease to expound its full meaning. When the trinity combines you are left with a complete whole. The picture is perfect and when they start to play, they play upon your senses.

As if this wasn't already enough, the repertoire also includes hand clapping - for percussion not applause. Hands became an instrument in their own right. There is no people on earth that can achieve the resonance or complexity of rhythm as the Gypsies when it comes to clapping. But again here, there is also specialisation and of course *arte*. It literally deafens you at times and there is no need to use microphones and amplifiers. Gypsies can turn their hand to extract a rhythm out of anything. Their 'drum' is a box - *cajón flamenco*, specially made, from which a player can exact a unique resonance. It originates from Peru.

Flamenco, naturally, didn't start out in life by gaining popular recognition filling theatres but instead first found itself in the public gaze by performing in brothels. Eventually it became respectable and reached the springboard it needed when it entered the *cafés*. They were known as *cafés cantantes* or *cafés flamencos*. *Cantantes* in this context meaning 'singing'. The first record of which dates from 1842 in Sevilla and then they extended to almost all corners of Spain. The great singer Silverio dedicated his time to the *café*, setting up the first of its kind, the famous *Café de Silverio* in *calle Taifa*, developing the art form and popularising such establishments along with its music. The first *cafés* were half-hidden almost clandestine affairs with an air of racial and clan exclusivity. The scene is roughly what must have greeted Prosper Mérimée when he wished the tale of Carmen into being. The women dancing among the men, the singing, the heightened emotion and the inevitable fighting that often ended in extreme violence, as a report in 1886 for the Institute of Social Reforms clearly indicates. It was written by one of the mine's engineers in the town of Linares in the province of Jaén:

"The last years of the 19th century were the years of the cafés, and in the principal Andalusian cities the cafés ended up being places where the flamenco song of the Gypsies mixed with their dance, and the visits that the gypsy women later made between tables, talking, drinking and breaking into dance, amongst jokes of their kind, which lead to drunkenness, discussions, and finished up very often in brawls, with shootings and knifings inside and out of these establishments."

With proprietors recognising the potential pull of the trade the age of professional Flamenco was born and with it their new home known as *tablaos*. This, however, meant that future songs would be severed from its original inspiration. Its origins of suffering and discrimination would now be sung and performed by a different artist with a different experience in life. Now it was the customer, keen for the Flamenco *fiesta* that would steer the direction of the music. The professional would have to give what was required and not what they necessarily desired. They would learn from other professionals and in turn be handed down a finely tuned ability as opposed to a living legacy. A little bit was lost and little bit was gained, but one thing was undeniable: the music had greater public access than ever before.

The *cafés* flourished alongside the emerging dance academies being filled with people from beyond Andalusia's frontiers. The same partnership is still in business today and trade is booming.

New songs were even absorbed from the New World washed up in the port of Cádiz. The main song arrived off the boat direct from the Caribbean and River Plate region. In 1922 a *Cante Jondo* competition was organised for the first time to try and preserve the roots of Flamenco. It was set in motion by the likes of Frederico García Lorca, the composer Manuel de Falla and the painter Ignacio Zulonga. But it was in the character of Don Chacón that Flamenco was first taken to the big stage and its complete theatricalisation was begun after the Civil War (1936-39). During the fifties there was a huge revival and then we arrive in the era of mass media. One could say that Flamenco hasn't looked back since, but it does all the time, always in the search for its ever elusive 'roots' - *raíces*, that so obsesses the local populace in everything they do.

Ironically, during Franco's time signs displaying *'SE PROHIBE EL CANTE':* 'Singing is forbidden' were posted in bars between the 1940's and 50's and some have stayed on the walls as a bit of tradition. The quick witted have even scribbled after the word *cante* the adjective *'malo'* – bad, so only bad singing is not allowed. The singing was banned, however, because of the disturbances that followed as the lyrics were charged with political sentiment. Today people sing in the bars without trouble and to great acclaim. There were also other signs such as: *'Se prohibe que los niños se sienten en el mostrador'* prohibiting the children from sitting on the counter or, *'Se prohibe escupir'*, where it banned spitting on the buses because of TB in the 40's. The same went for the rest of Europe at the time.

Further breadth was given to the expansion of Flamenco nationwide with the arrival and then return of miners from the north. In Linares alone the population exploded from 6,000 inhabitants in 1849 to a staggering

36,000 in just 26 years. When they returned home to their regions of Asturias and Galicia they took Flamenco with them. A reminder of what they had once shared down south. A part of history travelled within them, which would come to the fore each time they broke into song. *Farrucas*, a song thoroughly absorbed by the South, hails from the north as does *Garrotín*. There is a branch of Flamenco song (each type of song called *un palo* in Spanish) known as *Minera* and each August in the region of Murcía they celebrate *El Festival Nacional del Cante de las Minas* in the town of La Unión. The festival is one of the most important dates in the Flamenco calendar and all the big names are present.

Cante Jondo, the emblematic deep song of Flamenco, finds its original voice in three founding towns: Morón de la Frontera, Jerez de la Frontera and Ronda. It then expanded out to the smaller towns of Arcos de la Frontera, Grazalema (the wettest place in Spain), Lebrija and Montellano. The best singers are said to be from Jerez and the best guitarists from Córdoba, where every year they celebrate *El Festival Internacional de la Guitarra*. Córdoba University has the only Chair for a professor of Flamenco. Today anyone wishing to seek out Flamenco will find it alive and well in the main centres of Andalusia's provinces: Almería, Cádiz, Granada, Huelva, Jaén, Málaga and Sevilla capital. It is also present in the region of Extremadura.

Flamenco is a diverse art form and its song and music has been moulded to many different styles that will delight the student of music and perhaps frustrate the professional trying to master them all. The *fandangos* from Huelva alone have 68 recognised variations with many carrying the name of the author or that of their town of origin. They are divided into three groups, more or less, although once again it is difficult to obtain a consensus. Here follows a lose categorisation to give some idea of the assemblies and their names. There are more than 300 *palos* in Flamenco so the following is abridged, fortunately. But simply reading the words used to describe Flamenco variants also serves as a small step into its world. For the truly curious you'll have to seek out the sounds themselves to bring this list to life.

1. **Jondo**:   Caña, Debla, Martinete, Polo, Seguidilla gitana, Serrana and Soleares

2. **Intermedio**: Carcelera, Fandango, Liviana, Malagueña, Petenera, Saeta, Serrana and Toná

3. **Flamenco**: Alegrías, Bulerías, Caracoles, Farruca, Granadina, Mariana, Minera, Murciana, Rondeña, Sevillanas, Tango and Taranta

All Flamenco song is derived from the original Gypsy songs of *Tonás*, *Siguiriyas*, *Soleares* and *Tango*. The last being the only festive song of the group.

The very fact that some of these words ring familiar is tribute to the range and reach of Flamenco. The following are worth special mention due to their unique character or to the fact that we may have at some time come across the name:

Alegrías come from Cádiz and is divided into three parts the *preámbulo*, the *meollo* and *epílogo* with the central themes being festivals and gallants. It is said it is similar to the song *Fiori* from Sicily.

Boleras or *seguidillas* (not to be confused with *Seguirillas*) believed by some to be the 'grandmother' of modern day *Sevillanas* (the picturesque folkdance from Sevilla and popular throughout all Andalucía). The singing is *alegre* and accompanied by elegant dance.

Bulerías is the classic sound of Flamenco and the one most people identify the genre with. Some say that everything in Flamenco has something of *Bulerías* in it. It originates from the coastal towns and they say no one commands *Bulerías* like the Gypsies. The rhythms are so fast and complex that you need to have had a lifetime immersed in playing the guitar to feel at ease while performing it live to any degree.

Caña is said to be one of the hardest and the *'oro puro'* - pure gold, of Flamenco singing. It is the primitive expression of *Cante Jondo*.

Caracoles, translated literally as it is meant to be: 'Snails', gaining its name from its *estribillo* - bridge, in the song, where they sing ¡*Y caracoles... y caracoles!*

Carceleras, again as its name indicates, is inspired by the prisons. So, it is a slow and sad song.

Fandango from Málaga, but extended throughout all Spain especially in Asturias in the north, was originally a song written to accompany the dance of the same name. Today not only the voice - *el cante*, but also castanets - *las castañuelas*, clapping - *las palmas*, and *guitarra*, accompany the action to the extent that a *Fandango* is not performed properly if all elements are not present.

Martinete was created by Gypsy steel workers. The songs deal with politics and the social situation of the Gypsies and their historical persecution in Spain. The lyrics are profound and the singing is often stripped bare of percussion and instrumentation. A hammer on an anvil maybe the only accompaniment but more often than not it is the singer's family that stands alongside.

Nanas are basically Flamenco lullabies and change greatly in style depending on whether they are from Cádiz, Huelva, Málaga or Sevilla,

Saetas, literally meaning 'arrows', are sung throughout all Spain. This song finds its deepest expression in *Semana Santa*, while the procession grinds to a halt and silence descends over the throng. It is not so much homage to the image as a letting out of sorrowful feeling in the vain hope that it will fall on the ears of some deity. Its origins though are not Catholic and may well have Pagan beginnings.

Soleá claimed by many to be the 'mother' of Flamenco song or *Soleares* as it is also known, lends itself to the guitar like none other. The protagonism required of the guitar here and the complexity of the *falsetas* have meant many good guitarists have had to give up trying.

Tango was developed to accompany dance. The song has its roots buried in Cádiz.

Tarantas is a slow and desperate song whose themes are usually the stamp of Flamenco sentiment: a death, a disgrace, dishonour, lament or threat.

Temporera is an interesting format where the singers interact to each other as they take their turn to sing a verse. One starts and then a second will interrupt by saying, "¡*Voy!*" - I'm going! This alerts the others. The next will come in using the same method until the last singer enters saying, "¡*Fuera!*" - Out! And they will sing the last of the song together.

Vidalita is a popular Argentinean song that has been adopted by Andalucía as her own and now well integrated.

La Alboreá is a Gypsy song and tradition which requires special note. It was traditionally sung during the rite of checking a Gypsy bride's virginity on her wedding day. The deflowering through the use of a cloth known as a *diclé* and carried out by a matriarch or religious Gypsy woman was ended by the blooded *diclé* being thrown to the ground during the singing of the chorus:

> *En un verde prado*
> *Tendí mi pañuelo*
> *Salieron tres rosas*
> *Como tres luceros*

In a green meadow
I laid down my handkerchief
Three roses came out
Like three morning stars

The verse makes light work of the ceremony which until the mid-fifties had been a jealously guarded secret among the Gypsy clan and the song had never before been recorded. Now the ceremony is common knowledge.

There was an attempt not long ago to classify Flamenco song into two categories of *'Grandes'* and *'Chicos'* - great and small. Unfortunately, this gained some popularity but as anyone moved by Flamenco, or music in general, will tell you what makes a song great is the performer.

Even the names of the various artists are a world unto themselves with all their nicknames echoing the familiarity between the people and their music: Manolo *Caracol* (Manuel 'Snail'), *Tomatito* ('Small Tomato'), *Camarón* ('Big Prawn'), *Perejil* ('Parsley'), *Terremoto* (Earthquake), *Naranjito de Triana* (Little Orange from Triana) and *El Chocolate*. The list of artists is as endless as are the combinations of names.

They even have special names in Flamenco for singer, guitarist and dancer, separating them from the singers, guitarists and dancers of other music styles. They are *cantaor/a*, *tocaor/a* and *bailaor/a*. And we must not forget the great Flamenco families that have created a dynasty all of their own. Where would the world of Flamenco be without families? Morao, Farruco and Vargas are just the tip of the iceberg. They must have the only inheritance that the Inland Revenue - *Hacienda* here, cannot touch. What a family business to be handed down! A tradition preserved by a bloodline. A legacy of *arte*.

Sevilla is just one of the cradles of Flamenco - Madrid is its finishing school. There are home-grown products of the art from Madrid but invariably people learn in the provinces and then head to the capital to hone their talents and then abroad to even greater fame and fortune. The top foreign destinations are the States and Japan. In Tokyo alone there are 300 Flamenco schools more than in all Andalucía, a region as big as Portugal or Hungary. France produces a lot of its own talent and many of them also travel to Spain's capital to meet their heroes and further their development. The Gypsy Kings are in fact from France, from the Camargue region, and play *flamenquito*.

In Sevilla there is an abundance of academies for the novice to study at and a prolific number of offers for those who wish to learn a few steps of *Sevillanas* before *La Feria* in April. Serious institutions, which you would imagine abound in the city, are in fact harder to come by. And this is why many foreign students who come to start their studies in the home land, eventually migrate north to the nation's capital.

The Flamenco triangle in Andalucía, comprised of Cádiz, Jerez de la Frontera and Sevilla, is responsible for the greatest variety of the differing branches of music and song within Flamenco. The region of Murcía through its two cities La Unión and Cartegena and the south of the region Extremadura have also played an important part in influencing Flamenco. To a lesser extent the remote town of Almadén in the west of the province of Ciudad Real in the region of Castilla-La Mancha just north of Andalucía has also played a role. You could even go so far as to say that there is even a triangle made up from the most influential provinces those being the provinces of Sevilla, Cádiz and Huelva.

Around Sevilla, the nearby town of Utrera is the star in its Flamenco crown having produced more singers than any other place in the province. The towns of Marchena, Morón de la Frontera and Estepa are also of more note than the provincial capital.

Andalucía is to Flamenco what Wimbledon is to tennis – it just isn't the same when taken in elsewhere, even if the French invented the game.

The writer Juan Antonio Fernández Durán referred to Sevilla's soul as:

"...*inmersa en la carne viva de sus gentes y en la piel cálida de sus cosas.*"

That means to say, "...*immersed in the living flesh of her people and in the warm skin of her things.*" He also said that when Andalusians spoke of themselves and their artistic and geographic environment, just by uttering a few words their thoughts and expressions jumped into a poetic tradition, as his own description implies. This is part of their Arab cultural tradition: a poetic expression.

It is fascinating to consider that this poetic self-expression is more tragic than romantic and therefore, while showing positive aspects of their character, they can never fully escape their historical past. A history marked by tragedy even though it has been showered with brilliance at certain intervals along the way. Because they open their safety valve of emotions, perhaps they never let their darker nature get the better of them. There is always time to express *alegría* – joy. Like a drinker that is used to his drink it takes a lot to get drunk. Someone not used to expressing their sentiments, like someone not used to their drink, needs very little for it to get the better of them. *'Express not repress.'* As Meg Ryan said in *French Kiss*.

"The weakness of a soul is proportionate
to the number of truths that must be kept from it."
Eric Hoffer (1902-83) U.S. philosopher.

So, that is the history and theory but what of Flamenco in practice? There is only one way to explain it and that is to go and see some it. So, we shall start at *El Teatro de Lope de Vega*, named after Spain's most prolific playwright. The building is well set among some of the most splendid pavilions constructed for the 1929 Expo nestled among baying Platinus trees with their characteristic dappled bark. The time of year sets the mood with a gentle warm breeze and the Flamenco stronghold of Sevilla are out in force in their glad rags to pay homage to the occasion. This is no tourist *tablao*, but as polished and professional as it gets. It is more the way many of them carry themselves rather than their attire that impresses most. There is magnetism about the Flamenco fraternity, from the way they hold themselves to way the way in which they look into, not through, you. Flamenco allows a woman to be feminine and yet strong at the same time while a man could possess masculine virility without the need to resort to a simpleton's concept of a macho hardman.

Tonight's billing is *La Compañia Andaluza de Danza* - The Andalusian Dance Company, directed by José Antonio who has held the reigns of the Spanish National Ballet at one time. Many come to Spain eager to see the bullfight while others come desperate to see this. It is here in such a theatre that Andalucía will work her magic on you.

Amongst some of the figures who are present and whose lives evolve around the music there are also those studying the art from Japan, Israel and the States.

As you walk in you mingle with heads bearing long, tightly tied brunette hair and many of the men possessing even longer hair. Earrings, dark eyes, tanned skin, bright teeth, tailored clothing are everywhere and an air of youthfulness infects all ages. This is what it really means when they talk about the 'beautiful people'. There is of course the less refined field of Flamenco with its roots in the villages where dentists would be seen as a novelty and a tailor's a luxury. But Flamenco, having participated in the front seat of Spain's cultural and economic revival from the 50's, is also displaying its evident trappings tonight.

The lights fade, the audience keep talking and then a spotlight faintly lights a small focal point floating mid-air central stage. Then with one almighty *"¡Shhhh!"* from several people in the audience silence is at last achieved, if only momentarily. Slowly and unnervingly everyone's eyes adjust to a soft hazy image taking shape. Hanging in the still darkness, just about visible, are three pairs of intertwined hands. Choreography, like writing, is not spontaneous; it is weighted and fine-tuned to heighten its effect and depth. Flamenco, famed for its spontaneity, is now being presented under a staged light.

The hands move, mingle and then spin round before stopping and repeat over. As the spotlight widens, the eyes of the audience are hungry to make sense of the image and see if their understanding of what is happening on stage has been right. As the light grows stronger the lines of three women gradually appears. Mystery hangs on briefly until the shape of their dress dispels all doubts. With their backs to one another they are all wearing typical and yet different Andalusian costumes, each the representation of southern feminism in its folklore livery. One is covered by intricate white lace falling loosely down her back - *la mantilla*. It is held in at its focal point crowning her head by the all too familiar *peineta*, the fan-like high comb which distinguished *señoritas* wear. Her long flowing Flamenco dress tapers off along the floor behind her in a long tail - *cola de bata*. It has to be flicked expertly so as not to halter her progress. Next to her, another woman is adorned with a similar head garment cascading over her shoulders and decorated with small brightly coloured balls spread over an open latticed shawl, which flick up behind her as she goes. The third is more fashionably dressed, if such a thing is possible in folklore. Her polka-dot *Feria* dress is wrapped in her silk Manila shawl and topped by flowers tucked in her hair.

The lights focus and fill the stage. The smooth movements of the hands widen out and the characteristic body movements of a woman dancing Flamenco now commence. The arms extend out and drop, curve and ascend into the air again with effortless ease all the time drawing new lines in the air. Slowly but surely the feet start to mark the rhythm, *el compás*. At first faintly but ever more firmly until the audience depends less on the music and more on their footwork to understand the ebb and flow of the beat.

The introduction comes to a close but just then they are joined by the rest of the female troupe who flow in from the wings. The dancers are strong as opposed to frail, tanned not anaemic, curvaceous instead of stick-like and of course impassioned. The vigour and decisive force of the stamping is all channelled in the same direction, which is at the audience and while exhilarating, it verges on the frightening.

When the men finally show themselves they thunder onto the floor in unison like a stampeding herd. The rush of testosterone is unsettling but the purity of movement combined with its force played out by the dancers, is something touching the sublime. Ballet may be lost on most people but there is no escaping the impressiveness of this human movement. Power and masculinity is tethered to grace and perfect poise. The effect sends the blood rushing. The rhythms pound out unrelentingly on the boards and connect with a beat as deep rooted as that of the pounding heart.

Finally, the two opposing forces meet, the men with the women, and the experience goes into another dimension. The relation between the two is given new relevance and the audience is taken somewhere else within themselves. But then the music stops and the guitar beats a muted rhythm as hands hit onto the sound-boxes and rake across taut, silenced strings. Centre stage is now occupied by the company's best soloist and the audience is trapped between his ever-growing tapping on the hollow wooden floor while the guitars answer his complex, striking dance. Everyone wants release from the building anxiety and a chance to share in the rapture. But it only keeps building higher, increasing everyone's vertigo. Until quite unexpectedly, yet perfectly timed, the dancer slams his foot shut over the torment silencing the music and the theatre erupts into ecstasy. Clapping and outpourings of emotion are let loose in the theatre. *¡Bravo! ¡Olé! ¡Eso es! ¡Qué fuerte! ¡Qué arte tiene!* But no sooner has this been done than the whole thing is started up again and we are taken on another roller-coaster journey through our newly released passions but this time it is of staggering proportions. Again it finishes, mercifully, to allow us an opportunity to come to our senses but then... it comes again. You would have thought that your first exaltations had been enough of a rush but then to have them taken a step further, and then a step further *again* each time immersing you deeper within the sphere of your primitive impulses means you are entering into the realm of *duende*.

The night comes to a close by once again taking the audience unawares and letting the dancers show off their flare by giving them free reign over the stage. Flamenco was born out of spontaneity and although choreography tries to tame it, occasionally it is necessary to let it escape from its modern encasing and breathe freedom. The guitarists stand up and holding their instruments close to their chests form a semi-circular boundary with the dancers and dare one of them to step forward. *Alegría* fills the walls of the *Lope de Vega* and Sevilla is truly at one with herself. The audience claps out the music with the dancers and shouting their *alegría* and *arte*. Their artistic sentiment literally pours out of their voices. The company takes their final bow and then it starts. You won't be forewarned and will be delighted to discover a unique side of Andalusian culture, because it says so much about them in a simple and endearing way. They start clapping their familiar rhythm of: **ONE**-two-three, **ONE**-two-three, **ONE**-two-three, in appreciation of the dance company. It is their inimitable way of paying their respect by giving back a little of the emotion and music that the dancers have given to them. The hall resounds to Andalucía, positively throbbing with its heart beating out from the hands of her people. And of course the dancers dance as the theatre breathes Flamenco just a little longer.

Flamenco is one of the purest mediums that best expresses the culture and emotions of the ancient lands of Andalucía, where its heritage has been bottled up in the message of its music. It is the way people here, above all the Gypsies, express their joy and alleviate their anguish.

Sevilla lusts after her culture and when e*l Bienal de Flamenco* comes to town, as the name suggests every two years, you have to be quick to get those tickets if you want to see one of the 'Greats'. Surprisingly without the festival the city would be left a little threadbare for Flamenco of an international standing. The event pays respect to one of the art forms it has helped create and nurture and it is a time when Sevilla feels that Flamenco is the only consuming passion coursing through its veins.

From all corners of the country and globe Sevilla's finest return to their hometown.

The modern theatre built for the '92 Expo is a bright modern addition to the city's illustrious collection of architecture. Outside is the usual collection of heels and finely embroidered shawls - *mantones*, draped around delicate shoulders or casually hanging over arms for later use. There are jackets and slacks and tailor made shirts, pearls set off against dark *moreno* skin and shining hair. In the case of the men their hair is encased in a sheet of Brylcreem. And everywhere, as always, people are smiling and socialising, whether they know each other or not. Everything is: *'Como Dios manda'* - *As God intended*, as they say round these parts.

The auditorium is a little reminiscent of Glyndebourne all done out in designer wood. The stage is as in all Flamenco concerts left to the bare minimum, so as not to distract from the Flamenco.

Tonight's artist will make a token gesture to the purists and from then on in it is going to be his personal interpretation of the music that will be in charge. The audience take their places and there is an expectant buzz about the auditorium. It is after all the *Bienal*, this is *La Maestranza* and we are here to see none other than Paco de Lucía. This is the right place to be and most certainly at the right time.

The lights fade, the audience keep talking and a soft light gradually illuminates a small focal point mid-stage. Then with one almighty and customary Spanish *'¡Shhhh!'* from several people in the audience silence is at last achieved, if only for a moment. (That's how Flamenco, if not all concerts, start in Sevilla.) A guitarist comes in and sits down. People cheer and then immediately fall silent when they realise they have confused him for the great man. Paco de Lucia is still waiting back stage. He is already playing jokes with the purists. The guitarist sits down and starts up. One by one, artists come in and join in the playing. Another guitarist, back-up singers hand clapping - *las palmas*, a percussionist enters and sits on a Flamenco box, then another percussionist comes next to him surrounded by drums and strike up their respective instruments. After that more singers arrive and sit down together soon followed by a flutist, which leaves only one seat in the middle of the stage begging its owner. The distinct concave head of the maestro comes quickly onto the stage and sits down immediately joining the *juerga*. After a deafening reception we are able to hear the music again and it builds and builds and builds until we are hit by a gaping silence.

A Flemish Flamingo

The show is about to commence.

The late Paco de Lucia accompanied Flamenco's greatest singer Camarón de la Isla, known as *el Príncipe*. Together they recorded virtuoso performances that have become a benchmark by which all other Flamenco is judged. They were great friends during the singer's life and in 1992 Camarón passed away. Before that, the two artists had taken separate paths with Camarón hooking up with another great: Tomatito, whose daughters went on to world fame in the group Las Ketchup. When the great partnership of Paco and Camarón worked they broke the boundaries of the established order and it was something that Paco de Lucia did all his life and is still doing tonight before us.

His guitar solo which now strikes up is only a passing moment in the entire mix of music and talent that the guitarist wants to display. Flamenco breathes its vital life into the lungs of the flutist Jorge Pardo, who Paco de Lucía introduced to Flamenco to form part of his sextet. Then the Brazilian percussionist Rubem Dantas, who introduced the Peruvian percussion box into Flamenco, takes centre stage and releases the music in unconventional directions. All the while deep voices let out a spontaneous *¡Olé!* from the audience, which rolls out like a wave coming ashore at dusk. It isn't shouted, it is uttered in unison to underpin the moment, charge the atmosphere with Flamenco sentiment but never interfere with the playing. When the music stops there will be plenty of time to applaud.

In front of the group is a square block of wood. As the music climbs to its point of climax the other percussionist, who is seated quite contentedly on his *cajón de Flamenco* - Flamenco box, suddenly jumps up and pounds out the last few bars of the beat with his feet across the resounding wood, dazzling the eyes as he slashes lines through the air and punches a silence through the heart of the theatre as he cuts off the music the moment it reaches the end of its crescendo. The dancer is none other than Joaquín Grilo from Jerez.

Now we have been let in on a few of the surprises they take their time to develop their ideas at a more leisurely pace the second time round. When the exotic sounds of Flamenco take unexpected flight from that flute the whole place sits in restless rapture. We are all treated to something exquisite. For some it is almost on a par with the magic playing of the 'sacred' guitar. Then the pair of percussionists do battle between themselves letting one and all know why they are up there with Paco and not the budding enthusiasts sat watching with envy dripping from their hands and hearts.

The flute, the guitars, the clapping and the percussion have all had their moment with the audience to create a dimension of emotion oozing Flamenco character and charm. Now it is the turn of the *bailaor* to stamp the boards and take us once more up to dizzying heights of delirium. The sound of the wooden base is comparable to the temperate sound-box of the crafted Flamenco guitar. The musicians follow him as he gently raises his arms carving a pure contour before the expectant audience. The movements are slight, calculated to perfection and charged with masculinity. He has complete control over the space around him and total dominion over the sensation he is creating. The crowd hold their emotions in check for the time being. He never looks out to the crowd, never acknowledges their presence nor those playing behind him. The moment is his and we are fortunate to be present. Not a hair stays in place and yet not a line drawn by his body in the magnetic aura that surrounds him is anything short of perfect. And then the Cuban heels start to push syllables out from the wood giving birth to a clear, sharp beat to accompany the guitar. The sweat drops as testosterone is exuded and the tension pounds out ever more fervently on the wood. All the time the man keeps his movements slight, elegant and commanding. For a brief moment when his heel slams down demanding silence the whole theatre obeys and La Maestranza is suspended in time. Then suddenly everyone comes out of their senses, released from the tension and jumps to their feet and roars: ¡*Olé!* ¡*Bravo!* Too many things are shouted to remember but nobody holds themselves back now and everyone is out of their seats.

By the end of that concert his name is on everyone's lips, especially the *señoritas'* if not all the *señoras'*. And as far as 'real men don't dance' goes; there was more male hormone and vitality thrown out in those few glorious moments than an entire rugby team in a full-bloodied 80 minutes.

Then once again, and inevitably, it starts up: **ONE**-two-three, **ONE**-two-three, **ONE**-two-three the Andalusian hand clapping slowly lifts the roof. There is a Spanish saying, *'From Madrid to Heaven'* which the locals have changed to *'From Madrid to Sevilla and from Sevilla to Heaven'*. It feels almost true in that heady moment. Grilo has unhinged the theatre and Paco de Lucía has delivered what his faithful had come to feel.

The night ends in a bar among drinks, *tapas*, liberal conversation and much singing.

Then you get the chance to go to a *Peña Flamenco*, which is a

Flamenco club that are dotted all about town. One is down a back alley in La Macarena, a pleasant place with its own *patio*, fountain, bar and stage. They hold dance competitions and you see Isabel, half-gypsy, take the faithful by storm. She is a well rounded girl with innocent looks but turns the emotions of everyone upside down. She sets fire loose in the *peña* and everyone comes out burnt by her performance. Clicking her fingers by passing her thumbs across three fingers as opposed to the customary one, she has enough to surprise and the wherewithal to keep up the tempo. Her band of Gypsy supporters only increase her chances by transforming the atmosphere into euphoria of truly gargantuan proportions for such a small room. It is powerful and moving stuff.

There is even an American who has come to study Flamenco before returning to New York to join the ballet, brave enough to step onto the boards. She is technically good, better than good in fact, and has the nerve to stand up and be counted in front of the critical natives. But she doesn't have what Isabel has and what Isabel has inside her, that affects everyone the way she does, is priceless. Maybe it is *duende*, but whatever it is, it unseats the place.

The full-on Gypsy experience though must be had in the form of Farruquito, voted one of People magazine's top 50 most attractive men. For two glorious nights *el Teatro de la Mastranza* the young man, who is always accompanied by his family, dazzles the people of Sevilla and those of his own race. It is hard to find an audience that gives so much of themselves to any performance as the crowd that come to Sevilla to watch him perform. They clap, shout out *¡Olé!* as well as other words of encouragement during the whole act. Nobody holds back from giving an ovation and the characteristic rhythmic hand clapping that resounds louder than in any theatre: **ONE**-two-three... The emotion presses out on the walls not to mention in on the hearts and minds of the audience. The end of the show reaches near hysteria when the stage lights blink back on and at the front of the stage are all the dancers and musicians standing around the latest four-year-old addition to the clan as the young lad dances his heart out as if he were at home in the living-room and was just trying to impress his Gran. If the partisan crowd has been in a state of delirium until now, they are in a positively Flamencan Utopia.

If you only go to see Flamenco dancers once in your precious life time you would do your soul the world of good to experience what this man and his family are capable of provoking in you.

Unbelievably, and tragically, the star of the show Farruquito since writing this ran over and killed a man on a zebra crossing in Sevilla. He is about to know a little of the darker side of *cante jondo*, as his own suffering has begun.

El *Nuevo Flamenco* is the all happening scene on and off the stage now. It is the rage of discussion among the purists angered that the medium is being changed for the worse. The Gypsy nature for expression is something that lends itself to exploration and they are usually the ones that come up with something new before anyone goes ahead with it. Conflict with the purists is common. Flamenco has opened its doors like GM crops blowing in the wind: Divergent cross-breeds have grown up such as Flamenco-pop with the group Ketama; Flamenco-rock with the guitarist Raimundo; Flamenco and Blues with Raimundo again. The greatest fusion has possibly been with Jazz, where Miles Davis went on to record Flamenco variations. All of the above are referred to as *Fusión*. It is not welcomed by some, as much as floodlights and pyjamas are disliked by the M.C.C. or money at first in Rugby Union. But this is an art form and it is inherent in its nature to expand and branch out in different directions. Without that characteristic Flamenco itself would not have come into being in the first place. It is after all a *fusión* of different musics itself: Arab, Jewish, Gypsy and Christian.

The comparisons between Afro-American music and the Gypsies are all too evident and frequent amongst *Flamencos*. Both races have a don for rhythm and exteriorising their emotions. In short, they have less social complexes than most. It is a comparison that the people of Andalucía are very aware of and one they are proud to make.

If we want to look into the future for a sign of what may come of such multicultural and racial integration that characterises our modern times, especially in Europe; if we wish to know what hope lies for us in the future then we only have to look back to this great moment of multiracial fusion in times far more uncivilised than ours to find the answer. Here surely, in Flamenco, is at least one bright light burning in favour of the riches that can be gleamed for humanity when the influences and the best that each culture has to offer have been thoroughly sifted by time and taste, to leave something that no singular culture could ever have created in its isolation.

¡Ay-eee!

- SIETE -
SUN & *SOMBRAS*

*- Almost everything you wanted to know about 'bullfighting'
but weren't sure you should ask -*

'The composition of a tragedy requires testicles.'
Voltaire (1694-1778)

It is said by many that Spain looks like an outstretched bull hide, which was its symbol for its 2002 European Presidency. And if Spain does indeed take this form then maybe it was preordained for Spain to be forever connected with the bull, which is just how the local like it: fatalistic. No where is this side of their psyche better seen than in the bullfight. If Spain is the bull's hide then Sevilla is where its heart would have been.

Going to the bullfight for the first time? Haven't a clue what it's all about? Going with a beautiful *señorita* or attractive *señor* and don't want to fail to impress? Want to shed the shadow of ignorance and really know what goes on behind the scenes and what the locals think of it all? The following should be of some use then.

Let's start at the beginning. Back in the good old days when stadiums were full animals attacking each other as opposed to supporters doing it, one of the stars of the show from the earliest times was the bull. And with the bull being the symbol of the devil for some cultures, as well as a deity for others, this was an absolute must for the public. Bulls were worshipped in many religions especially as symbols of potency and for their horns which resemble the lunar crescent. The ancient auroch bulls were hunted and revered in Spain. Both the ancient Greeks and Basques believed that the first people were centaurs. In the Ancient Near East and the Aegean, the wild auroch bull was extensively worshipped as the Lunar Bull. It is quite typical for the god of one culture to be a demon in another. In many cultures the word 'cattle' also means 'money' or 'wealth'. The animals were one of the first and most exchangeable commodities. Hence the sacrifice of a calf was the offering of the most valuable possession that one had. The killing of the bull here then can be seen as a confrontation with an evil spirit or the sacrifice of a person's wealth.

The Romans were big on games and taking animals to their slaughter. So much so that they even denuded great parts of North Africa of their fauna.

'Bull' in Spanish is *Toro* and the bullfight *'La Corrida de Toros'* is the only remnant of the Roman games that we have with us today. It is a relic that has undergone a transformation leaving us only the original ring, a bull and human involvement with an animal. The rest is all Hispanic even though it had once been Roman in its deepest root.

Informally in Spain it is simply referred to as: *'Los Toros'* - The Bulls. However, it is not called a 'bullfight' but a *'Corrida'*, literally meaning 'running'. *La Corrida* refers to the moment when the bull runs at the *torero*. If it were strictly a fight then the bull would be killed as soon as possible, but it is not. Ironically in Pamplona, where they do run the bulls, it is not called a *Corrida*; but an *encierro*, from *encerrar* meaning to 'enclose'. They are run through the streets and then enclosed at their destination's end.

The title *'matador'* is used in Spanish but only in its full form: *'Matador de Toros'* - 'bullkiller'. The most commonly used name, however, is *Torero*, which has no direct translation and 'bullman' just doesn't have the same ring to it.

Next, one should know that it is not a 'sport' but an 'art'. One goes not to appreciate the killing as such, but more the manner in which it is achieved. If the *torero* does a good job it is referred to as *una buena faena*. The word *faena* is used in everyday language meaning – job or task.

> *'Bullfighting is the only art in which the artist is in danger of death and in which the degree of brilliance in the performance is left to the fighter's honor.'*
> Ernest Hemingway (1899-1961)

The bullfight as we know it didn't start to take shape until the 17th century in the ring at Ronda, a fine, classically colonnaded structure. Whether you like *La Corrida de Toros* or not architecturally it is well worth a visit. Ronda is believed by many to be the oldest *plaza* in Spain but that honour befalls *El Castañar* in Béjar c.1667, La Mancha. There is even an older structure in *la plaza de Las Virtudes* in Santa Cruz de Mudela, Ciudad Real. Curiously it isn't round but square and was built in 1643-5? but not used until 1722. The principal *plaza de toros*, however, is *Las Ventas* in

Madrid. The capital, incidentally, has two *plazas de toros* the second is covered and pleasantly named *La plaza de Vistalegre.*

Every *torero* wants to 'triumph' in Madrid; but curiously their dream is more than likely the desire to impress the crowd gathered in Sevilla during *La Feria de abril. Los sevillanos* are regarded by their Spanish peers to be the most knowledgeable about the art.

The Spanish Crown set up chivalric orders to encourage the nobles to train as horsemen, use weapons and be ready for action when called upon. *Las Reales Maestranzas* - Royal arsenals, were formed, five in total. Together they formed the chivalric order known as *El Real Maestranza de Caballería* founded in 17th century. Once their purpose had been served and fallen into disuse they turned their attentions to bullfighting and set up their respective rings. The five orders organized under Royal patronage are: Ronda, Sevilla, Granada, Valencia and Zaragoza. *La Real Maestranza de Caballería* in Sevilla (c.1671) doubles as a benevolent institution offering scholarships for university studies, organizes fine arts competitions and historical publications, they resolve social problems and help with the conservation of monuments. The Eldest Brother of the order is the King.

The *Maestranza* order demolished the original wooden bullring and made way for the present structure in 1758, which was completed in 1880. The bullring in Sevilla is not a perfect circle, as everyone here loves to tell visitors willing to lend an ear. Instead, it is more of an oval shape owing to the fact that they couldn't demolish all the town houses around the ring. So, they had to fit the ring between the buildings, hence the imperfect shape and the time needed to bring the project to fruition. However, they created one of Spain's fairest structures, painted *'cal de Morón'* white, ringed in red with a yellow *albero* centre and can seat up to 12,500 *aficionados.*

After Ronda it is possibly the most attractive bullring anywhere and it is strange that such a beautiful place has such a deadly purpose.

If you like a good argument then try and convince the locals it is a sport. To its many followers, *La Corrida* is an art - even a form of religious ritual. Then there are those - even among its fans - who openly admit it is barbaric. The decision as to whether it is a sport, ritual or art is obviously a personal one. The Spanish who take issue with it being labelled an art counter such claims with the following phrase:

"Si la tauromaquia es una arte, entonces el canibalismo es gastronomía."
(If bullfighting is an art, then cannibalism is gastronomy)

Hemingway and Orson Welles[1] were rhapsodic about the Spanish panoply of colour and found a meaning at every turn in the ceremonial death of the bull that no other walk of life could express.

"Either you respect the integrity of the drama the bullring provides or you don't. If you do respect it, you demand only the catharsis which it is uniquely constructed to give."
Orson Welles

But it was the hispanophile French, who were responsible for projecting the present romantic image of the bullfight. Above all it was the Prosper Mérimée's story handed down to him by a gypsy that another Frenchman, Georges Bizet, transformed into the world's favourite opera, Carmen. The cigar curling *femme fatale* from Seville's gypsy quarter of Triana toyed with a soldier but she fell for a *torero*. Her statue stands half-hidden across from the *Maestranza* bullring near the Guadalquivir River.

In August 2004 RTVE, the government owned TV and radio company, decided to halt transmission of the bullfight. Their motive, they said, was purely economical and not in any way political. However, the union of bull breeders believed the hand of animal rights was behind the decision. A spokesman for the union said, *"It has a political consequence that we completely reject for its contempt for a traditional and cultural manifestation of the highest magnitude and for its implications as a precedent reaffirming radical stances contrary to the fiesta."*

In August 2005 a scandal that rocked the bullfighting world took the debate one long awaited step further by those against the killing of bulls for viewing pleasure. Claims of bribery, unfair treatment of bulls before they reached the ring and other backhand dealings caused a stir. Many of the accusations were not new. Some bullfighters had even gone on record saying similar things had occurred at different times throughout their careers. Rumours that Vaseline had been used to blur the bull's vision and that horns

---

[1] *Welles was a revered hispanophile whose special love of the country saw him buried there in Málaga, in the garden of a friend... in a well.*

had been shorn so the animal misjudged its distances when trying to use them had been circulated for quite some time. What happened in August though was an *ex-torero* went on record and threw down all of these allegations in one go and the press lapped it up, leaving the bullfighting fraternity momentarily lost for words. This only encouraged the press to dig deeper. More than 20% of bulls analysed showed symptoms of having been drugged. Hearsay claimed that weights were sometimes hung around the bull's neck for several weeks before the *Corrida* so the animal could not lift its head high enough to defend itself properly. There had even been talk about animals being hit in the kidneys before taking to the *plaza*. The situation was a long way from it being normal to hear opposing opinions on a regular basis, but it did shake things up a bit. It may, however, ironically serve the better interests of the *Corrida* by returning the art form to its origins and ensuring that 'brave' bulls make it into the ring once more.

Spain's greatest living legend, Curro Romero from Camas just outside Sevilla, returned from retirement because he had said the bulls were smaller and less dangerous than before. With *los Toros* now having become the domain of big money and handsome faces perhaps going back to the old ways, which the purists have been crying out for, is about to happen.

To underline the extent of support for the bullfight and the regard with which it is held, suffice to mention the singular incident, which took place in the aforementioned town of Camas in 1999 when a fight between a bar owner and his client broke out when derogatory comments were made about the *torero* Curro Romero. The altercation took place in the home town of the *matador de toros*. What was surprising though about the unique episode was that the judge found in favour of the bar owner who had taken to his fists first, summing up that the admiration in Camas was *"a way of understanding life."*

Nonetheless, the bullfight does possess elements of spectacle, victory, blood and sacrifice and whether you love or hate it, living here you can't ignore it. It is a display of colour and pageant of music. It has the atmosphere and emotion of the crowd's expectations of the *Corrida's* age-old format versus the unpredictability of the bull and its sometimes unexpected outcome. The victor is normally the *torero*, seldom the bull and almost always the paying public. Everyone loves a winner and so the public bask in the *torero's* defiance of death. The blood connects everything to the vitality of life, because buried deep in our psyches, red is the colour of imminent danger.

The despatching of the bull after its methodical preparation for the ring is a quasi-religious sacrifice made in Spain. The norm is to dedicate the bull to the President. However, if there is another dignitary present such as the King then the *torero* will more than likely kill the bull in their honour. They won't kill it for their wife or mother, because it is rare that either is in attendance. Family do not want to sit through the half hour of torment waiting to see if their husband or son will survive the afternoon unscathed. It is not the winning that counts but the staying alive. But even coming out in one piece is seen as second best if the bullfighter hasn't demonstrated any valour in front of the animal and mastered its wild spirit. To kill and then walk away without having shown courage and contempt for your own possible demise will ensure any aspirant a very brief and fruitless career. Spain wants to see them confront man's worst fear with respect, control and passion by defying the transience of mortality. Above all, he must take his time, enjoy the moment and overcome the danger by turning the fear into fascination as the artist in the matador turns a possible death into a defiant sword dance. Only after all that has been achieved may the *torero* truly say that he has 'triumphed' in the ring.

The bullfight is a central part of any major Spanish celebration save *Semana Santa*, which is not a *fiesta*. *La Corrida* is called and regarded as *"La Fiesta Nacional"*. This in itself is at once believable and misleading. Some two million spectators attend the rings annually compared to five times that number who walk into football stadiums. Maybe because it's not so easy to kick a bull about. However, the culture of the ring and sand is Spanish, while the pitch and its turf is an import. In 1991 *La Corrida* was given an official seal of approval when José Luis Corcuera, the then Interior Minister, passed the law *Ley de Espectáculos Taurinos* where, for the first time, it was classified officially as a *'cultural tradition'*. A tradition that apparently takes in around €750,000,000 a year and maintains 170,000 in employment. It is even subsidised in part by regional governments. Three times a week a bullfighting school congregates in Alamillo Park in Sevilla so its youngsters can practice their cape technique. The school is maintained through money from *La Junta de Andalucía* because the activity is seen as a Spanish institution that should be maintained. One could argue, why then in a land of writers and poets is not poetry subsidised as well?

The rest of *La Corrida de Toros* should be unfolded *paso a paso*, that is step by step. We will look at the hard facts, history and traditions that go into its make up.

The full name of the Spanish bull is *Toro Bravo*, meaning 'brave bull'. The bulls that actually go into the ring (not all of them meet the grade) are called *Toros de Lidia*, 'fighting bulls'. The bull is labelled as 'brave' because, although it is punished in the ring with pain, it will keep on attacking. Most bulls would shy away after the first experience of it.

By the 16th century, there were established bull breeders called *ganaderos*, and the *Corrida* had survived as the most popular element of the ancient world's bloodthirsty games. A century later and the *toro bravo*, as we know him today, begins to take shape with the first 'official' bloodline: *La Jijona*. A hundred years on and the four main bloodlines were formed: *Raíz Cabrera, Gallardo, Raíz Vázquez* and *Raíz Vistahermosa*, just like the 'pure' bred English racehorse that can be traced back to one of three Arab stocks. The Spanish bull, as all domestic European cattle, is descended from the now extinct Auroch *(Bos Taurus primigenius.)* The last known example perished in a Polish park in 1627.

Today the principal areas that breed bulls are the provinces of Toledo, Salamanca and of course the region of Andalucía where the bull populates some of the most remote areas of Europe. One arguments given for defending *La Corrida* is that the animal lives well. Those that are kept as studs can live up to 20 years and in a season will mate on average four times a day with a herd of some 45 females. A bull is free to roam but then again the countryside is also a breeding ground for flies and mosquitoes that will pester the bull until he enters the ring.

Before a year of his life has passed, he is rounded up, separated from his mother and branded. Here, across the extensive Andalusian plains and expansive skies, come charging Western Europe's first and only cowboys - *vaqueros*, with lances in hands and the long manes of their Spanish horses dancing in the breeze. The riders gallop close as they try to separate cow from calf. The cow is quicker than her bull-calf, more agile and more determined. The lance - *la garrocha*, serves to knock the calf over by hitting its hindquarters as it turns. This running down of the bullock and then bringing him to ground is known as *acoso y derribo* and competitions in this discipline are held all over Andalucía. The rider, in flat cap and side-burns, draws the cow away from the young bull. When they finally trap him and take him to be branded, it is the last time the mother will see him. As the calf is immobilised and awaits his initiation, a large bonfire keeps the breeder's branding irons 'on ice'. As the initials and numbers are burnt in, the bull obviously cries out in pain. When all is done it is everyman for himself. The bull, now on its feet, wants to exact revenge. From the very moment the animal can stand properly it is prepared to charge anything. With good reason it takes its frustration out on the only thing that has remained behind and runs its horns through the centre of the fire scattering it in all directions.

Over time the selection process has bred the bull we are familiar with today. So familiar in fact that everyone knows the characteristic 40ft high silhouette from the Osborne sherry bottles and the great images the company has dotted around the Andalusian countryside to advertise itself.

They used to be seen in there hundreds but now only 97 survive, which started life in 1956 to promote their cognac. These remaining profiles have been declared a national monument after the Supreme Court ruled in 1997 that the bull sign: *"enhances the view rather than encourages consumption."* As the Spanish novelist Julio Llamazares observed, *"this was because, like mountains, castles, and villages, the bulls were landmarks. After seeing them for so many years beside our roads, after embracing them as part of our collective and individual iconography, it was hard to imagine life without them."*

Not all the bulls are black of course, though they do carry the same horns, broad shoulders and neck that even Mike Tyson would envy. The *Miura*, the most feared 'mankiller' tends to be light grey. This breed from Andalucía and Lamborgbini namesake, has killed more *toreros* than any other. Some are skewbald, others sorrel, many are dun in colour as well as roan. Times change even in such traditional institutions and today's most unpredictable breed is the *Victorino Martín*. *Miuras* have declined as *toreros* have refused to face them. Maybe they will be pacified or the breeder could be out of business. As the bullring has changed from the refuge of the working man to the arena of the gentry, bulls have, according to the well-informed, reduced in size and ferocity.

In order to look for the right characteristics in an animal that will be chosen for the ring they test the cow, not the bull-calf. If she, under 'light' punishment, continues to charge the mounted horseman then she is deemed to have *casta*, which is the 'determined spirit' and breeding that defines the bull in its relentless attack to defend itself against an aggressor. This trial and selection process is called *La Teinta*. From the mother comes courage and while the father merely bestows his good looks. The bull's broad shoulders hold up an immense pack of bulging neck muscle and the back tapers down to narrow haunches. The forehead is squared, as is the formation of the horns that turn out from the temple at right angles to face anything which is foolish enough to cross its path. It is awkward when seen from its flank but when admired head-on its stance is that of a seated sovereign in audience: noble, dominant and unmistakably powerful. There is no sign of danger from this apparently placid bovine. It does not roar, bare teeth nor rear up. Above all, what draws the viewer in, is the abyss of its black eyes. Dark as the night and soulless in their sinister emptiness, its eyes are as penetrating as its horns. It can seem serene in posture, wearing an expression of indifference, which at its most innocent verges on inquisitiveness, but all this changes the moment it charges.

Once passed *la teinta*, the bull born into this world is branded, tagged and named for posterity. From then on, it is left for anything from 3 to 6 years to lead the good life during which time it must not experience any cape play nor be near a man on foot. That is why those who work in the country with the bulls do so on horseback. This is done not just for the obvious reason of making a quick get-away but so the bull does not learn to charge the man instead of the cape.

Three-year-old bulls are taken for novice bullfighters - *novilleros*, and the six year olds, wise with age, for *toreros* wearing full colours. The day a *novillo* finally becomes a fully fledged *torero* is called *'tomando la alternativa'*. A bull may look like a dumb animal but it is an incredibly fast learner when it comes to working out who or what the real danger is - the cape or its carrier? This knowledge on the part of the bull is called *sentido* - sense. On average it takes 15 minutes to kill a bull in the *Corrida* and woe betide the man who takes any longer. During a bull's tragic 15 minutes of fame some do actually figure out who to go for and then the *torero* realises he's in trouble. However, if a bull has been practised on before getting into the ring it is an experience the animal never forgets. Then the man and not the cloth will be the animal's target from the very outset.

Capeas are 'anyone-can-have-a-go' *corridas* using experienced animals - often cows - *vaquillas* - which move faster. *Las capeas* are usually held in summer during local *fiestas*, and are attended by many participants. This is when the casualty list is set to soar. One bull was taken from *capea* to *capea* and gored its way through over 60 lives until it was eventually sent out to pasture.

Encierros are also another central part of many a local *fiesta* both North and South. From the verb *encerrar* meaning 'to enclose', this is the famed running of the bulls from a pen along the streets into the *plaza de toros*. Again, they are also common in summertime. The oldest is to be found in the town of Cuéllar in the province of Segovia and dates back over 500 years. The bulls are followed on horseback, run through a pine forest, then into open plains and finally through the centre of the town.

On the chosen day of a *Corrida* the bull, if it hasn't already been seriously wounded, lost an eye, or even killed in a tussle in the field, will be moved by using steers into a box and transported to the ring. Six bulls are required for each *Corrida* and one is kept in reserve in case a bull fails to charge in the ring. Sometimes a further bull is also taken. On the morning of the *Corrida* the bulls are off-loaded into a *corral* where they are inspected by a vet looking for physical defects that would in anyway inhibit them from playing their full part in the afternoon's proceedings.

Following the inspection there is a *sorteo* where lots are drawn for the bulls. They are divided into the three best and the three worst and then paired off, one from each group. The names of pairs are then picked out of a hat by either the *toreros'* managers - *los apoderados*, or one of their assistants who will also be in the ring with them that afternoon. Once that is done, the bulls are arranged in order through a complex system of gates and channelling and there they remain until their time comes.

The bulls have reached the final stage and within a few hours they will each take their turn in the ring with their respective *matador de toros* and an expectant, paying public. Here the *aficionados* - impassioned followers, will decide if the bull brought before them is 'keen', *celoso,* or *codicioso* that is if he runs in straight lines and is therefore easier to manage but still up for the challenge. However, if he does not take to the ring in the expected spirit and does not engage the *torero* properly, then he is *manso*, either cowardly or no good. Occasionally the problem is the bull's hooves do not support his weight properly and they fold as he turns. This has its own phrase in Spanish: *se doblan las manos*. In such cases the bulls are usually removed.

The day for the *torero* begins with the ritual of dressing, a process that takes up to an hour. Each *traje de luces*, 'suit of lights' (if one can translate it as that), costs in the region of €7,300 and is carefully laid out before each garment is put on. Here the rite becomes evident. The fine line between escaping unscathed and a goring - or at worst, curtains - is often luck. This tends to persuade even the least superstitious not to tempt fate and obsessive behaviour patterns become the norm. The suit is arranged in the same way for each event before the *torero* enters his dressing room, which is usually the hotel room. It is put on in the same order each time and then prayers and talismans are addressed. Superstition, religion and luck are called upon and respected. There is no apparent irony in the mixing of the three elements here; they are all one in the same trinity. Where once there may well have been humour there are now only nerves. The trousers, called *tallaguilla*, are possibly the most important part of the costume; so tight that not even the slightest wrinkle appears in the fabric. Loose fitting material could easily be hooked by a horn, carrying the wearer with it. The stockings are always pink and the slippers are dainty-looking but supposedly good for grip, except in rain. The frilled shirt is fronted by a thin tie harking back to those worn by the Mods. The jacket, heavily adorned with gold motif, is open in the underarm to allow greater mobility. It is made of silk but is as hard as board. Only the *torero* is permitted the gold braid on his jacket and trousers. The *picador* - the mounted horseman whose job it is to spike the bull in the neck during the *Corrida*, has gold trim only on his hat. The *torero's* 'team' in the ring, called *cuadrilla*, wear silver or black motif.

A false circular pigtail called *coleta* is attached to the back of the head, reminiscent of those worn by Roman gladiators. On the day of a *torero's* retirement the *coleta* is symbolically cut off.

A *torero's* greatest area of exposure is the inner thigh where a major artery runs. A goring here is the most common form of death. The blood loss can be so great at times that they are lifeless by the time they reach the infirmary inside the bullring. Padding is usually placed here to add some reassurance, if little else. However, for the first time spectator, the exaggerated bulge may lead some innocents to believe that such manhood is a prerequisite for entering the ring. As any Spaniard will be only too pleased to exclaim, the bravery is actually in the balls - apparently. *Hay que tener cojones*. A goring is referred to as a *cornada*, from *cuerno* meaning 'horn'. Here if you have horns though - *tienes cuernos*, or someone 'has given you horns' - *te han puesto los cuernos*, then your partner has been unfaithful. The symbolism, however, has nothing to do with bulls.

Once everything else is in place the hat, *montera*, is donned. After praying and walking to the ring the three *toreros* of the afternoon, who will each face two bulls, wrap themselves up in an exquisitely embroidered cape - *capote de paseo*, which may well bear the image of their patron saint. They are now ready to face what destiny has in store for them. Such allusions made to fate and destiny are no small matter here. Not only in the ring but right across the land that makes up Spain, fate pervades the attitude of the people. The lottery here is not just about winning to be rich. Every slight piece of luck that comes your way gains you status here. People's eyes widen when they hear of your good turn no matter how small. Death is out in the arena and somewhere with it is Fate deciding whether today she will be kind or cruel.

On 26th September, 1984 in the small town of Pozoblanco, Spain's most popular *torero* of the hour, Francisco Rivera Pérez, known as *'Paquirri'*, was gored by the bull *'Avispado'* from the breeders *Sayalero y Brandés* and bled to death in the infirmary while the television cameras recorded the whole gruesome spectacle of the man's rapid demise. One of the other *toreros* *'El Yiyo'* on the afternoon's bill was also killed in *la plaza* some years later.

Gored through the heart. The third, *'El Soro'*, after turning badly in the ring broke his ankle and could never return to the profession. The promoter of that fatal afternoon in Pozoblanco was also killed in a car accident soon afterwards. These incidents all have rational explanations but here the people talk of a cursed bill-poster. It is tradition that when a *torero* is killed in the *plaza* that the bull's body is burnt and his mother is sacrificed. The body burning could be for superstition but the killing of the mother is to ensure that a bloodline capable of killing once won't go on to kill twice. They like their bulls brave but not victorious. When one of Paquirri's *cuadrilla* of that afternoon learned recently that the head of *Avispado* had not been burnt but instead mounted and displayed in the bar *Hermanos Lora* in Gelves, Sevilla, he was shocked into silence. Superstition plays a very real part in and out of the ring.

It has been known on occasion to *indultar* the bull, where it isn't killed because either the *torero* or the public feel that the animal has never let up, always taken the cape *'siempre va al trapo'* as they say, and is therefore *noble*. The *cabestros* - tame oxen, are released into the ring and the bull follows them out to safe pasture.

Entering the *plaza* the *toreros* process in behind two horsemen, *alguaciles*, dressed in 16th century period cloaks with striking feathered caps. Traditionally these bailiffs cleared the ring of spectators but have remained for ceremonial purposes. They also act as the President's representatives in the *plaza*. Walking out through the entrance they parade towards the President's box high up above the main exit gate. This precursor to the main event is known as the *paseíllo*, from the word *paseo* - a stroll. On the President's right as he looks out to the *plaza* will be the senior *torero* - in rank not age - to the left the number two seed of the afternoon. Last, and in this case the least, in the centre will come number three. Behind the *toreros* will be their *banderilleros*, those responsible for placing the *banderillas* - the metre long, paper-decorated, steel barb-tipped darts.

Next in line are the rest of the respective *cuadrillas* - the team assistants. Each member is called a *peon* and they accompany the *torero* in the *plaza*. They're closely followed by the mounted *picadores*, whose job it is to weaken the bull by drawing first blood using the *vara* - the spear, by driving it into the nape known as the *morillo*. Alongside them are their assistants on foot called *monosabios* - wise monkeys, whose job with stick in hand it is to help maintain the horse on its feet and as calm as possible. All those who enter in the *paseíllo* will have their moment of protagonism in the afternoon's drama. Behind the 'monkeys' appear the carpenters whose role it is to carry out makeshift repairs should the bull destroy any part of the wooden *barrera* that runs round the inner part of the ring. Accompanying them are those responsible for levelling the *albero* - the characteristic sand floor of the ring which comes from the town of Álcala de Guadaira near Sevilla - after each bull has been dispatched. Then, last to arrive are the harnessed mules adorned with bells and flags and their handlers. They will complete the act in the *plaza* by dragging away the finished animal. With the parade over the *toreros* and their *cuadrillas* set to work preparing capes and swords while the *alguaciles* in time-honoured fashion hand over the key to the tunnel that leads to the bull-pen - *los torriles*, in readiness for the bulls' entrance. All this takes place accompanied by the sound of the *plaza's* band, occupying an area high up among the crowd.

The spectators are arranged into their corresponding shadings. The *plaza* is uniquely divided into areas and levels, unlike any other theatre. Those areas are: *sol, sol y sombra* and *sombra y sol. Sol* - 'Sun', are the cheapest seats owing to the hardship undertaken by the *aficionados* under the unforgiving rays. *Sol y sombra* seats enjoy a mixture of sun followed by shade as it swings west, and the most expensive tickets are found here. The two levels that the *plaza* occupies are the *tendido* and *grada. El tendido* stretches from *la barrera*, at the ringside, up to the balcony area. High in *la grada* you may have a bird's eye view of things; but unfortunately us humans were never equipped with a bird's keen sight to fully appreciate such a vantage point. *La grada*, is only worthwhile if you are near the President's box and right up against the balustrade that runs the full length of the *plaza*. Otherwise, behind this parapet you really are in the cheap seats with pillars in the way, binoculars often required and conversation bouncing off the ceiling above.

The *paso doble* being played by the band to lend atmosphere to the spectacle, suddenly halts and the trumpet playing turns official. This signals the commencement of the first of the three *suertes* that constitute the act of killing a bull in a *plaza*. *(Suerte*, translates literally as 'luck' and it is another telling sign that such a word should be used to divide the *Corrida* into its constituent parts) The President hangs a white handkerchief over his balcony and the *torero* salutes him.

La puerta de los torriles - gate to the bull-pen, swings opens and inside the depths of a tunnel waits a bull eager to escape its tight enclosure. As it stands bewildered, a ribbon bearing its breeders colours, called a *divisa*, is spiked into its neck through the use of a long pole. Another gate slams open and anyone left in the ring runs for cover. Over 500kg of purebred glistening muscle on the hoof thunders out into the light in a rush of testosterone that overwhelms the moribund air hanging in the *plaza*.

The *peones* of the *cuadrilla* will draw the bull towards their *torero* by throwing out their heavy fuchsia-backed and yellow-lined capes as they hide behind one of four 'escape routes', called *burladeros*, protruding from the red, wooden barrier. Sometimes the *torero* will go out and kneel down in front of the *torril* from where the bull will issue forth. This is called a *larga cambiada de rodillas* or 'a long knee change' if such a translation is possible. It is also known as *'a porta gayola'*, which roughly translates as 'bloody crazy' in any other language. If it is true that a woman wearing a stiletto heel applies the same pressure as an elephant then just imagine the force concentrated at the end of a bull's horn as it comes charging out with 500kg weighing in behind it. Then take it one step further and imagine that horn catching you full in the face. Well, Franco Cordeño didn't have to imagine it... he experienced it, at first face. Although his visage was left hanging by a thread and his body half-emptied of life, he miraculously survived. His bar in Sevilla is called *'Porta Gayola'*. The local punters go there to get off their face as well.

A great part of the atmosphere of the *plaza* is the proximity of the arena. This was partly why the 1992 Barcelona Olympics were such a success. The crowd form part of the spectacle by being included in its proceedings and not separated from it. Here you close the distance between you and the sinister yet enticing sense of death.

Once the bull is finally in the *plaza* the *torero* and his *cuadrilla* take over the reins. With their man-sized fuchsia serviettes they will play with the bull to determine with which horn it tends to lead. This is often the most colourful part of the three acts with all its dancing cape play. The long sweeps of the pink cape - *capote*, are referred to as *veronicas*.

The three *suertes* are also known as *tercios* - thirds: 1) *La Suerte de Vara* 2) *La Suerte de Banderilla* 3) *La Suerte de Matar*. Each *suerte* or *tercio* sees the bull in one of these three stages as the drama progresses. At first the bull's attitude is *levantado*, up for it. Then it is *parado*, slowed. Finally, it is *aplomado*, leaden or weighed down. The start of each *suerte* is signalled by the President draping a handkerchief from his balcony when the band sounds the change. A green handkerchief signals that the bull has to be returned and a *sobresaliente* - reserve bull, used. The signalling of the three *tercios* by the use of white handkerchiefs ensures that a time limit is adhered to. It takes an average of 15 minutes to kill a bull, in which time one hopes to witness spectacle and bravery in the face of death. For the first *suerte* the bull is fresh, unblemished by blood and the *torero* nowhere near a sword. This is, arguably, the *Corrida* at its most vibrant, lucid and popular height before things suddenly change completely. Then the *torero* will draw the bull to the mounted *picador* who will spike the back of the bull's neck and let the blood run. From here on in, things become more serious. The true nature of the meeting of man and beast in the arena becomes apparent.

As tradition dictates, the *picador* must engage the bull twice and not enter the inner circle of the two marked rings in the sand. If he does, the crowd will let him know. He sits atop a gigantic Breton horse sporting protective padding called a *peta*, which was only introduced in 1928 under a Royal decree for fear of losing business from tourists. It stipulated that the maximum *peta* would weigh 30kg and the *picador's* horse a maximum of 650kg.

Before then the spectacle was truly bloody with bulls ripping through horses hides and leaving them gutted in the sand. Some were even sown up with their entrails crudely shoved back in place and sent out a second time. Hard to believe but true and Goya's engravings in El Prado attest to this. Today the horses are padded and blindfolded but the internal damage done to these animals must still be great as the bull slams its pointed horns into the horse's side with all the force and pace it can muster.

If the *picador* punishes the bull too much it will be too weak to complete the remaining two *suertes*. The balance is a fine one. Some blood letting is required, as without it the animal would take far too long to finish off. The *picador* retires along with a reserve *picador* positioned at the opposite end of the *plaza*. The *torero* dedicates the bull by throwing his *montera* - hat, over his shoulder. Landing upside down is considered negative as superstition claims it will catch his spilt blood. So, if this happens it is turned over. However, in this case some say that this will empty his luck. The glass here is either half-empty or half-empty, there seems to be no room for optimism. His bright heavy cape is exchanged for the smaller, familiar red *muleta* cape and the *espada* – sword, in fact, another name for a *torero* is *espadas*. We enter the second *tercio: La Suerte de Banderillas,* in which a member of the *cuadrilla* will take on the bull by bearing his chest to it as he places three pairs of colourfully-decorated barbed darts into the bull's considerable neck muscles. The handkerchief appears over the President's balcony and the *tercio* changes as we enter the third and fatal act: *La Suerte de Matar.*

The obvious risk-taking and blatant showmanship have come to an end. Now the real subtlety begins and the measure of the man's metal is demonstrated by his willingness to allow the bull closer and closer to his body. Who knows at what moment the bull will finally identify his enemy as the *torero* and leave the red *muleta* behind? More often than not this moment never comes, but when it does it is always too soon. This last *tercio, la suerte de matar*, is the moment of the famed *'¡Olé!'* when Spain's identity finds its voice in the exaltation that rings out across the stained arena. This is also when the *torero* will decide whether to close the distance between his safety and that of mortal danger. In so doing he will intensify the fragile line between existence and extinction. It is what the true *aficionado* has come to feel, more than see.

The atmosphere always calms at this point, maybe as a mark of respect, or maybe because nothing spectacular will happen until the sword goes in. The *torero* returns to the *barrera* and changes his straight sword for a curved one handed to him by his helper known as *mozo de espadas*, so shaped to ensure an arched entrance into the bull's body. It is the *torero's* decision as to when he will go to the *barrera* to change his sword and take the act into its final stage by lining the bull up for the kill. The change of sword for the *estoque* is needed because the one he has been using up until then is blunt, so as not to cut himself. Permission is finally asked to kill the bull and formally given. Sometimes the bull's sacrifice is dedicated as the band plays a *paso doble*. Then he will pass the bull a few times with the cape until he positions the animal where he wants it. Taking up position he will dip the cape to the ground. This will lower the bull's head thereby exposing its nape, *el morillo*. The sword is lifted high as the *torero* peers down it like a sniper taking aim between the bull's shoulder blades and in almost one movement he jerks the cape over the bull's eyes, lets out a grunt of provocation as the bull hooks its neck forward to charge. The *torero* leans the sword into its target and in an instant there is a flash of *torero*, cape, sword, bull, sash, sequins, steel and blood-soaked hide. The onlookers wait for the confused parts to separate so they can make out where the sword and *torero* have ended up and what, if any, is the immediate response of the bull.

If the final blow, *la estocada*, has been dealt deep enough it should be a matter of only a few moments before the bull vomits blood. When it falls to the ground a *peon* will cut its spinal chord in the back of the neck, bringing an end to its life. Sometimes the sword is poorly placed and has to be thrust in again until it strikes home. Sometimes the blade is simply left there and the *peones* move in with their fuchsia capes, one on either side of the bull, flicking them in turn to make the bull move from side to side. This is to enable the sword to splice through more veins and arteries to bring the animal to its knees. The longer this takes the more the audience will whistle and jeer the *torero*. While hungry to see the kill they are angered to see the suffering drag on. If this fails to finish the *faena*, another sword with a crosspiece close to the tip, called *descabello* is taken from the *barrera* and used to sever the bull's spinal cord. This is done while the bull stands motionless. A quick jab behind the neck usually sees the bull jerk and drop dead. The moment this occurs a *banderillero* will stab a small knife - *puntilla*, into the same place delivering a *coup de grâce*.

With the snap of the nerves and the last rigid twitch of the bull's torso, it is over. The audience will applaud before it has its spinal chord severed if the animal falls to its knees soon after the sword goes in. They know that the *torero* has timed things right and the bull had had little left in him. The *torero*, delighted to see his foe felled and his own limbs still intact, will jump round with a youthful step and play out a social rite of the ring, which has infiltrated the imagination of the wider Spanish people. The man will go out to the centre of the ring or a place where he stands alone and draw in the attention of the crowd, holding out his arm with flat palm extended and then slowly turn full circle giving a peculiar pirouette salute and tribute to the people. More often than not he will finish off by wrapping both arms around himself and the hugging formality symbolising his bond of friendship and admiration for those who chant the three syllable adulation of the ring: 'to-**RE**-ro, to-**RE**-ro'. These motifs, very much from the ring, are found in everyday society. From the pop artist waving the audience and Almodóvar receiving his Oscar, to someone scoring a goal or a man being heckled by a group of girls. Those who receive a Spanish crowd's adulation will often hear the chant 'to-**RE**-ro' at some stage in the applause.

While the *torero* moves back to the *barrera* or *tablas* to drink water and store the sword, the crowd hold up their white handkerchiefs signalling the President to award the *torero* an ear, two ears or two ears and the tail. The importance of this will later be reflected in the annual 'rankings'. The more ears - *orejas*, he receives the higher up the ladder he is and the greater the demand for his services will be for the next billing of the national *fiesta*. If the President holds out the handkerchief once he concedes an ear, twice two ears and if three times he is granted both ears and the tail - *el rabo*. The trophies are cut then and there from the bull and handed over. The *torero* will give another characteristic salute and possibly throw the ears and tail into the crowd.

If the *torero* achieves ears when killing both bulls of the afternoon and brings a quick, successful kill after having brought the spectacle to a fever of excitement he is carried shoulder-high through the main gates come the end of the *Corrida*. This is called *'Salir por la puerta grande'* - 'to go out through the great door', similar to the common phrase we use: 'going out with style', but the Spanish also carries the added meaning that you are carried on the shoulders of others for the triumphant moment you have given them. As bullrings are divided into three classes, each will stipulate its own criteria for when a *torero* is carried out and it usually depends on the number of ears he has cut during the afternoon. In Sevilla the greatest accolade that one may receive is to be carried out through *La Puerta de Príncipes*, where the press and jubilant masses await.

Los toreros are supposed to be *otra raza* - another breed, and as such, they are often revered in Spain. This is believed to be because of their ability to face the bull again after having been seriously gored. Some try to stand up and finish the job while others need immediate surgical intervention and will have to wait their months of recovery before they can face a pair of horns again. *'El torero es otra raza'* is a phrase that you will often hear.

Madrid and its *plaza*, *Las Ventas*, is the Mecca of *Los Toros* and its *Feria de San Isidro* is its time of high pilgrimage, even though Andalucía is the birthplace of the art form. For many though, to triumph in *'La Maestranza'* - *La Plaza de Toros de Sevilla*, is the most sublime moment that the confrontation between bull and man may bring. The oldest bull ring may be considered to be Ronda and *Las Ventas* in Madrid the most important, but it is *La Maestranza* in Sevilla where all Spanish *toreros* wish to triumph.

For the visiting tourist the biggest pull is probably the social event itself, which is infectious and what the majority of the Spanish bullwatchers equally enjoy. The afternoon starts with people mingling in bars drinking *fino* or *manzanilla* wine, striped cushions unique to the arena swing nonchalantly from people's hands. Fine dresses, jackets and ties outnumber jeans and T-shirts in and around *calle Adriano* behind the bullring. Horse-drawn carriages pull up and *señoritas* that will be seated conspicuously in *la Grada* near the *puerta de los Príncipes* step down sporting laced *mantillas* cascading from ornamental high comb *peinetas*. The area around the entrance, giving out onto the Guadalquivir river, is awash with horses and carriages bringing owners and friends from the *Feria* celebrations. Traffic is diverted and crowds gather to see Spain's high, and not so high, society parade in. Cameras are suspended over the cobbled entrance to get a glimpse of a popular face and there are plenty about. The atmosphere is bathed in the bright sunshine as the flags of Spain, Andalucía and the *Real Maestranza* flutter floridly in the cerulean sky. Everyone wears sunglasses for practical and unpractical reasons. Mobile phones and other fashion accessories are prominent. The scenario oozes old money and newly made fortunes eager to rub their shoulders. Havana smoke fills the air and Cuban *aficionados* are two-a-penny, but not the cost of the cigars. This is a social buzz Sevilla style.

You don't get in cheap either and an *abono* - season ticket, for example in prime position for the 2004 bullfight season in *Tendido 1, Barrera, 1º Fila*, for: *"19 Corridas de Toros, 2 Corridas del Arte del Rejoneo y 8 Novilladas con Picadores"* weighed in at a hefty €2,745. The cheapest was €428 in the *Grada Especial*.

La Corrida expresses national qualities of bravery, pride, unity and euphoria as well as a potent Spanish cocktail of folklore, superstition and religion. It is an age-long popular event that not only ties Spain to her past but also keeps it mindful of its future, as does any tradition. So there can be no living icon more symbolic than a Spanish singer or dancer who marries a *torero*. There are several of these couples in Spain, who receive their due attention and blessing from the people. Byron wrote in *Don Juan* that:

> *All tragedies are finish'd by a death.*
> *All comedies are ended by a marriage.*

Perfect therefore is the traditional marriage that unites the *torero* to the world of Flamenco. He has avoided tragedy to be able to laugh freely at his wedding.

The bullfight did not begin life on foot but on horseback and such a form still exists and it is called *Rejoneo* in reference to the pole - a *rejón*, that is used to stab the bull while mounted on a horse. Andalusian riders turn their horses with their glistening manes tied back with interwoven ribbons astride grand armchair-like Portuguese saddles. They don the short jacket of the *vaquero* and what must be the world's most intricate chaps – *zahones*, strapped to their legs. The Domecq family that own the French-founded sherry *bodega* of Domecq in Jerez de la Frontera in the province of Cádiz are the most notorious in the *Rejoneo* circuit. The horses are piebald, bay, jet black or snow white in colour. These agile mounts have been trained to respond without thinking and are as faithful and sure as any police dog. One moment's hesitation would cost horse and rider dear.

The riders are referred to as *rejoneadores* and obviously because of cost, there are few of them about. Each rider takes several horses with them, all of which make an appearance during an afternoon's display.

In Portugal the *Rejoneo* has reached a more refined level than in Spain, a fact the Spanish bullfighting fraternity openly admit. The Portuguese tend use the Lusitano horse known for its bravery and the oldest mounted horse in history with 5,000 years of riding history behind it. The horse originates from Portugal where the locals do not in fact kill the bull but do, however, place tipped darts in its neck.

The equestrian bullfight dates as far back as 13th century. The *Rejoneo*, meant only for aristocrats, remained unchanged in both Portugal and Spain until the end of the 18th century, when Carlos II (1665-1700) of Spain died without an heir. The throne then passed to a grandson of Louis IV, who became Felipe V (1700-1748), and so the Bourbon dynasty entered Spain along with their French influence and disdain for bullfighting. The Bourbons prohibited the *fiesta nacional*. While the decree was adhered to by the governing class it was rejected by the common people and the bullfighters took to their feet leaving their horses behind. It wasn't until 1920 that *el Rejoneo* was again seen in Spain.

The process of training a horse for the *plaza* is a complicated one and in order to get the handful of horses they need they will buy anything up to a hundred just so they can extract two or three that will eventually enter the ring, but not after years of training first. What they do with the rest of the horses is anyone's guess. It is a costly business and those without a sizeable bank loan beforehand should not rush out and buy themselves a hundred horses.

The last Sunday of *La Feria de abril*, the great April Fair of Sevilla, is traditionally *El Rejoneo* in the morning, but you'll have to be early. The traditional *Corrida* that pulls the crowds is more popular because there is more risk. And in Spain, at times, if there is no risk involved there is no point in doing anything. Risk taking is in the blood here. Hence the running of the bulls in village *fiestas* and pedestrians taking their lives into their own hands when crossing the road, always seeing how close they can get to the passing cars. Sunday afternoon of Sevilla's *Feria* is always reserved for the notoriously unpredictable Miura bulls, thus leaving the best to last.

In the noteworthy town of Ronda, set over an impressive gorge between Sevilla and Málaga, is one of Spain's most beautiful bullrings. Each year in September they celebrate a 'Goyaesque' *Corrida* in homage to the local born *torero* Pedro Romero (1754-1839), who created the classical style of bullfighting. The riders dress in typical 18th century costume and recreate the atmosphere faithfully captured by the Spanish painter Goya, whose famous sketches are in El Prado in Madrid. In Portugal it is typical to see the *rejoneador* always dressed in period long coat and frilled shirt.

Another typical sight at a Portuguese *Rejoneo* are the *Forcados*. A group of unpaid men, who jump into the ring in unison and entertain the crowd by receiving the charging bull head on in a *pega de cara*. They have to wrestle *el toro* to a stand-still. They come into the ring when the *rejoneador* has finished with the bull. (In Portugal they don't kill it, remember) The team of men was originally employed to stop the bull from running up a staircase which linked the Royal box to the bullring. They had a *forcado* lance to repel the bull. They still carry the *forcado* when they enter the ring in the *paseíllo*. Broken bones are the norm for these elf-dressed bull tamers.

There is of course one last question to be asked after the long hot afternoon draws to a close and the people make their way out of the *plaza* and into the bars to wax lyrical, take *tapas* and drink a few idle hours away. What happens to the bull? The meat is sold on. Highly prized it is too, though strangely not of the highest quality. The tail finds its way into the best restaurants where *cola de toro* is considered a delicacy. The testicles are also highly prized but it has not been conclusively decided whether or not their properties can be passed on through ingestion. The well-worn *Corrida* anecdote breathes new life each time it finds an innocent tourist's ear and goes something like this: An American goes into a restaurant and asks for bull's testicles, *testículos de toro*, and when he is presented with the dish he remarks on their surprisingly small size. The waiter then leans in close and whispers, *"Sometimes señor... the bull wins."*

Michael Palin said something about the controversial matter of bullfighting in his video *'Hemingway Adventures'* which would make a fitting end for this, the oldest of Spanish themes:

"For me it's a Spanish thing. I will never feel about it the way they do. And that alone intrigues me."

- OCHO -
HOLY WEEK

*'I have a great mind to believe in Christianity
for the mere pleasure of fancying I may be damned.'*
Lord Byron

In Sevilla there are three sure ways to get yourself rejected by the resident population. One is not to take an interest in football, two is not to find their city beautiful and three is not to like their *Semana Santa*.

Semana Santa, meaning 'Holy Week' not 'Easter Week' as some may think, is a religious and social phenomena that has deep roots in Spain and has established itself all over the country in greater or lesser exuberance.

Most people who have a hazy knowledge of Sevilla will know about the *Giralda*, a barber, maybe something Byron said about the women and, of course, the oranges, which the locals consider inedible and so the English can have them. If the reader dusted off their history books then they might come up with the fact that the Inquisition started here, the city has the world's biggest gothic cathedral and was also the inspiration for the opera Carmen. There is one other lasting image of the city that the odd travel programme would certainly take time out to show us and that would be its Easter week commemoration. To the uninitiated it looks like a KKK procession with burning candles instead of a burning cross. *Semana Santa* for some reason seems to be the common denominator among all visitors. Maybe it is famous beyond its walls because it is seen by more tourists than any other celebration the city has to offer, which always coincides with tourists on holiday. The rest of the time, when Sevilla is kicking its heels up, the mass tourist trade is resting theirs.

When the first week of April arrives and *Semana Santa* is upon Sevilla you could be forgiven for thinking that the entire population had been forcibly moved out of their homes and into the streets. Intimidatingly large crowds spread across town, assembling outside churches and lining streets. They have come out to see the *Semana Santa* processions or *pasos* as they are called here, organised by the various church affiliations referred to as brotherhoods - *Hermandades*, which march as vast files of hooded penitents - *penitentes*. They are also referred to as *cofrades* or *cofradías*, which refer to the individual members. They lead the way from their neighbourhood church to

Holy Week

the cathedral, closely followed by a shuddering showpiece: their local baroque effigy of the *Virgen* or *Jesús*, or both. These are mounted high upon a rostrum, which is adorned with flowers, and a richly embroidered velvet drapery covers the base. Silver and gold threads are elaborately woven into it and the 'float' is borne on the backs of up to 30 *costaleros* or carriers. Bringing up the rear, but easily heard from the front, are the bands beating the march, shrouding the procession in an air of sombre and mournful music as the lamenting effigy steadily makes its way forward. The sometimes piercing music may stop to let the carriers rest or give way to a by-stander amongst the crowd who lifts their voice and sings a *Saeta*, literally meaning 'arrow', dedicating it to the Virgin or Christ.

The celebration reaches its climax with round-the-clock *pasos* on Holy Thursday, known as *La Madrugá*, starting around midnight and going through into Good Friday, finally coming to a rest on the Sunday. The city and its citizens are dressed for the occasion and even if religion isn't your thing, you'll certainly enjoy the ambience in the street where late night civilised drinking and fraternising continues at a pace. *Semana Santa* happens all over Andalucía and Spain but its pinnacle of colour is in Sevilla where its sheer size of *pasos* is a spectacle in itself. As there are seemingly as many churches as there are bars in Sevilla you get an idea of the scale of things when, around *calle Sierpes* in the old commercial centre, you can easily get stuck purely by the weight of numbers.

The most famous of all *pasos* is the one which leaves from La Macarena the night before Good Friday - *La Madrugá*. A boundless crowd gathers to see the procession outside the arch of La Macarena Basilica opposite the Andalusian parliament in the north of the city. The traffic is kept at bay and the resulting open space is swallowed up by the citizens. Cheri Blair came here to see the whole spectacle from a nearby balcony while Tony was off somewhere talking about a rock his ancestors had nicked.

There is nothing like this throughout the rest of Europe and that alone, in this continent of such diverse cultures, should be sufficient to hold your attention, if only for a brief while. Any event that sees some 40,000 people taking to the streets in a weeklong march of penitence is a sight to behold.

For some, *"Religion enables us to ignore nothingness and get on with the jobs of life."* Holy Week in Spain and especially in Sevilla has become for many a principal job in life.

Semana Santa flies the standard of Sevilla across the world and symbolises many things that she is and pretends to be. For that reason alone it is worth understanding its historical perspective and present reality. Anything that can survive nearly 500 hundred years and claim a clean bill of health is a living testimony of a people's belief in themselves.

The religious procession is festive and ritual; sombre and reflexive; elaborate and elegant; multitudinous and yet highly organised; passionate while being restrained; a show of civic pride and local achievement; the city is vibrant and its people united.

Semana Santa in Sevilla is said to have no equal in its passion, religious sentiment or emotive intensity. This is not only something that the local *sevillanos* will be happy to admit to, but it is generally believed to be true by the rest of Spain. It is something that the city is loved for by nationals and foreigners alike.

For a while after Franco's death Spanish symbolism was seen as out of date and *Semana Santa* was an event deemed as typical of his regime. But today it is alive and well with more participants than ever in its centuries-long history.

For one long and intense week of religious and (let it not be overlooked) civic expression, Sevilla like most of Spain is awash with fervour and sentiment from Palm Sunday to Easter Sunday. Commemorating the Passion of Christ, the citizens file out dressed as *penitentes* or *nazarenos*. The tradition started in 1518 when Fadrique Henríquez de Ribera, the first Marquis of Tarifa, started out on a pilgrimage to the Holy Land. There he participated in the procession of the Stations of the Cross, a procession commemorating Christ's last walk from Praetorium to Calvary, known in Spanish as the *Via Dolorosa*. Three years later on his return to the city he introduced such a procession into the social and religious fabric of Sevilla, having profound effects which are very much alive to this day. This he began in 1520 when he also constructed his lavish *Mudéjar* house, *Casa de Pilatos* said to be based on the design of Pontius Pilate's residence. The procession started at his house and went to a cross, *el Cruz del Campo*, so named because at the time the cross was found in open countryside on the road between the city and Carmona, a town to its north. The exact distance was measured out to be the 1,321 steps or the 997 metres that Christ took as he stumbled with his cross to that green hill far away. Every first Friday of Lent the origins of Sevilla's *Semana Santa* are commemorated inside *Casa de Pilatos*.

In the Parish of San Benito in *calle Luis Montoto* stands the brick monument *el Templete de la Cruz del Campo*, whose cross marks the spot of the original 'cross in the country'.

It may have 16th century origins but the basis for today's artistic outpouring is in fact from the Baroque of the Counter-Reformation.

Fifty-eight brotherhoods parade throughout the week, which means between six and seven each day with anywhere between 300 to 2,000 penitents on the move with one or two floats - *pasos*, being carried. Each procession, also called a *paso*, take anything from four to twelve hours to do the round trip. During this time the city throbs to the band beat of lament and the piercing cornet cry of sorrow. Traffic stops, the masses gather to line the streets and by night, candles mark the route as the votive penitents head out with the guiding cross, *la cruz de guía*, leading the way.

First comes an image of Christ carried by the church's strongest, bearing it on their necks and keeping time to the painfully slow rhythm of the drummers' beat. Then there are the hooded penitents with their pointed *capirote* hats, holding candles. Some hold silver staffs, some make up the guard of honour and others carry banners of the brotherhood. All this hierarchy, strange to find on an occasion like this, is determined by the amount of time each has spent in the brotherhood.

The main focus of attention is centred around the two *pasos* - floats. First there comes *el paso de Cristo* and then at a great distance trailing behind is the *el paso de la Virgen de palio*. The image of Christ is usually that of him on the cross or a scene from the Passion. While the figure of *María* is fully cloaked in the famed embroidery of the city and always depicted crying, an image referred to as *mater dolorosa* - suffering mother. These *pasos*, heavily laden with gold, fine wooden sculpting and costing in the region of €220,000, are borne on the shoulders of between 36 and 48 *costaleros*, so named for the *costal* material they wear wrapped around their head and neck for protection. The steam from under the *paso* lifts off in sheets each time someone lifts the cloth sidings and it is not unknown for a man to die of a heart attack under there.

The most striking feature that will first catch the eye of the visitor will inevitably be the tall pointed *capirote* hats covering the penitent's face, framing two menacing looking eyes. Their appearance usually reminds one of the KKK, so a little history is needed.

We will start as everyone starts the day by getting dressed. This also means that the hat will come last. In the case of the penitent we start with the tunic. The original tunics were only made in three colours: brown, black or purple of untreated, therefore rough, linen. Today though they come in many different colours with the most popular being white, black, scarlet and violet. The whole costume can cost up to €600, with its detailed embroidered badges, gloves, slippers, tunic, cloak and high pointed mask. The get up for the kids doesn't fall far short either. The act of filing out for the Passion procession has its own intricate history and significance.

In 1777 King Carlos III banned people from covering their face. This was not challenged effectively by the people until they refused to file out in 1831, when the ban was enforced with renewed vigour. Only one brotherhood - *Hermandad*, went out in *Semana Santa*, the rest remained in their churches in protest. There was even an attempt to make the long black morning suit, typical of the 19th century, the official attire for Holy Week, but the idea did not last and the tunic returned immediately.

Everything of note has some characteristic that separates it from the rest. Bullfighting has the distinct, turned down, horn-like hat; the bobby stands out through his ornate and unusual helmet, the Brit once had his bowler, the American still has the Stetson and *Semana Santa* tops them all with its 60cm tall *capirote* hat. There are even native born *sevillanos* that believe that this *was* influenced by the KKK. That is flattering the KKK with an historical past that it just doesn't have. *Semana Santa* has its roots in the 16th century and to think that the Spanish would have to turn to a marginalized group decked out in no more than ill-fitting rags is beyond the Pale. It is the KKK that took their dress from Spain if anything and not the other way round. First mention of the tall hats takes place in 1586 in the brotherhood of *La Hermandad de la Hiniesta* when the face was uncovered and not shrouded as it is today.

The idea of the headdress in Spain came about, like many things in Christianity, from an earthly, heretical source rather than a spiritually ordained tradition. Heretics about to be tried by the Inquisition - *El Santo Oficio*, were burned in *'the purifying flames'*. As the heretic was led out, their head was covered by a cloth mask, which had two eyeholes cut in it. It was this death mask that was adopted by the Spanish Christian masses when doing their public act of penance.

The present day tunic with its cape was designed by one Juan Manuel Rodríguez Ojeda for the *Hermandad* in La Macarena and introduced in 1889. There is, though, a mention in 1866 of *La Sagrada Mortaja* with its tunic and cape, which was eventually adopted by all of Andalucía and the greater part of Spain. Even then they were expensive at 91 *pesetas*. Steps were taken by another tailor to use less fine materials and thereby bring the price down considerably. There are in fact two types of tunic on show, for those tunic spotters among you who are keen to pick them out. There is *tunica con cola*, a tunic with a train which is furled up and carried over the arm. It's popular in the central part of the city costing anything up to €175. Then there is the tunic with cape - *tunica con capa*, which is more popular in the outer neighbourhoods and costs up to €600. Penitents cloaked in tunic-with-train belong to an *hermandad de cola*, as it is commonly known, while those in tunic-and-cape belong to an *hermandad de capa* related with the *barrio* or popular brotherhoods.

Sevilla takes not only religious imagery extremely seriously, but also its own self-image. Although clothes do not maketh the man, here it does go a long way, and up to the pearly gates one would hope. Quality, tailoring and attention to detail, which bring out the best in the wearer are conspicuous. As we are now living in a commercially competitive world, the need and pressure to maintain these standards, if not exceed them, is set to rise. Even in the act of penitence there is rivalry between brotherhoods to be the best turned out. They often talk about which brotherhood is the best.

Such is the nature of the city that vanity began to creep in as the penitents and Nazarenes started to decorate their tunics - possibly something from their Pagan past. Buttons, seen by many as functional are in reality purely decorative and once where rough linen braised the skin now lighter, kinder materials are paraded.

In Cuenca, a town to the east of Madrid and listed by UNESCO as a site of world heritage, men continue to take part in processions with faces uncovered. Here the *Semana Santa* resembles something closer to a rugby match as the wild side of things takes hold and only males need apply. The swathes of sweat lift into the air as evaporation gets underway on an industrial scale. It must rain some in the next village. The scene is one of pushing and shoving while the crowd is knitted tighter and tighter together as the sound of a drum pounds the ritual into a frenzy, if not despair, for some poor trapped individuals.

There is a lot of variety in Spain, not only in geography but also in cuisine, language, *fiestas* and customs. *Semana Santa* is no exception.

In the small town of Lora del Río near to the north of Sevilla the embroidery - *bordado religioso*, is of such a fine quality that it is of national renown and is even held in regard internationally. In the town of Pilas in the province of Huelva they have a moment where two *pasos*, one of Christ and one of Mary, charge toward each other representing their *encuentro* - meeting, in Heaven. In Málaga there is possibly the biggest *paso* of them all where the carriers, called *hombres de trono*, hold it high on their shoulders swaying as they go. Many places in fact don't carry their *pasos*, they pull them the modern and easy way by using a tractor, but this is frowned upon by the puritans in Sevilla where deep reverence for the occasion is seen as the essential ingredient. Holy Week is also commonly known as *Semana Grande* - the Great Week and there are many that spend all year preparing for this one event.

It is a complex web of history, religious ideals, tradition and local mores that go to make up the contradictions contained in *Semana Santa*: the idolatry with pagan origins; its masses with festive overtones; its artistic expression based in its Baroque splendour and its pomp and ceremony forming its Civic custom.

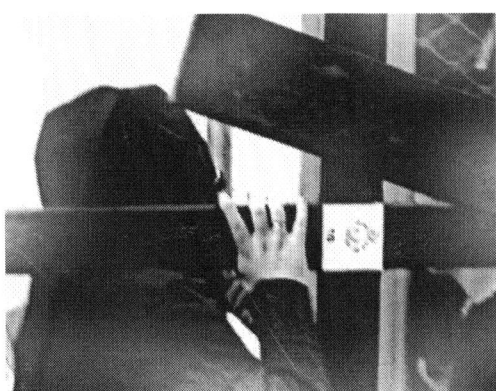

The week starts with Palm Sunday - *Domingo de Ramos*, then continues: *Lunes Santo* - Holy Monday; *Martes Santo; Miércoles Santo; Jueves Santo* - Maundy Thursday; *La Madrugá* - the night between Thursday and

Friday; *Viernes Santo* - Good Friday; *Sabado Santo* ending on *Domingo de la Resurrección*. The *Madrugá* written in full as *'La Madrugada'* is the twilight time between Holy Thursday and Good Friday when the night is at its most intense, far removed from the day before while still safe from the daylight waiting to break.

La Madrugá sees the greatest moment of mass participation. After that it's Wednesday. The *pasos* criss-cross the city taking agonisingly slow steps toward and then back from the cathedral. They weave in and out of the old streets, lined by onlookers and orange trees seep their intoxicating blossom into the night air. Candles flicker warmly, stretching shadows, softening lines, calming the sight and cooling the emotions until the band strikes up and the brotherhood marches forward. The central walkways are squeezed by biblical crowds, enhanced by the tight dimensions of the pedestrianised streets. People oscillate from side to side like a meandering snake, bottlenecking and strangling the flow like a boa constrictor. The 'massification' of *Semana Santa* is a recent affair. Everything was bumbling along quite nicely, as in the rest of the world at one time, until in 1900 the first blip appeared and the participation took a sharp rise. Things steadily rose until the Big Bang of 1970 when the participation rocketed and it hasn't let up since.

The *Hermandad de Nuestro Padre Jesús Nazareno* known to the locals as *'El Silencio'*, because it parades in silence through the streets, is considered to be the mother of all the *cofradías* in Sevilla. It has given the present form and distinctive customs to the brotherhoods in the city. The biggest *Hermandad* is *El Gran Poder* in La Macarena with more than 2,235 people filing out in Holy Week compared with the smallest, *la Sagrada Mortaja* and its modest 233.

So, why? Why do people bother going to such extraordinary extremes. Well, it's not so hard to believe that acts of faith should require such a show, effort and bring a city to a standstill. But when you ask people why exactly do they go out in Sevilla for *Semana Santa* they will say it's because it's a festive tradition and the religion has little to do with it. Then you'll meet person after person who will tell you, indignantly, that nothing could be further from the truth; religion and the Christian tradition are the sole motivating factors. So you are left with the question: is it one or the other or both?

The jury is split: half are motivated by religion while the rest are inspired by personal and cultural reasons. So, it's both.

For those who are religious it is a time to reflect on one's sins, to meditate and to be close to Christ.

On a cultural level there is a feeling that is awoken in the people provoked by the artistic beauty and mystic atmosphere. On a personal level it's a unique way to enjoy Sevilla and the company of your family and friends, as it affords you a moment to stop and take hold, which the mad rush of modernity does not permit.

So the principal reasons for so many processing in penitence are the traditional religious connotations as well as those of meditation and reflection. Half of all those out in the streets then are there for a reason other than religion.

What can we make of this? Something that was supposed to be simply religious suddenly has an undergrowth of religious complexes and secular complexities. We are now beginning to unearth another central, and in this case unique, piece of the city's selfhood. But are we able to join this with *La Corrida*, Flamenco, the family, *la Feria* and a modern lifestyle? Maybe they are separate parts but in such a small city of under a million inhabitants where everyone is willing and wanting to play a part in the city's life they must surely be interconnected.

One curious part of *Semana Santa's* greater whole is its myriad names displayed by the brotherhoods. Here are some of them along with their unfortunate translations. To put things into context translating such cultural items would be like a Spaniard hearing cricketing terms in his own language. They wouldn't have a clue what you were on about but they would at least enjoy hearing someone give it a try. There are too many to mention all the names so here is a selection:

La Amargura	**Bitterness**	*El Amor*	**Love**
El Calvario	**The Calvary**	*La Carreteria*	**The Lane**
El Valle	**The Valley**	*Los Estudiantes*	**The Students**
El Gran Poder	**The Great Power**	*Los Javieres*	**The Javiers**
Los Panaderos	**The Bakers**	*Quinta Angustia*	**Fifth Anguish**
Santo Entierro	**Holy Burial**	*El Silencio*	**The Silence**
La Soledad	**Solemnity**	*Las Aguas*	**The Waters**
El Museo	**The Museum**	*Los Gitanos*	**The Gypsies**

El Buen Fin	**The Good Ending**	*La Bofetá*	**The Slap**
El Cachorro	**The Pup (or Wagon)**	*La O*	**The O**
Las Cigarreras	**The Tobacco Girls**	*La Sed*	**The Thirst**
Los Negritos	**The Little Blacks**	*La Lanzada*	**The Spearing**
Las Siete Palabras	**The Seven Words**	*Pasión*	**Passion**

There are other curiosities and historical trivia concerning *Semana Santa* such as the origins of the *Hermandades*. They came into being alongside that of Spain herself. They were formed as the monarchs of the north, mainly *Castilla* and *León*, extended their territories ever southward in the slow but sure Reconquest of lands taking the land back from the long-established Moor. The *Hermandades* were left in place as a local defence and police force. They had to defend the town against any Moorish counterattack and control the newly liberated people.

Any brother who failed to complete his full penitence during *Semana Santa*, or did not turn up at all, used to have to present himself at his church and pay a *limosna* or donation.

A Royal Decree of 1777 banned public flagellation during the Easter processions, which still occurs in some places around Spain. You can even see people crawling part of the way on their knees, though this is usually frowned upon today. Officially it has been removed in Spain but there are some *cofradías* that keep up this tradition. At times, up until the 19th century, the need to do penitence became almost farcical and scandalous with some appearing dressed in nothing but a near transparent garment to protect them and with their private parts placed under some duress, by all accounts.

It is interesting to note that if today they have more people walking out in penitence in *Semana Santa* that at any time in its history then we are seeing a medieval tradition in a glory that it has never breathed since its very inception. We do not need to conjure up images of the past in order to savour one glorious forgotten moment in time when what we have before us has never been surpassed by its ancestors. Indeed, they would revel at the now not the then.

Semana Santa on Maundy Thursday and Good Friday are the only times when women will don the black lace *mantilla*, so characteristic of Spanish women, which will hang down over the high comb and then fall away at the back. As the image of the Virgin passes through *Plaza del Altozano* in Triana a group of girls dressed to the nines will often gather and shout out: *"¡Guapa! ¡Guapa!"* Exclaiming the beauty of the mother of their God.

The *paso* of the Virgin Mary, contained by a delicately ornate frame and supported an elaborately embroidered canopy, rocks from side to side. It has all the grace of a tall ship riding at anchor and all the sadness and mystery of a vessel lost at sea. The city is on the move and on the march leaving reality behind and giving a new meaning to things. The music, the masses, the spectacle, drama and singular *sevillano* Christian passion fills the faithful as the *paso* sways past. The crowd makes way and the city pays homage to her God and mother in this life and the next.

The town of Lora del Río is the only *Paso Infantile* in Spain in which some two hundred children process as penitents. Some children are even listed with a *cofradía* before they are on the civil register. Children also take part. They file out in the full garb but the very young ones keep their *capirote* open back and the face uncovered. The official age for the youngest to dress in the tunic is set around 14-16 years old, but it depends on the rule of each Brotherhood. There are also processions with children in May, which forms part of *Las Cruces de Mayo* celebrations. Easter gives the children and teachers a break and Spanish parents cherished time with their offspring, they really love kids here.

The *sevillanos*, surprisingly, are not willing puppets of the church by any stretch of the imagination. They used to pass under the balcony of the Archbishop's palace as a mark of respect but have dropped the habit, no pun intended. *Semana Santa* has pagan undercurrents and is more the people's week than the Church's. This is where the interests collide, historically - and in true Spanish style - painfully. No one is taking prisoners any longer; but in centuries gone by it did occur. On one occasion in 1782 the Church actually interrupted the procession of *La Hermandad de la Estrella* in Triana's *calle Castilla* and the Head Ecclesiastic Bailiff - *alguacil mayor eclesiástico*, marched four offenders, who had dared to cover their faces, smartly off to the Church's prison inside the Archbishop's palace. The local *Hermandad* got itself together and promptly broke their brothers out. The Church had to climb down after the incident while the four were taken back to their church and acclaimed as heroes. Then everyone carried on along the processional route to the Cathedral with their image of the Virgin.

The Brotherhoods have always resisted interference from the Church and if there is one place that knows what religious interference can be like, it is Sevilla. This was after all The Inquisition's HQ and they had a finger in every pie. The history of the *Hermandades* is littered with instances when they have had to resist losing their independence to the Church.

Relations were on the hot side recently until the Archbishop of Sevilla, Cardenal Amigo Vallejo, finally took a more tolerant view of the Brotherhoods and struck a conciliatory position on behalf of the Church.

But today the focus of attention is distinct and this time it is the controversy concerning women as *nazarenas*. Should women be allowed to go out and do penance in *Semana Santa* and dress in the tunic? Tradition - predictably - says 'no,' while reason and common sense say *'why are we even asking this question?'* At time of writing thirty-five Brotherhoods had included women while twenty-two still excluded them. But times are changing and it will not be long before it becomes the norm. Ironically, many cite as their reason for keeping women at bay the notion that their participation is a break from tradition and *Semana Santa* shouldn't change. However, let the truth be known that in the most formative years of Holy Week between 16th and 18th centuries women did complete the penance alongside the men. So, if tradition is anything to go by then the women should be reinstated, otherwise history is left incomplete and the true *Semana Santa* cannot be realized.

The first Brotherhood to accept women in recent times was *Los Javieres* in the conservative enclave of central Sevilla, as late as 1986. However, the brotherhood of *Vera Cruz* was the first to make their presence 'official' a year later.

La Saeta is also something that adds to the occasion. *Saeta*, meaning 'arrow', is seen as a personal dialogue between the singer and the Maker. From among the people in a crowded street; before the image in a bustling square or from a balcony hanging above the masses, a voice will soar out and a hush will fall over the multitude like a soft blanket. In a small town outside Sevilla there is even a school dedicated to the art form. It is not meant to be a spectacle, it is meant to be profound feeling. Each year though, it seems harder to calm the crowd and let the voice climb out from among them and be heard. And if you think Flamenco is unintelligible, you won't understand a single word when a *Saeta* starts up and like Flamenco there is nothing like the *Saeta*.

There is a poem called *La Saeta de Machado*, which was written as a hard biting criticism of the custom of worshipping a Christ figure sculpted from wood. Possibly to the writer's frustration, it was taken up and set to music by Joan Manuel Serrat, to be played in their *Semana Grande*. Today it is one of the most popular marching songs.

For the Brotherhoods at Easter their moment has come. In all the bars with connections to *Semana Santa* the numbers on calendars counting down the days, which begin with '*349 days till Semana Santa*', are turned for the last time. Capes will swirl through the streets as penitents make their way hurriedly to church. Friends gather in bars and houses in readiness to accompany their church or family member in the procession. The day is long and for many they will probably go right through the night before they make their weary way back home. Children will run among the crowd in an atmosphere of 'brotherhood' and good nature where candles flicker, music plays, silences are hushed from the crowds and impromptu ceremonies take place. The eyes are given a feast of colour, movement and spectacle; the ears are filled with music and silence and the nose senses burning candles and incense. Emotions receive new experiences. It will delight you, possibly enlighten you and may even inspire you. The sheer numbers of bodies in the crowd, the obvious pain from the burden for those involved may worry you as they press forward. The religious sculptures bob amid a sea of heads and the high hats of the Nazarenes ride above the waves of crowds like juddering ships' masts. Gold and fine cloths, embroidery and Baroque art abound. History comes alive by these very real experiences of the present. The people are caught up by the emotion of the throng and an energy that will keep them on their feet for up to 12 hours. The whole city is alive with the incomparable business of celebration. One thing is certain: you will not sleep through *Semana Santa* nor are you likely to forget it. You will never have experienced anything like Sevilla's *Semana Grande*.

If you are new to Spain you may well share the conventional wisdom that the Spanish are ultra-religious; but there is a dichotomy here. We have seen that even among believers, their primary reason for processing out into the streets is not religious and that presents us with a fundamental puzzle. How can someone be religious, form part of a religious event and not be motivated in the first instance by their beliefs? That is because *Semana Santa* goes beyond the religious and touches a vital human chord that has been in us since long before the advent of Christianity. It touches upon superstition and social bonding as well as tradition and identity. These things cannot be over estimated here.

> *'There is something Pagan in me that I cannot shake off.
> In short, I deny nothing, but doubt everything.'*
> Lord Byron.

If Christ hadn't died on the cross and Mary wept for him then Sevilla would still have its *Semana Santa*. It would have a different name and slightly different nature but the intensity and mass involvement, which today carry Sevilla's name around the world, would all be there. The pagan rites of this religious walk-about-town are all too evident to see. With the advent of Christ they were merely redirected into a Christian motif. The idea to pay homage to an image is pagan as is the act of parading it before the people. *Semana Santa* is manifest first in its citizens and second in its imagery. Dying has always played a strong role in the life of the people here. It is something that they are very close to. It is possibly this then that connects *La Corrida*, Flamenco, the family, *Feria* and their vision of modern living.

You may never get to Mecca but Europe does reverberate to religious fervour in its deep south. Every Muslim has to make the journey to Mohammad's birthplace at least once in their lives and anyone who revels in a city throwing off their 21st century shackles and getting back to their roots has to witness something like this, at least once in their lives.

- NUEVE -
VANITY FAIR

"Let us have wine and women, mirth and laughter.
Sermons and soda-water the day after."
Byron

Sevilla, however, is not completely versed in the writings of Byron and takes its *'sermons and soda water'* first in *Semana Santa* but with that out the way it thrusts itself headlong into indulging in *'mirth and laughter'*. After the somewhat sermonic proceedings of Holy Week the congregations are ready for something a little more on the secular side of life and that is when *La Feria de abril*, arrives. This may sound a contradiction in terms to be solemn and then almost at once festive but this yin and yang is a common characteristic of human nature. Spain's is a culture that does not hide from such nature, but rather embraces it.

Newton's Third Law of Physics or his Weak Law of Action and Reaction states that *'for every action there is an opposite and equal reaction'*. And strangely enough this manifests itself in social behaviour as well. Any swing in one direction is counterbalanced by a swing in another. It is all around us in nature and in our own character as well. The Reformation was met by the Counter-Reformation, Dictatorship is followed by liberalism. Puritanism is met by a loss of self-control. *'Where there is chasteness there is also liberty taken,'* as someone once said. Every country is marked by its contradictions and yet strangely we still feel surprised when we discover that a country famous for one trait also contains equal amounts of its antithesis. In a country like Spain then, it is no surprise that *Semana Santa* should be followed by an antidote: *La Feria*.

'I am always most religious upon a sunshiny day...'
Byron

Man cannot live by bread alone and however much he may try to lead a good and straight path his nature eventually gets the better of him and an escape valve is sought. He will take wine with his bread. So, a country fascinated by death will also be in love with life. After all, the secret of life is surely in the living not the dying.

The *Feria* is enormous. It is a bigger bash than Notting Hill and yet relatively unknown outside Spain. Pamplona is well trampled territory. *Semana Santa* has been seen by many and relayed through the international press. Many other local *fiestas* are frequented by summer tourists. And there are also those that know about the pilgrimage route to Santiago de Compostela, the oldest in Europe. So, one would think then with today's craving for information, and especially the tourist boom, that there are few corners left undiscovered in our world and certainly none in saturated old Europe. Here is one corner that finds itself at the very apex of Spain's *fiesta* culture easily outshining Pamplona in colour and yet it has been completely missed by the outsider's curiosity. It receives more visitors, drinks more alcohol and spends more money than Pamplona on preening itself for the occasion. It also kills as many bulls and not one person gets trampled in the process. The *fiesta* is a refined affair without the sole objective of getting drunk. The visitor here wants to remember the experience. It probably even offers up more photo opportunities than at any other time in Spain's exhaustive *fiesta* calendar. And this is only the Fair in Sevilla, every city and town in *Andalucía* has their own *Feria*. How is it with so many travel writers in evidence that this celebration has gone comparatively unnoticed? This is, after all, not *'a'* fiesta in Spain it is *'THE' fiesta*. Of course, due to Spain's multifarious diversity, it is impossible to name any one characteristic or any one *fiesta* as representative of the nation as a whole. But the rest have to go some to surpass the tradition and attention to detail that the *ferias* in *Andalucía* put on show.

So, *Los Encierros* - bull-running, such as those in Pamplona are to the North what the *Ferias* are to the South. And as the South has attracted more interest and visitors over the centuries and bullfighting is, in its origins, a southern tradition and also enjoyed in the North, surely the South's greatest *fiesta* must stand out in the traveller's imagination as Spain's *fiesta*. However, this has not been the case, so it is about high time to redress the balance and discover Spain's best kept festive secret: *La Feria de abril.*

Come the end of April all roads lead to the neighbourhood of Los Remedios taking with them hedonists in vast numbers, arriving on foot, by car, bus, by horse or by carriage with practically all the women in flamenco dress and a good number of the men traditionally turned out as well. But the first inkling that *La Feria* is about to get under way is the completion of the grand gateway. The first night is called *pescaito*, literally meaning 'little fried fish'. It underlines the fact that everyone eats fish fried in flour on the first night. Private dinners are held behind large closed awnings for the members of the private marquees that constitute the area where everyone unfolds their festivities.

So, the gateway - *La Portada*, stands brooding over the swaying mass that swarms around its base as they await the lights to blink into life on the stroke of midnight. This is known as *El Alumbrado* and is to the *Feria* what *el Chupinazo*, the starting rocket, is to *Los Encierros de San Fermín* in Pamplona. Inside the enclosure muffled music is already playing and at the far end of the temporary canvas town are the bright lights of the rides and big wheels dazzling the night sky. The seconds are counted down and then 22,500 light bulbs blaze into the night sky. The crowd cheer and when the euphoria finally dies down everyone realises that they are now stuck shoulder to shoulder along with hundreds of others who aren't going anywhere until the bottle neck of people clears. Gradually the crowd frees itself from its own grip and the people go their separate ways seeking friends, music and a place to dance.

Once inside the marquee area the boundlessness of the place becomes alarmingly apparent. Street upon street leads away into the distance all lined with alternating white and red lanterns creating a river of diffused light hanging over the yellow sandy walk ways. All the streets are cobbled and during the day they will ring to the sound of thorough bred hooves. The marquees – *casetas*, differ in size but all have paid great attention to their decoration. They sport either red and white or green and white stripes on their sidings and roofs. (The colours of the two local football teams oddly enough.) They are more *sevillano* than the *sevillano* style itself. They are a paragon of the city festooned in its folklore panoply. Everywhere people pour into the streets anxious to gets things going. Arriving at a cross roads and hanging in the air, framed against the black night, is a cobweb of bulbs burning away and shedding an almost painful brightness over the *rendez-vous* point.

The lights shine like pearly teeth, the streets are laid out for royalty and the *casetas* line them like oversized dolls' houses. It is a fantasy land made in the image of Andalusia's vision of itself. It is Valhalla for the living: where people feast, drink, dance, sing and walk the streets displaying their finery. Then the following day they are 'resurrected' to repeat the whole experience all over again. They feed their fill for seven days before the lights are put out until the following year. It is here that reality meets allegory head on. The eyes are given too much to take in and the mind doesn't know what to do with all the information. And all this is possible for the people to enjoy without coming to serious blows once the drinking starts. They obvioulsy have much to teach those cultures who can't take their drink.

Food is served up at all corners, gypsies walk round selling carnations and pieces of cane split down the middle with which they play the back beat of S*evillanas* music. Many people buy them yet few can play them like they can. There are kiosks selling ice-cream and information points distributing free maps. Fire engines are parked up in their own areas. The National Police are grouped at the far end where all the district *casetas* are huddlded together. People dance everywhere in the streets listening to the music flowing out into the young night.

The *casetas* have their pluses and minuses. As they are organised by paying members they are exclusive to them and their merry band. This would naturally exclude many but as there are over 1,000 *casetas* and a lot of people involved in each of them it is not difficult to find someone who is a member that will invite you in. For this reason it is said that *La Feria* is: *"The biggest party to which you're not invited."* Everyone *is* invited, though, to the street party. With so many thousands filling the *casetas* the word 'minority' seems ill-suited. The enclosure, known as *El Real*, is a place where dresses are flounced, horses prance, girls dance and men catch the eye as an elusive lover passes them by.

The first sign that *Feria* is coming is the sound of the jingle-bells borne across the flanks of mules clinking to the rhythm of the trotting animals as the conspicuous carriages appear on the streets. S*evillanas*

becomes the only music available on the local radio and in the bars, as people start to clap, the women spin and circle their hands in the air in the all too familiar dance. The men are elegant in their finest suits but a serious sight by comparison. DM boots and torn jeans twirl alongside the most furbelowed flamenco dresses. Wear whatever you want but you will always end up drinking and dancing just as much as the most experienced of the Fair's *aficionados*.

The *Feria* by day is very different to the atmosphere it creates by night. All around *El Real* is a traffic jam not of cars but horses and carriages. During the day time from about 12am-7pm the streets are open to horse drawn carriages and riders. The neighing replaces car horns and manure takes the place of exhaust fumes. Choose which poison you prefer. Carriages gleam and the feminine lines of the pure bred Spanish steeds capture the admiration of everyone. Wide brimmed hats, short jackets and intricate leather chaps give the riders equal standing in the folklore fashion stakes. Astride the backs of horses clinging to their riders are *señoritas* completing the typical scene in their flamenco dresses. The past is as present as never before. Hem lines may have changed with the times but here there is a constant classic of Andalusian identity. This parade is a glory of equestrian art and carriage craft and a free show well worth seeing at least once if ever down this way.

Manzanilla wine from Sanlúcar de Barrameda is the obligatory tipple. It is made just down the road on the coast and is exclusive throughout the world. It is a sharp dry form of sherry with the sea air giving the wine its distinct flavour and crispness. It is also *THE* drink in the *Feria* and when drunk elsewhere the smell alone transports you immediately back to springtime Sevilla and the atmosphere of a *caseta*.

La Feria goes full swing for one week, and adjoining it, if you have the desire and the adrenaline in you, is the infamous *calle Infierno* - Hell street, which has a fun fair that tries to rival anything Walt Disney has to offer with 55 principal rides. *La Feria* doesn't need it but here nothing seems ever enough for lifting the spirit.

The *Feria* is by day and night a photographer's dream and for the participant in the *fiesta* a time to let the senses breathe new life. Music, song, dance, guitar playing, improvisation, wine, food, friendship, tradition, a different way of life as well as horses galore. There are children dancing, all ages singing, food shared and new friends made. Women and men weigh up their chances while horses and carriages clip by. Riders hold up their mounts and sit back to drink in files. Gypsies perform flamenco while S*evillanas* is danced on all corners. Crowds gather and walk in concentric circles. The youth spend their money on rides with hotdogs, and candyfloss is never far behind. The great rides loom up into the black infinity of the night sky flashing their loud lights while girls pack their coloured frills into bumper cars. Groups sing in the street and join others they have never met before lending their voice to others that wish to dance. Friends meet by accident and then go their separate ways. High heels, polished footwear, fine silk shawls hanging from tanned shoulders. Delicate dresses accompanied by tailored jackets. Bright gelled hair reflects the street lights with ties well placed and women well groomed. Everyone watches and everyone is seen. The sun heightens the *fiesta* by day and the lanterns stir the magic by night. Photos are taken, ice-cream is purchased and the occasional foreigner strolls by shell-shocked from the revelation. Street theatre is born when the police and ambulance arrive, when someone famous is seen and when the *fiesta* slips into the sublime.

There is *alegría*, *bulerías*, bullfighters and flamenco dancers. There is bonhomie, frustration to get through the crowd and relief to finally get free. Expression, adulation and admiration. Feeling, hugging, greeting, laughter, joke telling and catching up on news. New alliances are made and old relationships broken. Tears of joy and few of sorrow until a little girl drops her ice-cream. Excitement, anticipation, participation and exhibition. Eventually tiredness arrives and all must leave.

Vanity Fair

> *April, April,*
> *Laugh thy girlish laughter;*
> *Then, the moment after,*
> *Weep thy girlish tears!*
> Sir William Watson (1858–1935)

The *Feria* had all begun in 1847 when two town councillors, neither of them from Sevilla as everyone here well knows, decided to organise an agricultural and livestock fair. (The oldest livestock fair in the province of Sevilla being Mairena del Alcor dating from 1441 and is also in April.) The two men responsible for getting the ball rolling were Narciso Bonaplata from *Cataluña* and José María Ibarra from *El País Vasco* - The Basque Country. The fair was one more try, in a long list of attempts, for Sevilla to regain her past splendour and kick start a flagging economy. In front of the old tobacco factory in the pastures called *El Prado de San Sebastian* the farmers and townsfolk met. Here the fair remained until the 1970's. During this time the pasture land was eventually transformed into a park of the same name and people were able to picnic under the shade of the trees.

The agricultural fair grew in importance and a *caseta* – marquee, for the Town Hall to regulate the trade, was set up. It was here that people had their first point of reference. And where *andaluces* meet, singing and dancing is always at hand. The municipal *caseta* soon saw guitars in people's hands and wine on the tables: *La Feria* was born. Once started there was no going back. In 1850 60,000 head of livestock were registered. In its wake there were 15 stalls selling *buñuelos*, a type of local doughnut cooked by gypsies, 34 stalls for selling hazelnuts and nougat, 43 offering games and 93 *tabernas* for drinking. In no more than four years the *Feria* was already transforming itself into what we have come to know today. In 1863 the circus came to the *Feria* for the first time and has come every year since. The next year fireworks were added. In 1870 the *Feria* was extended for two more days. Four years later and electricity was used for the first time. 1877, and we see paper lanterns appear in the festive streets and hot air balloons were brought to entertain the crowds. The first great *casetas* for casinos and various associations were set up. Then in 1896 they inaugurated the first permanent structure in the *Feria*: *La Pasarela*, an ornate raised walkway in iron, which acted as an official entrance. It was an innovation of the time and a lasting image of the *Ferias* of the 19th century. It was lit by 798 gas lights and stayed in place until 1920 when it had to be demolished and its 81,297 kilos of metal was sold as scrap.

Another tradition which continues to this today was also begun in the same year: the characteristic posters advertising the spring festivities – *La Fiestas de Primavera*. They have become collectors' items and copies of originals are released onto the market sporadically like diamonds from the mines of South Africa. In 1904 there was a *caseta* with a Japanese motif. The next year the same organisation's *caseta* was Arab. Walking around the enclosure were puppeteers and comedians. There were hundreds of stalls selling every kind of wares from fans to jewellery as well as all types of local foods from the surrounding towns and *sierras*. In 1914 the *Feria* now lasted 5 days. In 1927 two transatlantic steamers were used in the port of Sevilla as floating hotels. Then came the advent of the Spanish Civil War in 1936. The livestock fair went ahead but there was nothing to celebrate. In the 40's of the Post-War the *Feria* was back with music but was marked by the fact that many things were missing due to the country suffering from extreme hunger – *Los Años de Hambre* (The Years of Hunger). Even bulls were hard to find after most had been killed for meat or to deny the landed class their living. Cars had also been left at home due to lack of petrol.

In 1953 the *Feria* was now extended to 6 days. In 1964 the inevitable happened and the resulting fire killed one person and laid waste to 64 *casetas*. Two years later and the Prince of Monaco and his wife graced the *Feria de abril*. In 1972 *La Feria* closed its fireworks for the last time over El Prado and moved to a purpose built area in Los Remedios of 1.2km² in size, which had the capacity to produce enough electricity for a municipality of as many as 40,000 people. The number of *casetas* had now risen to over a thousand and the enclosure for the *casetas* excluding the funfair covered 40,000m² - the equivalent of 54½ football pitches. There were now over 1,200 wooden posts lining the *Feria* to support the illuminations, 500,000 light bulbs, 200,000 of which were used in the lanterns and 200 kilometres of electric cable not forgetting, of course, the 750,000 litres of wine that was put away. Today the success and extension of the *Feria* has been such that even that area is now becoming too small and it is planned to move to the area of *El Charco de la Pava* behind Triana in 2007.

The *traje de flamenca* or *de gitana* – the gypsy dress – is a central feature of the fair. Its origins are indeed gypsy. It was the popular dress among women in the 17th century, which later found favour among the more affluent who could afford better materials. It was finally accepted by more fortunate classes during the Iberian-Amercian Expo in '29. From then on the *Feria* became a public catwalk for fashions, and human nature's desire to stand out in the crowd has moulded tastes ever since. Almost as expensive, if not more so, are the famed intricate shawls: the *Mantón de Manila*, which adorn women's shoulders. Some wear them around their waist while others carry them over an arm ready to keep them warm when they return home in the early hours. It is so named because it was made with silk brought back from China via Manila when The Philippines, named after the Spanish King Felipe II, was a Spanish colony. From there to the motherland: *España*.

The men are not left out of it either. The wide brimmed hat is known as - *ala ancha*, and the short jacket - *traje corto*. The origin of the hat has its own history. In Córdoba during the medieval Caliph there was an Arab princess who had the unfortunate problem of a nose that protruded through her veil. You can imagine. So, a brim was placed around the Fez she wore under the veil to alleviate in the problem. In this way the Cordovan hat was born. The basic design is from Córdoba but Sevilla and Jerez have their own version. Only the trained eye though will be able to spot the differences. In Sevilla it is 10 cm tall and the brim 9cm wide. In Córdoba the dimensions are 14x9 and in Jerez 9x9. Women also wear this hat but theirs is slightly smaller. However, clients may of course choose their own dimensions. One must never forget though that the men must wear the hat lightly inclined toward the right and the women toward the left. Maybe it's similar to distinguishing between men that have just one earring in the right ear or in the left. So be careful not to tip the hat to the left or may receive uncalled for attention.

The 'short suit' was first used for working in the country and is still used by horsemen handling livestock. The principal descendant of the traditional *traje corto* is the *rociero*, which is worn on the road to the shrine in the village of El Rocío. The jacket has four basic variations, namely: *corto de feria, corto del rocío, corto campero* and *corto de ceremonia religiosa*. Subsequently it has inspired the short jackets worn for bullfighting. The jacket, however, that has been used most in *La Feria* is *el vaquero*, that of the cowboy. Yes, there are real live cowboys in this remote part of Europe. The most elaborate jacket, however, is without doubt *el corto de amazona* worn with the enigmatic *rondeña* hat, from the Andalusian town of Ronda. This a typical combination for the women and is familiar to us from the descriptions of the romantics travelling Spain in the 18th and 19th centuries and the drawings of the *bandoleros* who robbed the weary traveller. It was also a favourite of a former American bullfighter: John Fulton.

For the 'purists', and this city is famous for them, there are some rules that should be followed if Andalusian riding tradition is to be upheld. No tie should be worn, nor a scarf, gloves, belt or wristwatch. It is better not to wear long hair and be clean shaven. Hair in a tail should be avoided as well as sunglasses. Trousers should not have a pressed crease and shirts should be without frills. Black clothing is definitely out as are loud colours.

Religious brotherhood medallions around the neck are to be left at home along with the spurs. So, next time you are in *La Feria* take this list of rules along with you and go and tell everyone riding a horse to go home and get changed.

There followed a period when horse and rider were becoming less and less evident in the *Feria* until the 60's saw a drastic turnaround.

The carriages pulled by either mules or horses are the real spectacle by day while the women get the better part of attention by night.

'For the night
Shows stars and women in a better light.'
Byron.

Today you will no doubt see carriages that have been used since the very beginning of *La Feria*. High society arrives in English carriages but the majority of old money turns up in traditional *andaluz* colour and finery. Little has changed this spectacle over time. There are also a few that favour the Hungarian dressage. The horse and carriage suffered a decline in the 70's just as the horse and rider were starting to return. In 1983 to help stop the rot the Royal Andalusian Carriage Club – *el Real Club de Enganches de Andalucía*, was set up. The rot dried up and health was restored. There are 500 carriages alone in the province of Sevilla. *Andalucía* has the highest number of carriages in all of Spain. In 1984 the first exhibition of horse and carriage on the Sunday before the official opening of *Feria* in the *Real Maestranza* bullring was begun and has become an annual event. If you want to see the ring and avoid the bulls then this is your best opportunity. Carriages from all over Spain and especially *Andalucía* will trot out into *El Real Maestranza* and parade for all of Sevillian society to admire.

All combinations of horses and carriage will be turned out but none more spectacular, if you are ever fortunate to see it, than *cuartas con pericón*, which means four horses and one leading, which has been seen in *La Feria*. What is unique about the formation is that the horse leading – *el pericón*, is not actually attached to the other horses. It is completely free and yet goes where it is guided. In 2004 there were 3,000 horses and 1,271 carriages on show at the Fair.

The other catwalk the *Feria* has thrown up has been that of the stars. Apart from popular and national stars the Fair has been attracting big names for years. And this remember is not one of the richest cities in the world yet still they come. From Italy came Gina Lollobrigida, Brigitte Bardot from France, Anthony Quinn from Mexico, Richard Burton from Wales, from America Orson Welles and Hemingway, Eva Gardner and of course Jacqueline Lee Bouvier (no not the Simpsons, Bouvier was Jackie Kennedy) whose photo in *La Feria* was the front page of Life magazine in 1966. This is to name but a few. Even the Shah of Iran took time out, when he wasn't torturing opponents. Bo Derek, Mark Philips and very recently Michael Douglas and Catherine Zeta Jones have stopped by.

When the officials for the UEFA Cup were taken out in *La Feria* in 2001 they were so enthusiastic about their experience that they granted the city the final and asked if they could return the following year… just for the *fiesta*.

One of the most popular characters of recent times was known endearingly to everyone was *'Pepe el escocés'* - Joe the Scot. They are big on nicknames down here. Each year he would come dressed in full highland regalia much to the delight of the locals and add his own personality to the proceedings.

The gateway is a tradition in its own right and the first great entrance that was ever built measured 35m in height. Each design is based on buildings found in and around the old quarter of the city. Construction starts in earnest around January.

The *caseta* has its own design incorporating a dance floor and area to sing, a bar, a kitchen, toilets and an area for eating and drinking. Some even have private sections at the back though they are few and far between. Some *casetas* of note that are no longer with us have been: *'Er de 77'*, literally 'De one of '77', where 'De' is a simpleton's pronunciation of 'the', just as 'Er' is of 'El', which illustrates the good humour with which the locals invest in their *Feria*. They published their own magazine, had a piano, a circuit for mouse races, a well full of wine where everyone could help themselves and members all had nicknames like Count Custard – *el conde de natillas*. Another *caseta* called *'Esta es'* – 'This is it', had a miniature bullring installed where the *picador* mounted a donkey and the bull was no more than a calf. Another even had its own orchestra. The oldest *caseta* to be still within the same family is *La Machacante* and dates from 1927. In 1983 regulations for the construction of *casetas* were finally introduced. Although everything looks as if it would go up in smoke at the mere puff of a cigarette everything must, of course, be made of inflammable material. It'll go up gradually but at least the fire brigade will be able to get there in time.

Small fortunes are spent behind the bars in these *casetas* and €5,000 on entertaining friends and family wouldn't be an exaggeration for some.

> *"The presence of ladies generally adds considerably*
> *to the expenses of the party."*
> Baedeker (1894)

This would not be Spain, of course, nor the South if there were no room for involuntary irony and this comes in the form of the weather. In the land of sun and in its brightest *fiesta* you are guaranteed rain. Don't ask why they celebrate their fairest fair in the rainiest season when they have so much sunshine to make use of. But the expression 'March winds, April showers' is poetically echoed in Spain in the rhythmic words of:

'En abril aguas mil'

Exercising an evident lack of artistic licence it literally translates in the following fashion:

'In April a thousand waters'.

The *Feria* will give you a taste of it when you are least ready to have your spirits dampened.

When you first arrive in *El Real de La Feria* your senses will be reborn again as they rediscover their infant beginnings and what they were originally intended for. Your eyes will become sponges for colour while your ears will gather you melodies from all quarters. Your chest will feel the pound of clapping and stamping feet and your blood will carry your emotions a beat faster than before. You will be disorientated and at a loss as where to look. The image you have just witnessed you will never see again even though it will stay with you forever. *La Feria* gives the adult the excitement of a child entering a fair ground and that is exactly what it is: an adult fair ground. For the native born it is their identity, their culture. This is quite normal for them although surreal for those that have come from further afield.

Come 8am things have finally run their course. Those that have stayed the distance collapse out of *casetas* pushing past the heavy plastic awnings over the entrance. They stumble into the cool morning air and meet the sun coming up and other stragglers making their way home. Girls are now tightly wrapped in their Manila shawls. Bottles clank as people stumble over them while they shuffle away to have breakfast in one of the many bars serving *churros y chocolate. Churros* are long pieces of fried dough meant to be dunked into thick chocolate and a big favourite here. Many drift off to the more traditional gypsy *caseta* enclosure where the *casetas* are given an even fuller decorative treatment. Here they fry up *buñuelos*, a type of light doughnut served with chocolate. The whole operation is a gypsy family affair and the atmosphere and characters are another attraction that the *fiesta* creates, even if the prices do sober you up somewhat sharply.

There are so many things in the *Feria* that a book alone would not suffice to cover them all. *Feria* is for living not reading though, and it should be experienced first hand. It is in short, an immense sensual show that tells you that spring is finally here by throwing all the senses into overload. The scent of the night air, the sight of the lanterns hanging above you, the taste of your first glass of Manzanilla, the sound of distant dancing and laughter as well as the emotion of horses and carriages thundering close by. It is unique.

By day the *Feria* is dust, riders, the brilliance of colour, the iridescent light, the lanterns against the blue sky, the air blowing the sound of the *fiesta*, the screaming from the roller coaster, the spin of the big wheel, the sea food left on the floor, the heat pressing in from the *caseta* ceiling, people sitting down to lunch, the glitter of jewellery, children groomed for the day, hair gel worn as if it were a hat, folds of flamenco dresses furling and unfurling in the dance, girls dancing with girls, old men dancing with young things and cameras click while foreigners try their hand at *sevillanas*. The catwalk is in full flow with the horses parading and carriages trundling past.

By night the streets are taken over by the masses and the *Feria* becomes a scene of the flashing lights on the big wheels, people dancing salsa and *sevillanas* outside *casetas*. There is the smell of broth, the chink of whisky glasses, the fall of ice across the bar, the singing in the street, the police to one side, the children bright-eyed and bushy-tailed, the fluffy toys from the funfair, flamenco groups carrying their guitars to a *caseta*, the gateway lit in its glory, the singing, the eye contact, generosity, humour, the unexpected, new friends, old acquaintances, gypsies in their finery attracting a crowd as they dance among themselves, the smell of *churros* and finally the fair ground subdued.

The celebration for many also means: the circus, the bullfight and the fair-ground rides. Despite all that it represents, however, you will either love it or loathe it. It is too intense an experience to inspire indifference.

The Japanese are also in force at *La Feria*, along with the Israelis and French, who best appreciate this art form beyond its frontiers. Previously hidden in the shadows of the flamenco dance studios the Japanese now appear in the streets of *El Real* to express the artistry in them. They are welcomed with open arms and the flamenco atmosphere that they and their tutors strike up in the *casetas* has to be seen to be believed. Take all the photos you want but it will be the music ringing in your ears and the spontaneity raising your spirits that will be the lasting image you take away with you.

If Japan is the land of the Rising Sun then Spain is the land of a resonant one with *Andalucía* at its zenith and *La Feria de abril* its brightest light.

Vanity Fair

To give you some idea of what's involved here, the following figures were registered for *La Feria* 2000:

- 10 public *casetas*
- 1,000 carriages
- 3,000 cleaners
- 2,000 streets lights
- 1,000,000 litres of Manzanilla wine was drunk
- 5,000 rubbish bags, each with a capacity of between 40-60 litres
- 15,000 people helped to prepare it by putting up *casetas*, lights etc
- Profits in 2000 were 28,000,000 pesetas and in 2001 expected to be around 30,000,000 pesetas
- 6 district *casetas* were closed at 5am to avoid mass concentrations of people & consequent problems

In *La Feria* in 2003:

- €70 million on rides in *Calle Infierno*
- €90 million on food and drink in the *casetas*
- €27.5 million spent on hotel accommodation
- €213 million in total for the economy was made
- TUSSAM (bus company) registered 1 million customers
- 600,000 kilos of gunpowder were used in the fireworks display
- Lost children were collected from the Red Cross on average after 30 minutes

> *Alas! How deeply painful is all payment!*
> Byron from *Don Juan*

La Portada (The entrance gate) in 2004

- 165,000 kg
- 3,800 kg of paint
- 22,500 light bulbs
- 3,000 hours of painting
- 3,000 man-hours in carpentry
- 4,000 man-hours in construction

o   4,000 hours to mount and check components
o   Cost: €369,755.66 (The 66 cents was for matches and a candle in case they couldn't switch the thing on)

    Some countries if they wanted to organise such an event as this would have to open a whole new governmental department and employ an army of civil servants along with it. You might be able to organise a 'Pamplonesque' *fiesta* elsewhere if you really want to run in front of 500kg bulls, as has been done in the States, but *La Feria* can only be had here in *Andalucía*. Where else would you find the hundreds of guitarists and thousands of singers and dancers to fill its streets? And for free?
    When a society has lost its ability to celebrate with its own song it has sadly lost an essential part of its soul and here the *Feria* fills the soul with singing.

Sevillanas music, which will keep your feet tapping and a smile on your face for weeks afterwards, will become inextricably linked to your experience of spring in the city. *La Sevillana* should speak for itself and describe *La Feria* in its own words. A little bit of dictionary work might be necessary but it shouldn't prove too difficult to extract the basic meaning. To translate it, would only destroy the rhyme, the feeling and the expression imbued in the lyrics.

<u>Allí en La Feria</u>

- I -
Ya tengo los zapatos
llenos de albero
de bailar con la niña
que yo más quiero

- Chorus -
Es cosa seria
como baila mi niña
allí en la feria

- II -
La caseta del Pepe
vaya salero
Tiene toda la gracia
del mundo entero
Es cosa seria
La caseta de Pepe
allí en la feria

- III -
Un mar de farolillos
y de bombillas.
Y de cañera fresca
de manzanilla
Es cosa seria
Manzanilla fresquita
Allí en la feria

- IV -
Chocolate con churro por la mañana
entre cantes y bailes
por sevillanas
Es cosa seria
Chocolate con churros
Allí en la feria

Sevillanas is actually an adaptation of a style of dance music from the central region of Castilla-La Mancha, though not a lot of people know that even down here. It comes from the music variation *la Seguidilla*. Its golden age was in the 18th century when the dance was popular throughout all Spain's cities. However, in Sevilla and in several towns of Huelva, they adapted the music to their own style and festive needs. So, *las Seguidillas* were transformed into *Sevillanas* in music, song and dance. Then a *Sevillanas* boom took hold around the 1850's and since then it hasn't looked back. There is such a demand at present that a whole legion of groups that specialise in *Sevillanas* and its festive companion *la Rumba* has grown up. Typical themes predictably include women and love as well as drinking, eating, celebrating, history, homage to the people, the city and Triana.

It is odd to note that the first time that *la Seguidilla sevillana*, also known as *la Seguidilla bolera* now known simply as *Sevillanas*, was first performed was in Barcelona in the Liceo theatre in the same year as the very first *Feria*, 4th April 1847.

The following S*evillanas* will let us see how the *andaluces* see themselves. It may not be the best of S*evillanas* but it does lay bare their traditional mores.

- I -
Andalucía es mi tierra
Yo soy del sur
Yo soy del sur
Andalucía es mi tierra
Soy del sur soy andaluz
Me gusta el mosto en noviembre
Y mirar al cielo azul
Y mirar al cielo azul
De aquí fueron mis abuelos
Se formaron mis mayores
Aquí nacieron mis padres
Y nacieron mis amores

- Chorus -
Yo soy así
Y tienes que comprender
Y tienes que comprender
Que mis costumbres son estas
Y no las quiero perder

- II -
Me gusta dormir la siesta
Yo soy del sur
El gazpacho y el buen vino
Los caballos bien 'domaos'
Y la charla de casino.
Me gusta el cante 'sentío'
El baile de cuerpo entero
La guitarra bien 'templá'
Y los olivares nuevos

- III -

Me gustan los toros serios,
Yo soy del sur
Y los toreros del arte
Los buenos banderilleros
Y las murallas de arrastre
Me gusta ver la vendimia
Y beber con los amigos
Y las mujeres bonitas
Y las siembras de buen trigo

- IV -

Me gustan las romerías
Yo soy del sur
Las ermitas de mi pueblo
Las Vírgenes bajo palio
Los Cristos nazarenos
Los jardines con geranios
Las casas blancas y con tejas
Los miradores con arco
Y las ventanas con rajas

You may think that all this expense is absurd and there are better things to be spending money on. But *everyone* has a possession or expense that may be deemed as capricious by another. If you have money to spend then why not use it to drive dull care away and invite your friends as well?

All who joy would win
Must share it, - Happiness was born a twin.
Lord Byron from *Don Juan*

The *Fiesta* reminds us that our lives were not supposed to be spent in continual economic pursuit and social strife. The West is tied to its wristwatch and the East resists being strapped to it. *Andalucía* throws off this restraint as often as possible and embraces the traces of its Eastern past. For some brief moments each year we may rid ourselves of 'the ordinary business of life' and get down to reaping its rewards and let our other human aspirations take hold. Music, dance, song, colour, food, drink; the fruits of our labour are now laid on the table ready to be enjoyed. We briefly live as Gods do: without a care in the world. All pain is forgotten, all care of debts vanish, stress is subdued and rivalry put aside. Let celebration have her day and happiness its release on a grand day such as this in *La Feria de Sevilla*.

To the uninitiated *La Feria* is a revelation in its spontaneous merry making, its transcendency of colour by night, its outward display during the day and the fact that it possesses an undying desire to ride its wave of adulation for as long as the lights stay on.

To conclude *La Feria de abril* then, it is best to leave *El Real* with the uplifting words of Byron:

On with the dance! Let joy be unconfined;
No sleep till morn, when Youth and Pleasure meet
To chase the glowing hours with flying feet.

- DIEZ -
LIDS & OTHER APPETISERS

Man, being reasonable, must get drunk;
The best of life is but intoxication.
Byron from *Don Juan*

Not all intoxication of the senses is alcoholic. Here the orange blossom intoxicates, the heat changes perceptions and the *fiesta* acts upon you. Food also offers its own reward and hedonistic pleasure.

Sevilla has two claims to modern fame. It is home of the song, 'Macarena', sung by *Los del Río* - 'Those from the River'. The second claim, although doubted by many, is that Sevilla is the home of the humble *tapa*. No book on any Spanish city could be complete without a mention of its food and Sevilla would be saddened if we did not devote time to honour her *tapas*.

The bar *Café de la Iberia*, which no longer exists, apparently invented the dish. And even its oldest bar 'El Rinconcillo' dating from 1670, (beyond the Church Santa Catalina as it leads to calle Sol) could have come up with the novel idea. Either way it became customary to place a lid over a beer glass to keep the flies at bay. Bar owners decided to place food on the lid as they served out the beer. This was in an attempt to cut back on problems of drunkenness.

However, all this is predated by a more popular tale that in the 13th century King Alfonso X, the Wise, after recovering from an illness where he could only cope with small meals decreed that wine could not be served without it being accompanied by food. But this is not the only royal origin of the *tapa*. A more recent patronage was started when the king Alfonso XIII, on an official visit to the province of Cádiz, stopped to rest at the still-standing Ventorillo de Chato. He ordered a glass of Jerez wine. To stop the wind that was blowing from filling the glass with sand from the beach, the waiter had the bright idea of covering the glass with a slice of *jamón serrano*. On being asked by the King the reason for putting the *tapa* - lid, over the glass, the waiter apologised and explained his reasons. The King ate the *jamón* with the wine and asked for another glass and a *'tapa'* as before. On hearing this, the court ordered the same and a legend was born.

Once it had taken hold there was no stopping it. The *sevillanos* gave it full rein it and it soon spread throughout all *Andalucía* and northwards around the rest of the peninsular.

'Tapa' comes from the Spanish meaning 'lid', from the verb *'tapar'* meaning 'to cover'. The *Real Academia de la Lengua* defines the *tapa* in the following way: *"cualquier porción de alimento sólido capaz de acompañar a una bebida"* - which means 'any portion of solid food able to accompany a drink.' With the typical drink being wine, although beer is very popular. The word *tapa* has other derivations depending on the region; for example in Aragón and Navarra it is called *'alifara'* and in País Vasco (Euskadi in the local tongue and Basque Country in English) it is *'poteo'*.

Regions, provinces, cities and bars have their own specialities. There are variations in the way it is served and the range of *tapas* available. In the province of Granada, for example, it is not possible to choose the *tapas* you want. There, they are given free with the beer, so if you want more *tapas* just keep drinking.

Tapas aren't normally specialities in themselves. Anything on offer as a *tapa* is usually available as a main meal, but fashions are changing. *Tapas* are supposed to be inexpensive and they are, but some establishments can be pricey. So, if your *tapas* bar has expensive, specially made *tapas*, it is nothing to do with the real McCoy. *Tapas* do not exist to breed exclusivity but rather 'inclusivity'. Everything on the *tapa* menu should be within everyone's price range and reach.

There are many great advantages of *tapas*:

o You can afford to eat out every week
o You fill up on food, and not empty out your pocket
o It's 'fast' food
o The variety is extensive
o You can eat while you drink, making the occasion more sociable and it helps safeguard against getting drunk
o It develops a nation's cuisine and maintains a healthy cultural interest in food

It is very clear that here they live to eat. They spend an average 11% of their earnings on eating and drinking out, the largest in Europe, so there is no doubt that food is high on their list of priorities.

Their *tapas* culture is enviable because it gives them such readily available, good, cheap and in most cases healthy food. Few countries, if any, have such a system to equal it. Finding a place to eat where both food and prices are at least reasonable will not be a difficult task as the majority of bars serve food.

There are several ways you can order:

Firstly, there is the *'Menú del día'*, a meal often including wine. Prices are easy on the pocket but can vary depending on the bar and menu. This could be your best option of filling up on the cheap and cheerful.

Secondly, there are *'Raciones'*, which are full plates of individual dishes. Some *raciones*, for example the Spanish cured ham, can be a bit steep, but well worth the extra expense. Half *raciones* called *'Media Ración'* are also available in most establishments.

Finally, there are the *'Tapas'* themselves which are snack-size samples of some or all of whatever is on the main menu. The price reflects their size (about a quarter of a *racion*) but more often than not several *tapas* are enough to suffice.

The following is a very basic guide to the typical foods you'll find awaiting you in Sevilla:

Tapas *(for vegetarians)*:

Espinacas	Slow-cooked spinach and chickpeas with paprika
Tortilla de patata	Spanish potato omelette - the one and only!
Patatas a la brava	Fried potatoes in a thick and sometimes lightly spicy sauce
Gazpacho	The classic cold soup of the south with garlic, olive oil, cucumber, green pepper, vinegar, bread and tomato, always served in a glass.

Patatas aliñadas	Cold potato salad in olive oil, vinegar, peppers and onion
Patatas fritas	Chips (If you must!)
Pisto	Very much like ratatouille; but Spanish style
Calamares del campo	Onion and peppers fried like *calamares*

Fish *(Pescado):*

Gambas a la plancha	Grilled prawns
Gambas al ajillo	Prawns fried in olive oil and garlic
Puntillitas	Small squid, deep-fried
Paella	Paella! Rice, chicken, seafood etc.
Calamares fritos	Fried *calamares*
Merluza	Hake
Mero empanado	Grouper fried in breadcrumbs
Chipirón a la plancha	Grilled squid in garlic, olive oil and parsley
Pez espada	Swordfish
Pavía	Cod in batter
Boquerones en vinagre	Anchovies (unsalted) marinated in olive oil, vinegar, lemon, parsley and garlic
Brocheta de mero	Grouper kebab
Cóctel de mariscos	Prawn cocktail (again - only if you have to)

Meat *(Carne):*

Albóndigas	Freshly made meatballs
Pinchitos	Kebabs
Chuleta de cerdo	Pork chop
Filete de ternera	Veal cutlet
Chuletón	Beef chop
Churrasco	Barbecued steak
Morcilla	Black pudding with onion (or rice, if it's from Burgos)
Serranito	Fillet of beef, roasted pepper, cured mountain ham in a sandwich. Very filling and cheap.
Solomillo al wisky	Sirloin steak cooked in whisky
Carne mechada	Meat in a sauce of wine and spices

Lids & Other Appetisers

Filete con Roquefort	Fillet with Roquefort blue cheese
Carne a la brasa	Barbecued meat
Jamón York	Cooked Ham
Jamón Serrano	Spanish mountain ham. Very similar to Parma ham but better. Can be seen hanging in all the bars

Other:

Ensaladilla	Potato salad with hard-boiled egg, tuna, red peppers in mayonnaise
Caracoles	Snails. If you can avoid thinking about what you're really eating, you'll luv 'em!
Potaje de garbanzos	A type of meaty chick-pea stew
Habas con jamón	Broad beans cooked with *jamón serrano* and onion
Queso	Wide variety of cheeses *(Oveja:* sheep's or *Cabra:* goat's)
Empanada	A savoury pastry with a tuna, tomato and onion filling. Often served cold: but you can ask them to warm it up
Empanadillas	Smaller fried versions of empanada
San Jacobo	A slice of cheese sandwiched between two ham slices then deep-fried
Filete de pollo a la plancha	Grilled chicken breast

Montaditos: (In almost every bar - small toasted sandwiches)

Pringá	Cooked pork and its fat. A local specialty
Roquefort	The blue cheese again
Morcilla	Black Pudding with rice or onion
Anchoas	Anchovies
Salmón y queso blanco	Salmon with soft white cheese
Atún con pimientos	Tuna with red peppers

You will discover a hundred and one things besides this list; but at least with such a guide in hand you can avoid having to order the same plate of chips time and time again during your first few days.

During the summer months the diet here turns full circle and throws off its heavy winter eating habits of the northern regions of Spain. *Andalucía* makes no effort to hide its Mediterranean influence and nowhere is that better illustrated than at the dinner table.

Where once you made the rounds of the supermarket stockpiling hard cheeses, meats and carbohydrate rich foods, now in the height of Andalusia's arid summer the only thing you have on your mind is thirst, thirst and parched thirst. Where once you had eyes bigger than your tummy now you have sweat glands bigger than your bladder. You fill your trolley with bottles of water, cartons of fruit juice, yoghurt, beer, milk, *Casera© Blanca* (to be mixed with red wine), gin, tonic and a large bottle of cola. You never drink cola, can't really stand the stuff but now you're gagging for it, can't do without it. You have ice in the fridge but you buy a couple of bags just in case you run out during the night, such is the heat affecting your body and such is the desire to drown yourself. Before you would frown at a person drinking beer midday but now you find yourself rushing in the bar on the way back home with the shopping to dowse your mouth with cool, crisp *cerveza*, wiping your forehead with the ice cold glass for good measure. Bars now become regular watering holes, which you now depend on to get you from A to B. They supply you with a quick blast of air-conditioning and relieve that parched mouth for at least an instant. You now understand why when a dog has a dry nose it is an indicator that he is not well. You have to keep your mouth from drying out because if it is not moist it will make the heat unbearable.

But a Spaniard cannot live by liquid alone, even if many an Englishman has tried to. Food must be attempted. This is where the genius of the *andaluz* comes to the fore as they have produced a food that is 100% natural, excellent for your health and delicious at the same time. Believe it or not, it is also refreshing. And no, it's not a vitamin-based beer but none other than the famed *Gazpacho*. Foods become as light as possible and eating *al fresco* is only an option after 11 pm. Salads and cold meats become the order of the day.

Gazpacho moved out from *Andalucía* and throughout the rest of Spain as the result of Eugenia de Montijo, wife of the French Emperor Napoleon III in the 19th century. There were even some areas in the north of the country where the dish remained unknown until as late as the 1930's. The recipe probably originated from Spain's Islamic Middle Ages, when it was a cold soup today known as *ajoblanco*, containing garlic, almonds, bread, olive oil, vinegar, and salt. *Gazpacho* turned blood red in colour when Colón disembarked with tomatoes and peppers in his pouch from the New World. Etymologists believe that the origin of the word might be derived from the Mozarab word *caspa*, meaning 'fragments' or 'residue' hinting at the small pieces of bread and vegetables in it. *(Caspa* in Spanish today means dandruff, but you won't be getting that in the mix) However, it could well be a pre-Roman Iberian word modified by the Arabic. There is even the theory that it is derived from the Hebrew *gazaz*, meaning to break into pieces, alluding to the chunks of bread that are added.

So, *Andalucía* has its two faces of *fiesta: Semana Santa* and *Feria* and its two distinct obsessions; life and death, plus its two cultures; European and African. It also has its two climates, cold and hot and therefore its two cuisines, heavy and light.

The Italians may have great variety, the French fine quality, the Turk and Thai, exotic experience; but the Spanish will put on a spread where the only risk to health will be indigestion. Not even the bill could give you a heart attack.

The greatest smokers in the world are the Greeks, the Spanish are second. The greatest consumers of alcohol are the French and the Spanish are second. One would imagine then that they must have a horrendous heart problem, when in fact we discover that they have some of the longest-living citizens in Europe. In Italy life expectancy is an average 83 years as in Spain and the British can look forward to 81, according to data published by WHO in 2015. How can that be? The simple answer is diet. If they cut down on the smoking and drinking who knows how much longer they could live?

The Spanish cuisine is so full of antioxidants, especially the number one item containing antioxidant: tomato, whose lycopene dissolves the animal fat in many foods stopping the hardening of blood vessels. If they are cooked and a little oil added they can become doubly effective. When combined with vitamin E it prevents oxidation even further. Fish is so popular in Spain that the second biggest fish market in the world is to be found in Madrid - a land-locked capital. (The biggest is Tokyo, if you were wondering.) The benefits of the oil from fish, especially blue fish, are almost legendary.

Very little frozen food is used here, although habits are changing, when compared with other industrialised countries. Quality is demanded and provided in most restaurants. Some may be below par; but the majority at least have some respect for what cooking is all about. Desserts are few and far between, though. They are seen as a frivolous afterthought for those who haven't filled themselves on good fare beforehand. *Fruta del día* is on all menus across the land as a dessert. Even the finest four fork - *cuatro tenedores*, restaurants of the country will pay little attention to puddings. Perhaps it shows their no-nonsense approach to cooking, which will delight any visitor who loves simple food. *Gazpacho* and *Paella* are rare exotic exceptions. Spanish food is basic, full of taste, simply presented and always good value for money. And the added bonus about it is, you can be sure that it is good for you. The province of Almeria, known as the *La Huerta de Europa* - the vegetable garden of Europe, alone produces three billion kilos of vegetables, the largest output in the world.

So, in summertime the work routine and eating habits change but there is a strict daily eating timetable that never alters. You will never see a Spaniard eating in the streets while they are walking or on a park bench and it is an even rarer occurrence in Sevilla. This is because there is a strict, socially enforced eating code. The fine is a frown and drawing attention to oneself. Among friends the penalty is to be thought less of. In puritan countries cleanliness is next to godliness; but in Spain, it is eating correctly which will bring salvation. Breakfast is always light here and taken at any time between 7am and noon. It involves *torrefacto* coffee, made from toasted coffee beans with added sugar, or freshly squeezed orange juice - *zumo de naranja*, and *tostada* - toast, with *foie gras* or *manteca colorada*, which is coloured lard or olive oil and accompanied by fresh tomato. It may well be washed down by a glass of the local tipple: *anís*, from the hills to the north in La Sierra de Cazalla. Many have nothing for breakfast. Lunch is heavy and taken very seriously indeed. It is to the Spaniard today, what the breakfast was to the English of yesterday. Lunch is at two and not a minute before.

The point is well illustrated of just how rigidly enforced this social custom is. Just ask your Sevillian friend to go to lunch at 1:30 and they will answer,

"*Are you all right? You want to have lunch now? At 1:30?!*"

"*What time do you want to have lunch?*" you'll respond.

"*At two o'clock, of course! When else?*"

What difference can half an hour make you'll wonder? Here, a world of difference.

The evening meal is late, extremely late. Maybe not as late as in Greece, but still late. When Samuel L. Jackson was asked once, back in LA, if he liked Spain, he replied to the effect of, "*Spain, yeah. That's the place where they sit down to dinner at ten at night. Crazy! Yeah, I love that."* Don't bother going at eight. You won't be late - you'll be alone. Nobody likes being alone here. And on a Sunday evening nowhere opens before 9:30.

Conversations evolve around food. Here you literally are what you eat. People ask you if you are more of a meat, fish or veggie man. *¿Eres más de verdura, pescado o carne?* This is as common as asking which football team you support, but much more telling as it reflects on your physical, not mental state of play.

Every national cuisine seems to depend on some good old faithful staple around which most main meals are planned. In the British Isles it is the spud, Italy it's pasta and rice in Asia. But Spain chooses not to depend upon a single foodstuff, opting instead for three: meat, fish and vegetables. They do not have pasta every day although it is very popular, if simply done. Rice is common, but not prepared daily either, such as fish and meat.

Potato puts in an appearance but nothing like as often as it does throughout the rest of Europe. There are heavy, meaty stews that saw the nation through poorer times and still keep them warm through the winters. There are big cuts of meat untouched by sauces, retaining as much of their natural flavour as possible. Fish is lightly fried and served up in great quantities. Eggs play a key role as well, creating one of the pinnacle national dishes - the Spanish omelette - *la tortilla española* also called *la tortilla de patata*, which is made with just potatoes, eggs and onion. The omelette with *chorizo* and vegetables is known as *tortilla campera*. It may not be the most diverse cuisine in the world, although there is quite a spread, and the restaurant menus may offer the same meals over and over again with annoying regularity at times, but on a daily and weekly basis you will have your required intake of minerals, vitamins and nourishment. It offers you proteins, calcium. fish oils, antioxidants and roughage. If a dietician were to create a national cuisine they could do a lot worse than to settle for Spain's - pork products apart, of course.

Early evenings are marked by queues standing outside their local chip shop. Fish is lightly fried in flour thereby retaining its own flavour and reducing the fat intake. Baby squid - *puntillitas, boquerones fritos* - whitebait, *calamares,* cod - *bacalao, merluza* - hake, fried fish eggs - *huevas, croquetas de jamón* - ham croquettes, dogfish fried in vinegar - *cazón en adobo, tortillitas de camarones* - fried shrimp pancakes plus much more besides.

It is heart warming to know, though, that people who take their eating very seriously go mad for fried egg and chips. They are a favourite among all strata of Sevillian society.

Not all popular dishes go down well with everyone here; such as snails - *caracoles* when they are in season. They begin to appear on menus all over town in spring and continue through into summer

'Caracol, caracol saca tus cuernos al sol'

There are also *callos* - tripe, *sangre frito* - fried blood (which is just that: slices of fried blood not to be confused with Black Pudding) *seso* - brains and *criadillas* - bull's testicles. Not big favourites with foreigners, and not all of the locals either.

Sunday lunch is time for everything done on the *plancha* – grill. Grilled meat and fish are the weekend and restaurant staple. Families and friends pile into cars and head off to the hills to prop up the rural economy.

Restaurants or *asadores* - 'roasters', are the destinations for a multitude wishing to escape their urban surroundings, if but for a day. To the west of the city among the green hills behind Camas is Salteras, which has a host of *asadores*. The best among them for its setting is probably *La Resolana*, which means 'suntrap', hidden away but well signposted once in the village. The building is 100% *andaluz* but only 75% authentic, as a quarter of it is a recent extension but looks as old as the original core. Chairs are upholstered in the familiar striped material found on cushions in the bullrings. The walls are hung with characteristic memorabilia of the area's agricultural heritage and bull-breeding past. Waiters are dressed in well-pressed, black and white uniforms and are as courteously efficient as they are smart. The high ceiling covers a beautiful, dark brown clay tiled floor and equally hard starched table cloths. The food is good, the tables packed, the place unfalteringly rural *Andalucía* as families and friends drink and eat to their hearts' content. Work has been forgotten by everyone especially you... you're on holiday.

To the north west and en route to Portugal, in the high rust-red hills of Aracena populated by red gum eucalyptus trees brought in to combat the constant summer forest fires, are some real earthy *asadores* where hunters bring their prey to be put in the pot. To enter here is to know that you are a city boy after all. Unless you come this way often you really will be out to lunch; but certainly made to feel welcome. Those who show a willingness to learn and appreciate are accepted almost anywhere and if you can talk the talk there is conversation to be had at the bar. The air will be heavy with the aromas of burning wood, roasting game and the countryside that surrounds you.

The Spanish are MFT, positively Mad For It, they can't live without it and nobody sits down to eat without it. They prefer it fresh and try their best not to have to buy it out of the packet. Every day they queue for it and even have it delivered or set aside for them in the shops, namely bread. In the *hornos*, literally translated as 'ovens' but the name is given to the corner shop. They have a glass-fronted counter where they display the morning's intake from the bakery. Each has its own small in-house oven where they will heat up baguettes etc. offering you piping hot bread if you get there early enough.

The Spanish can't understand how someone can eat their meal without a hunk of bread to hand, or serviettes for that matter, and the Italians agree with them. Spanish bread comes in all shapes and sizes. *Baguette* is baguette, *andaluza* is the same bread only shorter and wider and therefore ideal for making sandwiches. *Bollos* are compact, oval affairs that are dry on the outside and thick and doughy on the inside. They are best broken up and used in small pieces. *Mollete*, now this is a whole different thing. So popular is this bread that Japanese visitors have been known to take the recipe back with them. There is in fact a website for it at www.mollete.com. It's either rounded or oval in shape, light on the inside, tasty and great for sandwiches or toasted for breakfast. It is one of the most popular breads so don't arrive late at the *horno*. There are also *molletes integrales* using wholemeal bread and while they fail to have much taste when cold, they are something else when toasted.

Here there are two types of sandwich. There are those we all know, with the square sliced bread which the Spanish call *pan de molde* and really don't consider to be bread at all, because it comes in a packet and is not delivered fresh from the baker's, plus the fact it is full preservatives. Then there is the full-blooded, no-nonsense Spanish version of the sandwich, called *Bocadillos*, taken from the Spanish word *'bocado'* meaning mouthful. It could loosely be translated as 'jawbreaker' because of the strength needed to get your teeth into the crust and force through what seems an impenetrable layer of dough. After achieving that, your jaw will come to rest on something edible, such as cheese, salami or a piece of Spanish omelette. There is no butter or olive oil to moisten the bread; it is left dry, which gives your saliva glands something to get to work on. The bread, which is used for the ubiquitous *bocadillo*, is usually *viena* or *bollo;* but any bread will do - *barra* is also common and even *sanwich* [sic] if there is nothing else left.

Coffee is taken in the afternoon to stop you from nodding off at work. Lunch is at home but dinner may often be *tapas* in a nearby bar if your lazy ways get the better of you... and they usually do.

Tapas are one of the great attractions of this city for the foreigners who come here and possibly one of the reasons that has helped persuade some that have chosen to settle in Sevilla. Such is the variety, interest and profusion of the *tapa* in Sevilla that *'En Sevilla se come mejor de pie que sentado'* - In Seville you eat better standing up than sitting down. Few *sevillanos* would disagree.

Rudyard Kipling once wrote that, *"The first condition of understanding a foreign country is to smell it"* but forgot to add that the best condition is to taste it. So, what better place is there for someone who loves their food and drink than the land of the *tapa* and possibly the city that invented it?

¡Buen provecho!
(Take good advantage!)

- ONCE -
PRIMAVERA

La primavera la sangre altera

-Spanish Proverb-

The spring, the blood affects you

The image of Spain that first travelled out from its shores and has hung in the world's collective consciousness ever since, was that of a French initiative under the leadership of such writers as Theophile Gautier and their painters. The best way to sing your praises is to get a foreigner to do it for you. It gives your claims substance and credibility if they can stand up to the third degree from a third party and imitation is always the best form of flattery.

> *"Andalusia is what for a century or more the foreigner has understood to be Spain. It is the Spain of the romantic legend, as Castile is the Spain of the 'black legend',* la leyenda negra. *We see in our mind's eye the Córdoba hat of the feria, the women with the high combs, the proud carriage, and the rose or carnation in their hair; we see the dangerous gypsy dancer, the long-toothed, narrow-hipped bullfighter, the figure of Don Juan. We see the cool tiled patios of Córdoba, Seville and Granada, hear the lazy talking of the guitar, the electric crackle of the castanets, as the twisting arms swing down. We are in the heart of the Moorish kingdom and have one foot in the East. Flowers, singing, sunlight, black shade and the rustle of water."*
> V.S. Pritchett in 1954.

Paris is the City of Light and Las Vegas the City of Lights, according to the Romans Alicante was the City of Light. L.A. is the City of Dreams or Angels as its name indicates and Auckland is the City of Sails. Rome the Eternal City and the City of Seven Hills and Florence the City of Lilies. Jerusalem is the City of David and ironically the City of Peace, with Ciudad Juárez having become the city of impunity. Hawthorne in California on the other hand is 'the City of Good Neighbours', maybe because all the other good names were taken up. San Francisco is the 'City of Complications' and Memphis 'the City Elvis Ruined' and Oxford is 'the City of Dreaming

Spires'. But everyone that has ever visited Sevilla is under no doubt as to what it is the city of... *Alegria*. The city positively invented the word and to this day we use the Spanish word *alegre* in our diction because 'joy' just doesn't seem to quite fit the bill.

'La ciudad, alegre y brillante.'

If Sevilla could export anything to the four corners of the globe then her citizens agree they would take spring to those that need it most. The seasonal changes here are strongly marked by the changing temperatures. From the emotions of contemplation in autumn to the irrationality and madness of summer. From sombre shades and parades to the jubilant colours and the time of lovers. The arrival of spring is palpable in the streets of Sevilla. People wait for the warmth to return after its 'hibernation' and the build up to the summer to begin. The season of *fiestas* is just around the corner and that of holidays and weekends at the beach. Now comes the time for youth to rejoice and the reserved colours of winter to make way for a new lease of life. Sevilla, as they say in Spain, has its own colours in spring - *'Tiene colores propios'*. The sun turns briefly gold before it glows white in summertime and the bright colours are sharpened as the damp is chased away. Red becomes carmine, yellow becomes ochre and white regains its brightness. The oranges swell in the trees, jasmine and orange blossom intoxicate the imagination as the tension grows. Nature is playing its strongest hand.

The light opens the eye and alleviates the mind. The hard work of the autumn and winter is almost behind us and it is time to reap the fruits of that labour. Fortunately, you find yourself in a city that understands this and encourages its citizens to go out and play.

One may come to the conclusion that the intention of English Hispanohile writers has been to add an even thicker coat of varnish to seal in the illusion of what Spanishness is or try to strip the whole thing off and leave it bare. But one thing is certain; many have passed through here to discover the city and Andalucía for themselves and gone home more than contented. Some have even returned for more. Perhaps they found a part of the illusion they were looking for.

Don Juan is the perfect figure for us to learn from and lead us through the paradoxical character of Sevilla. If the introverted personality of Sherlock

Holmes could only have come out of Britain then such a character as Don Juan could only have been born in Sevilla. We have this suave cut of a man swaggering along the narrow exotic tracks of this southern city and yet his image is the very opposite of his true self. He is an opportunist and unscrupulous scoundrel. A man further removed from his conscience would be harder to find. He is a player and definitely no gentleman. Sevilla does have her romance but as the tale of Don Juan warns us, it is deceptive. You may win the momentary affections of Carmen but she will despise you for it. And while under the sun seems the perfect place to be, here it will scorch you. Yes, this can be a romantic place if you associate romance with ruse. If you believe that love brings you nothing but pain and suffering then this land understands such concepts to its very core. Its folklore, known the world over, brings this aspect to the fore. Don Juan and Carmen that offer passion, of a dangerous nature, to incurable romantics are not in need of it themselves.

Romantic notions then are dangerous to entertain in this city but difficult to resist when spring pulls on those heart strings, hence the above proviso. So, don't say you weren't warned.

It is precisely now, in *primavera*, when the greater part of the foreigners decide to come. They have heard that it is best to be in Sevilla in spring and they have not been misinformed. They arrive to experience spring as Sevilla has created it, as Andalucía perceives it and how they have never felt it before.

> *O, Wind,*
> *If Winter comes, can Spring be far behind?*
> Percy Bysshe Shelley (1792-1822)

Every year there are expats that consider leaving the city but then decide to stay on at least one more year but suddenly grow restless as soon as the winter kicks in. They begin to regret their decision of not having left. The euphoria of the intense summer months now seems like a distant memory, but this change of heart is at once turned around the moment the sun takes its first tentative steps to wake the local population from their slumber. The growing light and intense smell of orange blossom soon dispel all thoughts of leaving. Spring in Sevilla is about to come again and nobody wants to miss it.

- DOCE -
SEVILLIAN SUMMER

*What men call gallantry, and gods adultery,
Is much more common where the climate's sultry.*
Lord Byron from *Don Juan*

La Feria de abril fades, although the gate will stand tall for several more months until it is eventually dismantled. The *casetas* are taken down in no time and before any sadness can take hold the *plazas* all across Sevilla are being decorated in readiness for May and a further round of festivities. Spring may be short lived but there is no harm in stretching it out a little. The light is bright but not harsh yet. The colours are still vivid but not washed out and the air fragrant not stifled. Spring is still very much in the air and with it, the people's aspirations.

May hosts the singular celebration of *Las Cruces de Mayo* – May Crosses. Every weekend for one month crosses, adorned with flowers, are set up in public *plazas* and *casas de vecinos* - communal houses, along with a stage, bar, bunting and decorative lanterns. The scene is set and each community that decides to celebrate a *cruz de mayo* in their *plaza* gets ready for a weekend of *fiesta* where all are invited.

While Sevilla is decorating its *plazas* Córdoba is getting ready for war - *La Guerra de los Patios*. Private patios open their doors and reveal their spectacular flowers to the wandering visitor. 'The War of the Patios' is no war of the Roses, rather a war of carnations. A prize is given to the annual winner and it is the best time to see the city.

Once Sevilla has opened the door to spring all of Andalusia's towns and cities take their turn to celebrate their own *feria* and *corrida de toros*. Jerez's *Feria de Caballo* - Horse Fair, lets those unfulfilled by Sevilla's explosion of colour get another dose. June stands in limbo with everyone poised to jump into July and begin their holidays. It feels as if the whole point of the year has been building toward this one moment. The last ten months have been anticipating this change. Finally, when the heat seems to have reached its limit and can go no further it suddenly doubles in intensity leaving you trapped by its lethargic fall-out. Meat eaters become lotus eaters and only *gazpacho* excites the appetite now.

Sevillian Summer

When the African wind blows the Saharan heat across southern Spain, Andalucía gently readopts her Moorish roots and gradually leaves behind her Castilian culture. Her temperate nature becomes sharply southern, acutely African. The heat steadily rises, the colours grow clearer and the attitude of the people changes in step with the lengthening days.

The streets are filled with a different people who have emerged from their winter hibernation. Andalucía slackens the reigns and returns to her old self. The timetable changes and the people turn their attentions to leisure. The children are off to camp, the beach or the unlucky few abroad to learn English, but they too will return to spend a month by the sea. The skin takes on its full-blooded Arab brown and then there will be no mistaking the ancestors of these people. The air becomes heavy, the mind freed from worry and the body calmed by the transforming cocktail of light, temperature and atmosphere. The streets in the afternoon will be deserted and the townspeople shut away sleeping the *siesta*.

The sun turns the day into a deserted night. The street is on fire and life put under threat. By three o'clock no one is seen walking the streets except tourists and stray dogs. Even the Englishmen that live here have learnt the hard lesson to keep out of the raw sun. The soles of your feet burn from the heat coming up off from the pavement. In the Sevillian town of Ecija 'the Frying Pan of Spain' - *La Sarten de España*, they cook an egg on the road for the news cameras each year. T-shirts with the graphic **e = mc²**, which under it reads: **España = mucho (calor)²** are everywhere in the shops.

> *'Only dogs and foreigners walk in the sun.*
> *Christians will walk in the shade.'*
> Roman Proverb

The old are under great duress from the heat and you emerge from trips to the supermarket with water, fruit juice, beer, yoghurt drink, G&T and melon. Your appetite for heavy foodstuffs has long since gone. You can't get enough of salad and no one dares to use the oven. Now you know why *gazpacho* came into being in this part of the world; it was a necessity not a luxury. The only thing you want to do is drink not eat so what better way to take your vegetables than to have them on ice. Even the red wine is drunk with ice and mixed with lemonade and this 'summer wine' is known as *tinto de verano*. The kilos drop off and so nature takes care of preparing the body for the beach.

The *siesta*, which one would think is also a necessity is more than that: it is obligatory. The weight of the heat forces your eyes to close. Fighting the encroaching tiredness will only weaken you further. Like a computer overheating, your body shuts down. You sleep three long hours, slowly awaking around six or seven and seven hours later at two in the morning you're more than ready to sleep again.

By three in the afternoon everyone has shut shop until the next day. In the centre the streets have been covered by tarpaulins throwing shade over the main shopping alleys. The streets of Sierpes and Tetuán breathe but beyond their shrouded protection they positively gasp. The streets are quiet until ten and then they come out from their houses: the children, babies in prams, couples holding hands and whole families strolling. The bars fill quickly and empty just as fast. The riverside, although not much developed, is heavily sought by the local population as the only place to cool down. It attracts the crowds like a waterhole draws in the wildlife. Late open-air bars, called *terrazas*, are reopened for their summer season converting the area into what locals know as *La Costa del Guadalquivir*.

Time slows, the light grows and soon you forget what life had been like without so much heat and time on your hands. You've long shed your winter overcoat and now your jacket for spring makes way for lightweight clothes before the summer strips you down to the bare minimum in the dizzying heights of August. The colours of autumn seem as far away as the moon and something that may never return. Fashions, skin colours, music and attitudes have all changed. You are now living in a different city, a different country with friends who have also become different people under a different sun that now rages like a bull above you.

Seville is urban Spain at its best but its sizzling summer makes it its worst. There are days when you can't go out because you just can't breathe and are dependant on your fan and air-conditioning as if they were dialysis machines. You become cut off by the heat as if the town had been plunged into darkness and no one dare venture out. The day becomes night. A curfew has been imposed. You phone your friends to see what has become of them. Your TV really has become a window on the world. It shows you images of your city that you haven't seen first hand for several weeks because you daren't go out there. The simplest things become impossible. You rise early because you want to go shopping and prefer to do it before

12am. However, that doesn't give you enough time to clean your flat even though you will be at home all day. You can't bend your back to household chores too late in the day because the heat is suffocating and you will be covered in sweat from the slightest effort. Like a trip through space it is better to sleep through it. It is better to keep your mind off the heat in any way you can. It is not hibernation in winter that you want but 'estivation' for the summer.

Outside nature has also gone off the rails and while the intense buzzing of the cicadas give noise to the falling waves of heat, plagues of insects finish off the weary wanderer in the streets. From midges and mosquitoes to grasshoppers and cockroaches, they positively thrive in the high temperatures.

No matter what the class, the money or the background, going on holiday here means one thing and one thing only: the beach. *Matalascañas* is the buzzword. The next mass migration from Sevilla is found in Chipiona where people say that you even get a suntan in your underarm because you spend the entire day lifting your arm up to wave hello to the people you know from Sevilla.

Whole communities move *en masse* to the sea. People who come down from the North are reunited with old friends. New communities meet up every year at the beach. Here people escape the city traffic jams to join the congested rows of cars by the sea. They get away from the masses in the town and then club together again on the sand. They elude the crowds in the supermarkets and reunite with them in the queues in local shops. The beaches that were half empty in *Semana Santa* are now overflowing and bars that were not there before have now been specially put up as every year.

The '*Chiringuito*' bars on the sand are the focal part of any Andalusian beach. Some people drink continuously, others come and go. Music pumps out and food sizzles in the background. Children run to them to buy ice-cream. Their are impromptu sellers who trudge up and down the sand pushing, pulling and carrying their stands, trolleys and boxes selling chilled drinks, cakes and ices. Here the summer is one big feast and if you're not eating, then you're drinking and if you're doing neither it means you're waiting to be served.

Things you have never seen before now become the norm. Life takes on another rhythm and moves in another direction. The beach towns are overflowing with helmetless moped riders from grandmothers to granddaughters. Whole families move about piled up on a single Vespa not forgetting the family pet. Local police, used to having a quiet time of it, now earn their money twice over. The summer here is like a scene from the film 'Groundhog Day' where everything repeats itself exactly as it was the day before. The beach routine is quickly learnt and soon adopted and then your city life becomes foreign to you. There isn't even time to contemplate whether any of this is good in the long run, you just go with the flow of the rising heat and the wind blowing across the straights of Gibraltar. Who wants to compete here? Those that do try and tackle the sun head on soon wish they hadn't. Here, there is only time for one thing and that is to lay back and take it easy. You'll do yourself a mischief if you don't.

But the heat also brings out the Mr. Hyde in the natives and lunatics are replaced by 'solartics'. The system breaks down and fuses blow. Sevilla sees its fair share of summer madness - *la inclemencia veraniega*. One summer a 77 year-old man who couldn't stand his two neighbours living below after year long threats poured petrol down the central staircase in his block of flats and then set light to a gas bottle. The three of them died and eleven families lost their homes. As one of them said on the news the old man had argued with everyone in the block apart from the intercom. The next day an 83 year-old drove his 4x4 36km in the wrong direction along the A49 motorway that links Sevilla to the city of Huelva. Fortunately, only the old man died. All over the country the number of crimes increase, especially the number of cases of women killed by their partner. The summer sees previously controlled conflicts and passions boil over. The next altercation to hit the headlines days later was that of two friends both in their nineties found dead together. The subsequent investigation concluded they had beaten each other to death. The summer goes to the head round here.

One of the first signs of the things that the summer will change is the opening of *los cines de verano* - summer cinemas. In the 18th century building of the *Diputación de Sevilla* in its enormous patio a large screen and bar are set up. The film list changes and details are posted in the papers and on Internet. Many of the cinemas are usually makeshift and some are constructed on waste ground just for the summer months. In the villages some are permanent structures and on the coast they are set up on the beach. With a blanket of stars and gentle breeze blowing the public crunch away on their sunflower seeds as if stamping on cockroaches. Families at the back come early to reserve a table where they eat dinner. The bar serves up the best *tortilla de patata* and drinks galore and the films on offer are the blockbusters from the previous 12 months. It is a characteristic and endearing summer scene.

For the visitor, however, not only does the temperature transform but also the social calendar. Spain literally explodes into *fiesta* with *Andalucía*, as always, leading the way. Accompanying the *fiestas* is a great number of concerts. And despite the summer chart topper, Flamenco reigns supreme in the South. As if it had been waiting especially for the summer, Flamenco takes over and can be found at every turn. All bullrings are fully booked as well, as the stars of the sand abandon the North. Granada in the Alhambra and Sevilla in El Alcázar host a wide range of musical concerts. No *andaluz* city is left without its summer spree of festivities and flamenco. The Alhambra holds the most emblematic Flamenco festival while the city of Almeria further to the east has one of the oldest.

The first big *fiesta* of the summer is Triana's moment to invite everyone across the river onto its streets. *La Velá de Santiago y de Santa Ana* takes place in the middle of July and *casetas* are erected all along *calle Betis*. Lighting and flags as well as a large gateway are erected on Triana Bridge. By night thousands pack the streets and the lights burn brightly. No neighbours are keen to call the police. In *la Plaza del Altozano* a large stage is put in place where by night music, singing and dance entertains everyone. Hanging in the air against the background of the night sky are pearl strings of lights bringing the stars within touching distance. Leading off in all directions is even more decorative street lighting. The whole area has been cordoned off by the police and taken over by the people. Triana is in *fiesta*.

By day the crowds are fewer but the spectacle no less for it. Eating and drinking need not be hurried and the real show is out on the river. A boat rides at anchor facing *calle Betis*. The spectators gather to watch the confident young men of Triana demonstrate their balance and flexibility. A pole runs out over the water from the bow of the boat. A green grease has been heavily applied to the pole and at its end is a flag. A youngster stands prepared, breathing heavily and going through his particular ritual. He crosses himself, everyone laughs and he holds onto the two outstretched arms from men standing either side to give balance as he launches himself into the inevitable. He gets a third of the way, runs out of steam and gravity and grease cruelly take over. He comes to a stop, maintains his balance momentarily and then realises he has lost all momentum. The only direction he can go now is down. He lets his body fall forward and somersaults into the water. No sooner has he fallen from grace than the next is up and a similar fate awaits him, as well as most of those behind him. Some meet comical ends while others take a more painful exit from their cylindrical stage. It is river theatre. One lad launches himself while the others behind are busy pruning their spiked hair and flexing their muscles. He lurches forward and just keeps going and when finally the grease gets the better of his legs he stretches out as he falls away taking hold of the flag just as he passes the pole on his way down. The crowd cheers, cameras whir and the boys and men on the boat jump into the water to cool off until the pole has been prepared again. The victorious flag bearer gives it to those in a white boat which now makes its way out to the moored vessel. In the centre of the white row boat is a fixed ladder. It cruises up to the pole and while the rower maintains his position another climbs up the ladder and greases the pole again. The flag is now placed further out and the young aspirants take up position. The papers in Sevilla will always show at least one image of the *cucaña* as it is called, on its leading pages.

La Velá is the face of Sevilla in summer. It is the week that Triana gets to play host to its citizens and let those not fortunate enough to be at the beach to forget that fact and remember that the *fiesta* is here on the *Costa del Guadalquivir* and not on the coast by the sea.

In the first week of August Huelva celebrates its Feria popularly known as *las Fiestas Colombinas*, after Colombus. When 15th August clicks up on the calendar the nation is united in its festivity again. *El Día de la Asunción* - Ascension, takes on local character and is especially popular along coastal areas.

But it is not just the South that is gripped by the fervour of *fiesta* in summer. The rest of the peninsular demonstrates this characteristic admirably. In Asturias in the North a 19km canoe race is held along the river Sella. People from at least 19 different countries compete and the race is at least 70 years old. For *El Día de la Asunción* in Madrid they dance *Chotis* in their elegant *Plaza Mayor* wearing typical dress in honour of their patron saint *La Virgen de la Paloma*. In Alicante they grow enormous basil plants for the day and process through the town. In the town of Peñafiel in the province of Valladolid they have Spain's most refreshing *fiesta*: a water-fight, called *Chúndara*, not to mention *los encierros* - running of the bulls and *capeas*. They also hold a balcony auction for those who want to get a closer seat for the local *corridas*, with the highest price one year reaching €1,200 Euros.

The ring is in their *Plaza Mayor* with its castle standing above it. As one person said, *'If you haven't got a balcony you haven't got a fiesta.'* In Bilbao, in the Basque country, there are big celebrations with traditional music and folk dancing. *'La Virgen de Agosto'*, as the collective images of the Virgin Mary are commonly known, celebrates the patron saints of each of these towns. In the Basque capital, known as Donostia in Basque and San Sebastian in Spanish, a jazz festival strums into life. In the *Barrio de La Gracia* in Barcelona after months of preparation the streets are finally decorated and the celebrating begins. In the city of Gijón in the Autonomous Community of *Asturias* are major fireworks by the beach as well as *toros* and music. Once again in the South in Cádiz a night of feasting is held on the beach during *La Noche de San Juan (Bautista)* - The Night of St. John (the Baptist), on 23rd June which coincides with the pagan celebration of the summer solstice - the shortest night of the year, though the Spanish make seem like the longest. Sevilla is quiet for once by comparison and solemnity is observed as a procession files around the cathedral starting in the early morning. *La Virgen de los Reyes* is the patron saint of Sevilla and her *paso* encircles the church. The image became the first canonised image in *Andalucía* in 1904.

No sooner is that weekend behind you than Málaga begins her week long *Feria*. 500,000m² dedicated to 367 *casetas* (open to all the public unlike Sevilla) and funfair attractions. The Feria by day is celebrated in the sheltered streets of the historic town centre. It is known as *'La Gran Fiesta de Verano'* - the Big Summer Fiesta. No wonder the country is renowned for people that are out to have a good time. Here they go back to work for a rest.

The archetypal coastal town of Sanlúcar de Barrameda in the south-western province of Cádiz standing at the mouth of the Guadalquivir river has a unique atmosphere when it hosts the nation's oldest horse races.

While many come at the weekend for the races the majority are there for the night time revelry. First impressions are usually traffic jams, teenagers of all ages on scooters curving through the mayhem and police sweating their way through their shift, trying to put some semblance of order into something that has no desire to be tamed, namely the Spanish out on a summer Saturday night.

Sevillian Summer

You park in local tradition: wherever you can, the motto being: '*He who dares parks*'. There is safety in numbers and the police are not going to write out fines for hundreds of cars in one night.

Once out of the comfortable confines of your air-conditioned cocoon you are hit, not by heat, but by the famous humidity coming off from the sea. Down on the beach the horses of the Guardia Civil can be seen close to the shore line keeping watch as the jockeys, with their colours gleaming, kick up spray as their steeds canter down to the starting gate. An area on the wet sand some 10-15 metres wide from spectators to the sea has been cleared for the horses to run. A makeshift plastic net, acting as a barrier, has been erected to mark off the onlookers. All along the beach are lines dug into the sand. Then an ambulance passes down to the start followed by a car of the Guardia Civil, which swings around and then turns its lights on. Once it receives the signal its engine roars into motion and the sirens scream. Within a few moments the thundering hooves race the jockeys past as cheering top hats and binoculars are replaced by swimming costumes and beach umbrellas. Before the horses have been they have gone and you are left with only their hoof prints in the sand and some elated children screaming as they run off to a small box behind you.

Out to sea a huge ship that was moored in Sevilla, 50km inland, just the day before is now coming out to the Atlantic. There is a handful of small pleasure craft out on the calm sea framed by umbrella pine trees and the shifting dunes of Europe's most diverse natural park: Doñana. In the far distance following the line of the charging horses is the *meta* - finishing post, where the stand costs €10 a piece to get in.

The races began in the first half of the 19th century when the owners of the horses that had transported the fish and shellfish from the beach *Bajo de Guía* held informal races. The first race officially organised was in 1845. Their President is the King and in 1997 the races were officially declared by the Spanish government to be of international tourist interest.

The horses are all pure English thoroughbreds and have been brought over from the USA, Ireland, France, England and of course from all parts of Spain. Today's prize money is minimal but it is reward enough perhaps to have a holiday in the sun for horse, jockey, trainer and breeder. The money increases though in the second and final meet two weeks later. The races take place along Sanlúcar's beach from *Bajo de Guía* to the finishing post in *Piletas*, with more than two kilometres of fine sand for racetrack. There is always television coverage.

However, the most interesting part of the whole event is what the kids are up to. There are no bookies 'officially'. Anyone who wants to place a bet on the outright winner has to go to *Piletas* and place it there. Anyone wanting to put down a bet here has to go through one of the kids. Lining the whole length of the two kilometre course, children set up homemade 'stalls' which are little other than boxes with a racing theme where they receive the bets. *'Minimum 0,05 cents and maximum €1'* reads the sign. Any winner is paid triple which is in fact their bet back and then double, so to cut a long explanation short the odds are 2-1 on all horses. Basically, the bets are for children but the really interesting part is yet to be seen. The youngsters once having put up their 'stall' go out onto the course and draw a line in the sand. This is their own personal finishing line and the horse that crosses that mark as it bolts towards *Piletas* counts as the winner. That makes it interesting for those who can't see the eventual victor. The line is watched carefully by friends and family before anyone pays up. Unknown to outsiders the children are actually competing for a prize, which is given out at the second meet for the best decorative stall. And surprisingly some of the kids do not bring out their best decorations because they don't want the competition copying their designs before 'judgement day'.

With the last race done, the barrier is pushed down by the families as the children take possession of the beach and shallow water. The sun begins to set into the sea while the snow white moon begins to rise above it, framed by a delicate blue sky. A few horsemen trot by, one in a top hat, jodhpurs and tailed riding coat soon followed by the mobile starting gate. With that done the races are over until their second session a week later when the tide will return to its lowest ebb and the jockeys will be out in their colours once more.

But Sanlúcar is famous for more than just its races and an exploration of its historic district reaps its own rewards. Strolling down the *Calzada del Ejército*, a huge yellow sand covered walkway where bars and the municipal brass band are the central attraction by night, you eventually arrive in the heart of the old town centre. On balmy summer evenings the area is an army of prams and families out to dinner and those making their way back from the beach. At the end of the promenade to the right is the grand 18th century bodega of La Guita with its white walls, grand windows and doorways framed by characteristic deep red lines.

Keep on going straight and you soon enter a warren of streets packed with chairs, bars, restaurants and punters of all ages and one colour: tanned.

The town looks as if it is anticipating carnival but it is just the typical summer scene of the Spanish taking their holidays. Eventually you come out in *La Plaza del Cabildo*, an open air reprieve among the crammed and humid pedestrianised lanes. The *plaza* is swarming with people, though, who fill tables and chairs while children run in all directions. Traffic jams of coffee, ice-cream and cold beer are moving slowly to and fro. The narrow streets are good for shielding you from the sun but a killer when it comes to humidity. They are peaceful cloisters out of season no doubt, which then become rabbit runs in high summer with so many people vying for space.

Crayfish is the town's local delicacy and that speaks volumes for a country mad about their seafood, and many establishments uphold Sanlúcar's just reputation for having the best. The local drink, however, is what really put the town on the map and not the fact that Christopher Colombus had set sail from here on his 3rd journey to the New World in 1498. Sanlúcar is famous above all else for its *Manzanilla* (fortified wine not infusion tea) and along with Jerez and Puerto de Santa María forms an important corner of the Andalusian sherry triangle. The old wine cellars of the town are as any good *bodega* should be: a place where time has stood still. A place very much like the wine they serve: once inside it is unchanged by the atmosphere of the outside world. The locals like their *Manzanilla 'pasada'*, that is to say matured eight years or more. The distinct flavour of *Manzanilla* is achieved by the fact that the humidity from the sea breeze lets the protective *flor* yeast grow thicker and live longer than in any of the other sherry regions hence its distinctive taste and unmatched dryness.

There are 64 brands of *Manzanilla* from the different *bodegas* and in Sanlúcar alone there are 9 different *bodegas* - wine companies, of note. The total sales in 1999 were 1,049,000 nine litre boxes. Although the first vines were introduced into the region by the Phoenicians as early as 1100 BC, the oldest winery in Sanlúcar is Delgado Zuleta and dates from 1719. The company now has 14 of its *bodegas* dotted about the town. The wine, taking advantage of the high humidity in the area to mature, also needs a lot of circulating air hence the great structure of the *bodegas* is an entirely functional design. They are grand Spanish buildings from its imperial heyday, now enjoying a more local viticulture revival. The *Manzanilla*, classified as unique in the world by the European Union in 1996, is perhaps an acquired taste and could be described by a heathen novice as a clear dry acidic sherry. It is above all *the* drink of the Andalusian *fiesta* and also excellent when used in cooking.

"I didn't have any food on land during my stay in Seville, but I tried different vintages of Manzanilla *wine in the cafés. It's a type of very dry sherry, served as a general rule with a small piece of smoked head of boar. The flavour of the inferior quality brands remind one of the smell of the evening newspapers, but that of superior quality is refined and delicate."*
Evelyn Waugh

You will wine and dine well in the overflowing festive side-streets of Sanlúcar de Barrameda, that is after first having enjoyed a typical day at the Spanish races.

'I shall soon be six-and-twenty. Is there anything in the future that can possibly console us for not being always twenty-five?
Byron

Byron could have consoled himself, had he stayed a little longer, instead of rushing off to meet his destiny in Greece. Had he stayed he may have enjoyed at least once the passion that these people have for the *fiesta*. A passion that each year reminds them that the ideal of life that so infects us at twenty-five is with us always, only sometimes it needs a little coaxing out of us now and again.

Time plays her hand and nature obeys her. The sky begins to close its doors earlier than usual asking the summer to finish up and with it ushering in the autumn through the back door. The change in temperature and the growing number of calls from the office shuffle everyone off the beaches and back to work. It will all come round again though, but it won't be quite the same. A year will have aged us, a little of our health will have been chipped away and some of our perceptions changed while the paint on the beach apartments will have weathered.

The grind of the rat race takes over for another long 11 months and it takes a true optimist to be able to look ahead with faith. But Oscar Wilde loved autumn above all seasons, a time when its slight chill breeze brings the world to rest and deepens personal reflection. Fortunately, Sevilla has much to look forward to and after so much summer heat it can afford to welcome in a brief cooling off period. It is happy to have a time of introspection, especially after its summer madness, just as long as the strong sunshine comes back to tan their skin. And it always will.

The last of the summer wine is finished up and everyone looks forward to the first of the autumn beer.

- TRECE -
'WINE, WOMEN AND SONG'

The man that hath no music in himself,
Nor is not moved with concord of sweet sounds,
Is fit for treasons, stratagems and spoils;
The motions of his spirit are dull as night
And his affections dark as Erebus:
Let no such man be trusted. Mark the music.

Shakespeare

In 1904 the German critic Oscar Adolf Hermann Schmitz notoriously claimed that England was *'Das Land Ohne Musik'* (the land without music). He was referring to the composing aptitude of the nation, or rather the lack of it. The slur was made at the absence of any great masters and not at the absence of a popular love for music or passion for singing. The smear came just at a moment when England went on to produce Elgar, Holst, Britten, Vaughan Williams, WH Reed, Algernon Ashton and Gerald Finzi. They arguably left the Germans in their wake and that is not to mention the rise of English popular music in the second half of the twentieth century. However, it is still possible to claim that England is still a land without music, in part. But it is probably the most important part. Were you to stop the average Londoner and ask them to rattle off a tune, how many would be capable of such a feat? And yet, do the same in Seville and you would have better luck in a city a tenth the size. And why is that you may ask? It is simply because the music is in the people. They are not wholly dependant on a music industry to provide them with all their musical needs. Where the *sevillanos* congregate there will be song and they will be singing from the same songsheet with no need for words to be provided. England may have more world famous bands but we are left speechless in such a situation.

Where is all this leading? To the inevitable conclusion that Sevilla possesses a different way of life that is worth taking the time to get to know.

No book on Sevilla could close without covering its musical tastes, traditions and themes. Sevilla is more renowned for its music than its oranges and has more than likely inspired more operas than any other city in the world. The list is short but in the world of Opera it is extensive: *'La Favorita'* by Donizetti; Beethoven's *'Fidelio'* his only opera and set in a prison near Sevilla; *'La Forza de Destino'* by Verdi; The Barber of Seville - *El Barbero de Sevilla* or as Rossini knew it in 1816 *'Il Barbiere di Siviglia'*; Mozart's *Le Notte di Figaro (The Marriage of Figaro)* and *'Don Giovanni'* (Don Juan). Not forgetting, of course, what is supposed to be the world's most popular opera ever: *'Carmen'* by Bizet. And they are all set in the same place. Bizet, Donizetti, Beethoven, Rossini, Verdi and Mozart all wrote to the greater glory of Sevilla.

Such a collection of operas means that in a provincial city they will be repeated again... and again... and again. And the same people will go and see them each time.

Sevilla and especially *Andalucía* has been attracting outsiders for centuries. When the English writer Richard Ford turned up in the 19th century he chose Sevilla as his base and reiterated an old Moorish expression when summing up how he felt about the place, *"He who has not at Seville been. Has not, I trow, a wonder seen."* (The original Moorish expression - in Spanish - is found at the beginning of chapter 2) From Sevilla he set out to explore the south of Spain and document it, creating as he did the forerunner of the modern day travel guide. However, his original work, still a classic despite countless works since, ran to more than 1,000 pages, covering 140 itineraries with a 50-page index. The *'Handbook for Travellers in Spain'* first appeared in 1845, when people probably had much bigger hands. Fortunately, the following year he published a more manageable book under the title of *'Gatherings from Spain'*. He had spent three years between 1830-33 travelling Spain on horseback. His name is still one of the foremost among the Anglo-Saxon writers to have ventured out here and express their art by venting their passion and satisfying their vision. Richard Ford described Spain as: *'A land bottled up for antiquarians'* and *'hovers between Europe and Africa, between the hat and the turban.'*

Sevilla is one of the planet's most enchanting, historic and mysterious cities. It has always been its own inspiration and in Europe it holds a unique place in its history and culture. Byron, once notoriously described Sevilla as, *"A pleasant city, famous for its oranges and women"*. He may have been here in 1809 and stayed in *calle de las Cruces*, 19 but England's most prolific romantic writer didn't say the place was 'romantic', even though it was much to his liking. And Sevilla is not romantic, she is sultry. She is not a Juliet but a Carmen. She inspires romance with but a fleeting glance and is only too aware that love is often a bitter pill to swallow. Nowhere does Sevilla more clearly lift the varnish off romance and express the hidden depths of despair and cruelty than in its two universal characters: Carmen and Don Juan. They were made for each other yet never met; if they had it would have been poetic justice for both. Instead they found other prey. 'Carmen' in Latin can mean 'song, poetry or a magic spell' very much like the city she has come to represent.

To Mrs. Byron, Gibraltar, Aug. 11, 1809

... We lodged in the house of two Spanish unmarried ladies, who possess six houses in Seville, and gave me a curious specimen of Spanish manners. They are women of character, and the eldest a fine woman, the youngest pretty, but not so good a figure as Donna Josepha. The freedom of manner, which is general here, astonished me not a little; and in the course of further observation, I find that reserve is not the characteristic of the Spanish belles, who are, in general, very handsome, with large black eyes, and very fine forms. The eldest honoured your unworthy son with very particular attention, embracing him with great tenderness at parting (I was there but three days), after cutting off a lock of his hair, and presenting him with one of her own, about three feet in length, which I send, and beg you will retain till my return. Her last words were, "Adios, tu hermoso! Me gusto mucho." - 'Adieu, you pretty fellow! You please me much.' She offered me a share of her apartment, which my virtue induced me to decline; she laughed, and said I had some English amante (lover), and added that she was going to be married to an officer in the Spanish army. ...

Carmen was also entangled with an officer from the Spanish army, and the general description above is well-aimed and still valid today in part.

Carmen has often been taken to be a romantic figure, but this was a northern European interpretation. Carmen, of course, is a *femme fatal*, which doesn't mean she's a nice person, quite the contrary. She is not going to make any man happy, but rather momentarily satisfy the insecure nature of someone that needs to possess that which cannot be owned. Flowers and joyous singing apart, there are dark undertones moving in the bottom of the opera. Undertones that have come from Andalusia's past, a past the rest of

Europe never shared. She is a local gypsy girl killed by her lover, but not her love. Carmen should always be seen in her Flamenco context more than her operatic version if she is to be seen in her true temperament.

The French Hispanophile Theophile Gautier (1811-72) said of Sevillian women,

> "They possess in a high degree what Spaniards call la sal. This is a thing of which it is difficult to give an idea in France: a mixture of nonchalance and vivacity, of daring retorts and childish wiles, of a grace, a piquancy, a ragoût, as the painters say, which may be found quite apart from beauty, and is often preferred to it."

The French writer Prosper Mérimée travelled through Andalucía in 1830 and was completely enrapt by a story told him by Countess Montíjo of a gypsy girl killed by her jealous lover. Through further travels and experiences in the south the event transformed in his imagination and in 1845 the story of Carmen was finally published. Thirty years later it was produced as an opera. Its first reception was cool to say the least, both the production and theatre ended up in financial ruin. It wasn't until two years later when it was actually sung in Italian in St. Petersburg before moving on to London and then New York, that it eventually received the acclaim we have come to associate with the work. According to at least one survey, the *Toreador* song is the most known of all operatic arias and Carmen the most successful opera.

The tobacco factory where Carmen rolled the cigars on her thighs still stands, now used as the city's university. The building which served to inspire Rossini's famous barber shop exists in Triana as does *La Plaza de Alfaro* where one can find the balcony of Doña Rosina in *'The Barber of Seville'*. However, the town 'Aguas Frescas' Fresh Waters, in *'The Marriage of Figaro'*, supposedly 14½km outside the city, never existed though there is a town in the province called Aguadulce - Sweet water, at 99km.

Italy had Casanova and Rudolph Valentino while Don Juan is Spanish and from Sevilla. He was this city's first great figure to capture the world's imagination, but was not conjured up by music but by literature.

Don Juan has many historical derivations: Don Pedro, Don Juan Tenorio and Miguel de Mañara. He was first given life by the Spanish friar Gabriel Téllez, who, under the pseudonym Tirso de Molina, wrote *El*

Burlador de Sevilla y Convidado de Piedra in the first half of the seventeenth century. His character was later made further famous by the Spanish writers Juan de la Cueva and Zorrilla as well as foreign writers such as Byron (whose poem '*Don Juan*' runs to over 700 pages!), Dumas, Goldoni, Mérimée and Moliere have all lent the character weight. And in the world of opera there was none more formidable than Mozart to compose his praises. Why such interest when the original character by Tirso de Molina is such a detestable individual? Once the seed had been sown the thorns were removed by the Romantics and a flower was brought to bloom.

'As to "Don Juan," confess... that it is the sublime of that there sort of writing; it may be bawdy, but is it not good English? It may be profligate, but is it not life, is it not the thing? Could any man have written it who has not lived in the world? And tooled in a post-chaise? In a hackney coach? In a Gondola? Against a wall? In a court carriage? In a vis-à-vis? On a table? And under it?'
Byron

But as George Bernard Shaw remarked, *"the lesson which the moralist wishes to teach is not always the lesson his hearers choose to learn."*

The psychoanalyst Austen observed,

"In no other country and in no other age, could the stage have found such a hero as in Spain of the sixteenth and seventeenth centuries: and few other races would have received so naturally the legend which so completely expresses this character. Spain's racial history, her climate, religion, and social life produce the very type which the legend demands at a time when this legend, older than her history, had become one with all the religious instincts of her people."

With so much writing and talent invested in the man it begs the question 'Who was Don Juan?' and 'Was he ever real?' People have speculated over possible names of real noble families in Seville such as those of de la Mota, Tenorio and de Ulloa. However, there are no historical records that actually chronicle the exploits of a noble quite like Don Juan. The most likely candidate to have emerged over time, in people's obsessive need to believe there actually was a Don Juan of Seville, is that of Miguel Mañara but the man in question was born too late, 1626. He is also quite uncharacteristic of Don Juan becoming guilt ridden over his past libertine lifestyle. This is not in keeping with the nature of a psychopath, as was Don Juan. He displayed all the hallmarks of the condition: no feelings of guilt or remorse, oblivious to punishment, insincere, a lack of insight, impulsiveness, loveless as well as possessing a tendency toward bravery over fear.

Tirso did have, however, literary models very similar to the character of Don Juan to inspire him in the plays of Spain's 'Golden Age' of literature. There was Leucino in Juan de la Cueva's *Infamador* (1581) and Leonido in Lope de Vega's *Fianza Satisfecha* (1612) yet both fall short of the character that was to burst forth from Tirso's pen and pensiveness.

'One can imagine that the effect of the Don Juan character on the young caballeros of el siglo de oro (Golden Age) may have been somewhat different than Tirso intended. Arrogant and fearless before even God and king, proud, quick to resort to the sword to defend his own honor, making no apologies for his behavior, like the conquistadores of the New World, Don Juan took what he wanted as if by right.'
Gordon Banks.

Love him or loathe him the man is here to stay. He is with us in both his forms: as initially intended: to shock us into acknowledging his existence and to act as counsel to those who wish to emulate him, and secondly, in his less offensive form as a lost romantic at the mercy of emotions more overpowering than flesh and blood themselves.

Another central song to Andalucía is *La Copla*, also known as *La Canción española* - Spanish Song, which has spawned many native stars and boasts a long history. The typical image of a busty, sturdy dark haired singer giving it her all and an *¡Olé!* at the top of her lungs will be a *Copla* singer. They have a big following not only in Spain but also the Americas and with their *paso dobles* add even more to the rich music fabric that covers this land.

Sevilla will surprise any individual with its range, intensity and size of its festivities. But just when you think that you have finally exhausted the city's supply and worn out your will for more *fiesta* you suddenly discover to your disbelief that the biggest occasion has yet to be seen. The event this time will unite people from all corners of *Andalucía* including people from other parts of Europe along for the ride, as well as even some from as far away as Argentina. It is the second largest pilgrimage in Europe after the four-yearly trek to Santiago de Compostela and the largest to take place annually. From Sevilla, Cádiz, Jerez, Huelva and surrounding villages people set out on a week long pilgrimage. Sounds arduous? A pilgrimage? Not when you see what *los andaluces* do to it.

Around the middle of June brotherhoods - *hermandades*, from Triana, Salvador and La Macarena set out in the early morning with rockets exploding in the air, guitars strumming, hands clapping, voices singing, drums pounding and pipes piping. Crowds gather at seven in the morning to watch the pilgrim train head out of town. The entourage is headed by riders with their short jackets, wide brimmed hats and ornate chaps with those in the lead holding silver staffs bearing their church's insignia.

In Triana the first ceremony of the morning is held in front of the church Santa Ana when the embroidered pennant of the Virgin, *el Simpecao*, is taken from the church and installed in an over-elaborate silver gilded wagon that will be pulled by two oxen to the shrine of *La Virgen del Rocío* in the village of the same name: El Rocío. As they push their way out from Triana a file of highly decorated painted wagons with oxen pulling, trundles its way to the shrine 55km away. Behind them come the foot soldiers, those who will walk the distance. All wear a hat and carry a walking stick with a twig of rosemary attached at the top. They also wear a silver medallion of their brotherhood hanging from green and white chord around their neck.

The atmosphere is festive. People have breakfast in bars while others sing, play music and dance *Sevillanas* in the street. Balconies with Mantila shawls draped over them are packed with onlookers decorating the way. Those still in bed are stirred awake from their slumber by the sound of the characteristic exploding rockets. The wagon trails hold up traffic all over town. When they are finally out of Triana and on to the open road they are joined by less traditional means of transport: 4WDs and tractors pulling large trailers. Huge water bottles and layers of mattresses are piled aboard for the nights they will spend sleeping out under the stars and the time they will spend in El Rocío. Some will even sit down to starched table cloths and champagne on their way through the sand dunes to the sacred town.

People take out bank loans for this *Romería* and banks even advertise for this unique trade. By the time the *rocieros* arrive, all well-documented by local and national TV cameras, they will meet up with the rest of the estimated 1,000,000 people there. It is the biggest gathering of horseback riders in Europe. El Rocío is a town purpose-built to host the shrine of the Virgin, *la patrona de Andalucía*, and everything else built around it has grown up in readiness for this annual event, which reaches its climax on Whit Sunday. Apart from the odd weekend, a full house at Christmas, the horse meeting of A.I.CAB in August and the small pilgrimage on 19th August to the Virgin for protecting the nearby village of Almonte during the War of Independence, there is no other use for the town apart from feeding the steady stream of annual tourists. With this in mind it is difficult to comprehend the scale of the construction.

El Rocío is a small, but complete municipality. There are streets upon streets of houses and outbuildings with balconies, patios and aesthetic detail in its architecture. The position of the shrine right alongside the marshlands where wild horses graze next to flamingos is enough to satisfy any eager visitor in search of a unique environment. No expense has been spared and the ornamentation on the buildings, what for most of the year is a ghost town, is astonishing. It also has the feeling of a Wild West town. A very quiet one, out of gold digging season that is. The odd member of a brotherhood or private house owner may have come to spend the weekend but their fellow brethren are not with them for most of the year.

Long, straight, wide sandy streets (there is no Tarmac anywhere), are lined by closely-packed buildings of differing sizes; but mainly large, self-catered boarding houses owned by brotherhoods from all over Andalucía. Hitching rails for the horses are in front of every house.

When the problems of foot & mouth disease, *fiebre aftosa* arose in Britain, the *Romería* and other popular *fiestas* involving the use of livestock came under threat. Horses escaped controls because they are not cloven-hoofed and were given free oats at the festivities (don't ask why), the oxen, on the other hand, were not so fortunate.

Representatives had to approach the European parliament to allow some of the beasts of burden to participate in El Rocío otherwise the *Simpecao* would have been towed by tractor which has never happened before. Fortunately, the event went ahead. Who would have thought that 'Farmer Giles' could have had an influence over such a *fiesta*. Several years later and they were not so fortunate. An outbreak of blue tongue among oxen meant that they had to resort to using mules.

Pilgrims set out from Triana mid-week and arrive back a week later. As each *hermandad* arrives the oxen pull the *Simpecao* up to the doors of the shrine where they are made to kneel down and the crowds burst into applause. Then the pennant is pulled to its resting place in a large niche in each brotherhood's main building, which are dotted about town. Then it's time for the celebrations to begin anew. As the people gather on Sunday night, the time-honoured rituals including the insignia and *Simpecaos* from all the *hermandades* are paraded out. The men from the nearest village, Almonte, gather in the church and congregate in droves against the grille that separates them from the statue of the Virgin. So many are assembled there, waiting for hours, that clouds of sweat literally billow out from the church entrance. Only those from Almonte are allowed into the building. They alone may lift and carry the statue around El Rocío. Woe betides those who try and get near the grille. The *almonteños* will make sure any intruder changes their mind. Suddenly, and no one knows how this is really supposed to work, the villagers will scramble over the bars in a mad dash to lift the heavy statue over and out of the church. Agonising minutes pass by while sweat and frustration fill their faces. The weight of the crowd and statue press down on them. Just watching it makes you feel the anguish of the moment. It is usually in the early hours after midnight that the order is given but it varies. It is, as the Spanish say, *'un caos total.'*

Fourteen hours later after being carried through the masses on her ornate silver-gilt plinth the Virgin finally comes to rest. In the year 2001, for example, they jumped the railings at 3:30am and returned the statue at 12:45pm. When they return home Triana receives the sun-blackened pilgrims on the Wednesday night as they arrive with a band playing their triumphant entrance into the *barrio*.

El Rocío though is not the oldest *Romería*, that honour goes to Andújar in the province of Jaén. *La Virgen de la Cabeza*, is Spain's oldest *Romería* and therefore that of Andalucía. An apparition of the Virgin Mary was seen there in 1227. A multitude gathers to receive mass from a modern open-air pulpit with Guardia Civil in regalia standing in attendance. The President of Andalucía is also present, as are the familiar oxen pulling the pretty painted wagons.

Strangely enough the one event that much of the European Mediterranean celebrates but Sevilla doesn't is carnival. Carnival is traditional in towns by the sea, such as Cádiz, whose musical march-past is famous throughout all Spain, along with that of Tenerife. Both burst into carnal celebration. In this corner of the world the next carnival of note is that of the modest coastal town Chipiona. With the Atlantic as its background, like Cádiz, it goes full swing for a whole week. While Tenerife reflects the Brazilian form of celebrating carnival, Cádiz is faithful to its roots and does it in true Spanish fashion. Everyone in Cádiz sings. Theirs is a singing carnival. For 11½ months they write and practice their satirical songs. They work hard on their *couplets*, *paso dobles* and *tangos*. Here is a place that holds no fear of self-criticism, unlike Sevilla. The groups are called *Chirigotas* and they spend good money on costumes which they wear proudly for two weeks as they compete in their city's theatre *Gran Teatro Falla*. The singing is televised nationwide.

The week-long carnival sees the cramped streets of Cádiz bulging at the seams with life and careless abandon. Large floats weave their way through the throng while singers impress the crowd with their humour and wit. The party-goers drink, dance and make merry while listening to the occasional improvised song. For seven days the place hardly sleeps a wink and Andalucía is once again alive with music.

'Fools are my theme, let satire be my song.'
Byron

Sevilla has not only been the scene for opera but also the background in celluloid. It has been a popular location for film-makers. *'Lawrence of Arabia' (1962)* directed by David Lean, was partly shot here. Peter O'Toole arrives at British HQ dressed in his robes and shocks the cloned officer class. This was shot in the central pavilion of *Plaza de España*. *'That Obscure Object of Desire'* by Buñuel (1977) was also based here. More recently the city has been used for Ridley Scott's '1492 - *the Discovery of Paradise*' (1992) and *'Episode One: The Phantom Menace'* when *Plaza de España* was used again and a bit of artistic licence exercised. The *plaza* really is that fantastic and it delighted the locals when they saw it bounce onto the big screen.

A lesser known homage to Andalucía was surprisingly made by The Doors after their visit. The song which reflects their impression was *'Spanish Caravan'* from the album *'Waiting for the Sun'*.

Carry me Caravan take me away
Take me to Portugal, take me to Spain
Andalusia with fields full of grain
I have to see you again and again
Take me, Spanish Caravan
Yes, I know you can

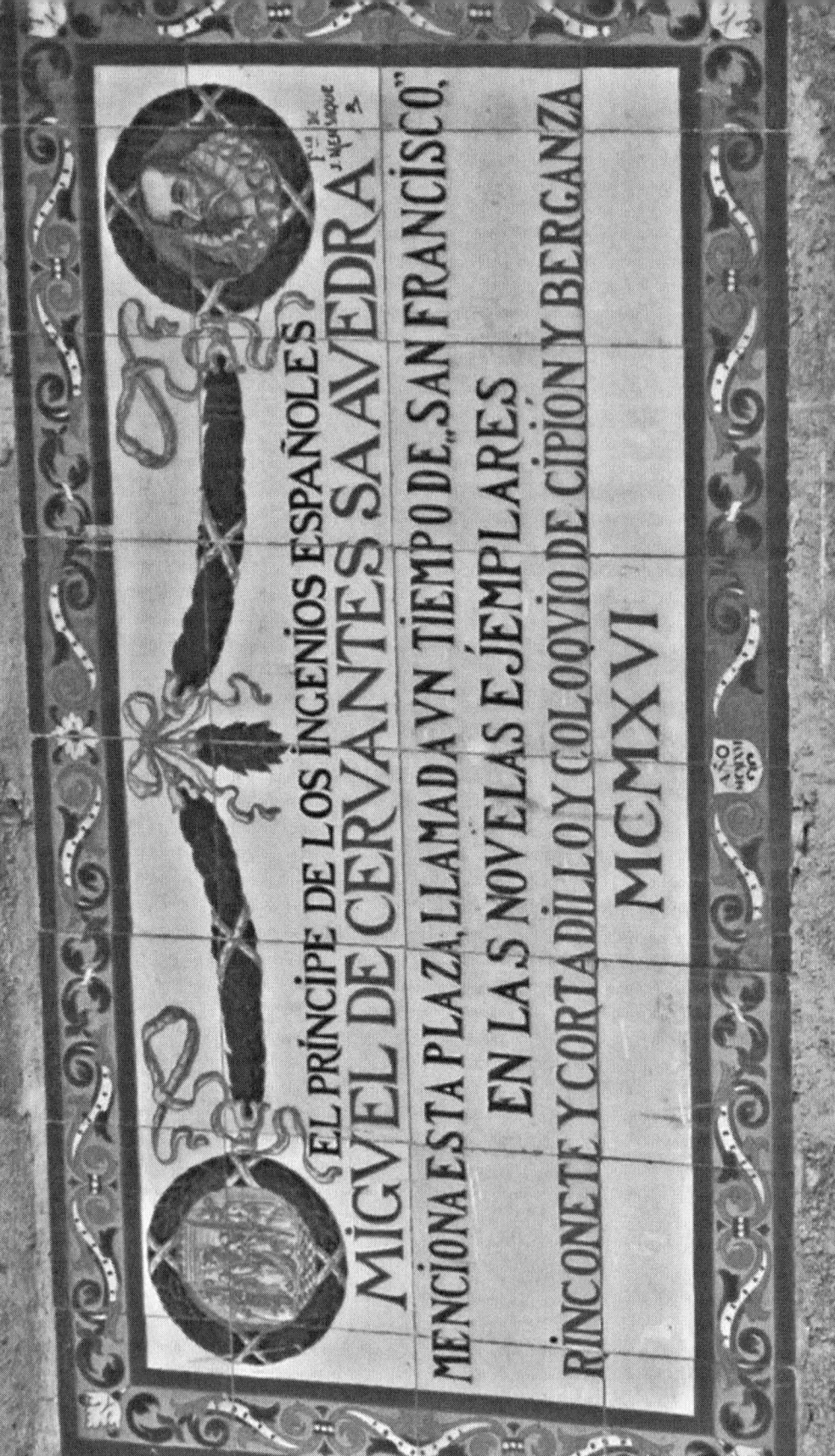

"EL PRÍNCIPE DE LOS INGENIOS ESPAÑOLES
MIGUEL DE CERVANTES SAAVEDRA"
MENCIONA ESTA PLAZA, LLAMADA UN TIEMPO DE "SAN FRANCISCO",
EN LAS NOVELAS EJEMPLARES
RINCONETE Y CORTADILLO Y COLOQVIO DE CIPION Y BERGANZA
MCMXVI

- CATORCE -
OIL MASTERS & PAPER MENTORS

'One picture is worth ten thousand words'
Chinese Proverb

Foreigners have always found food for thought in Sevilla's folklore, which has provided a background and emotion for European operatic material but outsiders have also been stirred by Sevilla's artistic vision, sparked by her home grown talent.

Spain's *Siglo de Oro*, the nation's renowned 'Golden Century', roughly began with the discovery of the New World in 1492 and closed around the mid 17th Century. It does not refer to some imperial peak but rather an artistic apex. It sings, surprisingly, not of blatant territorial domination but instead of the triumph of acute academic sensitivities. Seville played an integral part in the construction of this cultural edifice to Spain's noteworthy artistic achievements. The city's greatest contribution to her nation's aesthetic attainment is without doubt the painter Diego Rodríguez de Silva y Velázquez (1599-1660). The man needs no introduction as his surname has rung out down through the past four centuries. No nation's art gallery is denied their corner honouring the brush strokes of an artist that had no equal in his day. His realism greatly influenced the later great masters, above all Édouard Manet as well as paintings recreated by Picasso, Dalí and Francis Bacon. His *Portrait of Pope Innocent X*, was considered by Sir Joshua Reynolds as the greatest painting in Rome and many of the art world's great and good believe it to be the greatest portrait ever created. The artwork was executed just ten years before his death and Velázquez was a painter that continually matured throughout his life despite the confines of his position as court painter to Felipe IV. Sadly, little of his production is on view in the city of his birth. His *Vieja friendo huevos* (Old woman frying eggs) is in Edinburgh, *Pope Innocent X* is in Rome whilst his *Surrender of Breda, the Triumph of Bacchus* and his magnum opus *Las Meninas* are all housed in Madrid far from Seville. He was not a prolific producer and his output amounted to around 120 canvases. Manet referred to him as the *'painter of painters'*. Remarkably, little of Velázquez's national notoriety and artistic prowess was known outside his native lands until the advent of the nineteenth century. Since his discovery the subtle realist has found a permanent place amongst the Great Masters of universal art.

The painting *Las Meninas* is to Velázquez what *Don Quixote* is to Cervantes. The unexpected composition of court dwarves and the prominent figure of Margarita Teresa, the second queen's eldest daughter, also features a self-portrait of the painter set to the left of the canvas. It may not be his most emotive manufacture as there are others that express more intense moments of fleeting humanity. *Pope Innocent X*'s pitiless glare, for example, so concerned members of the Vatican that they feared the sitter's reaction to the finished piece. As history has proven though, the Bishop of Rome approved of his image reflected on the canvas and neither excommunicated Velázquez nor had the painting destroyed.

The prominence of the *Meninas* masterpiece lies in its arrangement, while its mystery resides in the moving sands of differing interpretations. The contest surrounds the painting's point of convergence. Is it the obvious personage of the Infanta in the very middle of the composition? Perhaps it is the artist himself to the left, the largest figure in the work bearing the unmistakable mark of the elite Order of Santiago. This aristocratic distinction has lead to the painting being wrapped in fable. The story runs that King Felipe on viewing Diego's handiwork took the brush from the maestro's hand and painted the striking red cross of St. James on the breast of artist's image in the painting in recognition of his gratitude. This version of events has reached the four corners of the realm but has been dismissed as the painter did not in fact receive the nobilic title until three years after the painting had been accomplished. It was unheard of for a member of such low mercantile rank to rise to such vertiginous social heights. However, his unique patronage removed that obstacle. Under the employ of the royal household meant he didn't 'sell' pictures to make a living and therefore could be accepted into the rank of file of the Spanish gentry.

In the background one can distinguish the faint figures of the King and Queen reflected in a wall-mounted mirror and this has lead to diverse interpretations, amongst which it is said that the painter predicted the coming demise of his royal patron. What is clear from this parallel image though is the depiction we perceive, which is the precise view that the two monarchs observed while having their portraits painted. In so doing the artist has uniquely taken the viewer's point of sight out of the painting and thus breaks the 'fourth wall'. It was the first of its kind and therefore a revolution of perspective.

Las Meninas means *'The Maids of Honour'* but could easily be subtitled *'Sovereigns Sitting for a Portrait'*. The English Romantic painter of the Regency, Thomas Lawrence, referred to it as *'philosophy of art'*. What it is without question though, this is Velázquez's most recognisable work and with that Sevilla's greatest contribution to world art.

The city has other brush masters to its name. Riding in the wake of Velázquez's greatness came his lesser peer and fellow citizen Bartolomé Esteban Murillo. While attaining renown Murillo did not fare so well as his mentor in the financial stakes. There were only two main benefactors at the time, the monarchy or the church. While the latter ensured secure patronage the former guaranteed superfluous prosperity. His replicate and realist style reinforced the influence and bearing of Velázquez. He documented daily life. Now the poor would be reflected in the paintings of a great artist and not just rich patrons. Murillo's collection stands as an image-rich memoir of Baroque street life and such examples enlighten the globe's most important art galleries. The likeness most people possess of seventeenth century Spanish street life is that of Murillo's Sevilla; an urban scene of *picaros*, waifs, peddlers, beggars and flower girls.

Murillo founded the Sevilla Academy together with his colleague and friend Juan de Valdés Leal. While a contemporary of Murillo, Valdés painted more dramatic compositions forgoing the calm and dulcitude which are the hallmarks of a Murillo canvas. He is best remembered for two works displayed in the *Hospital de la Caridad*, where they were originally created. They are *Finis gloriae mundi* and *Jeroglíficos de las Postrimerías*. His name soon becomes familiar on any tour of Sevilla's historical landmarks.

'The Master Painter of the city of Seville' was Francisco de Zurbarán as he referred to himself. Originally from the province of Badajoz he trained and worked in the Andalusian capital before moving to Madrid. His time in Sevilla enabled him to enjoy the benefaction of the numerous religious houses that had followed the New World prosperity and flooded the city. His effective *chiaroscuro* style earnt him the designate 'the Spanish Caravaggio' and his stern aesthetic manner lent itself matchlessly to Sevilla's affinity for Baroque religious expression. On moving to Madrid he joined up with his friend Velázquez and soon received royal commissions.

Few of his works, however, have remained inside Sevilla's city walls. One noteworthy exemption is *Santo Domingo en Soriano*, which is to be found in the Church of Santa María Magdalena. Although Zurbarán was not from Sevilla he is overtly tied to the lively locality. Without Sevilla and its moment of high Baroque perhaps the master painter might not have found the dark depth of inspiration that made his name, placing it alongside Velázquez, El Greco and Picasso in Spain's hall of fame. His statue stands in *plaza de Pilatos*.

If an image is worth manifold words then how many images can be borne by suggestive language? Seville has provided paintings of intimate importance to the national stockpile and it has also penned a substantial amount of its most memorable phrases and literary works. From the classrooms on both sides of the Hispanic Atlantic and the secluded literary cafés of Spanish speaking capitals to the restricted recesses of academia, some of Sevilla's literary sons have established an opined presence.

The name Lope de Rueda (1510? - 1565) is inseparable from Spain's theatre. He is considered the founder of the national fashion by not only Cervantes but also Lope de Vega one of world literature's most limitless writers with some 1,800 plays to his name. Lope de Rueda headed a travelling company in the 16th century and followed the lines of contemporary Italian dramas adding his genius to the dialogue and prose. He gained popular acclaim for his fierce humour and keen social scrutiny. His works, like Shakepseare, were gathered together by a friend and published posthumously. Unlike the English bard his works, which were published in 1567 by Timoneda, were toned down. Perhaps Timoneda wanted to polish the legacy of de Rueda or save the audience from blushing, in the same way Hansard safeguards its speakers from turning red when they re-read their selfless words.

Gustavo Adolfo Bécquer (1836-70) is another name that will ring out in the study halls of literary apprentices that dedicate their wits to discover the rythmic depths of *castellano*. The greatest romantic poet from Spain's *Siglo de Oro*, who took his father's Flemish surname, is considered the author of modern Spanish lyricality. The illustrious poet worked in tandem with his brother publishing a book under a *nom de plume*, which satirised the life of the royal family and was accompanied by erotic illustrations. It was titled *Los Borbones en Pelotas*, which loosely translates as 'The Bourbons Butt Naked'. On his death a group of friends gathered his surviving works together in order to raise funds to fend for his widow and children. His writings enjoy intercontinental distinction due to its lack of precisely the quality that characterises his native region of *Andalucía*, namely rhetoric and in its absence it exudes an unaffected beauty. His most acknowledged works are 'Rhymes' and 'Legends' (*Rimas* and *Leyendas*). The former consists of 98 rhymes and runs to just a thousand lines, which was enough to act as the foundation stone of current Spanish verse. Rhyme 21 is one of Spain's most recounted poems:

> *¿Qué es poesía?, dices mientras clavas*
> *En mi pupila tu pupila azul*
> *¡Qué es poesía! ¿Y tú me preguntas?*
> *Poesía... eres tú.*

> What is poetry? you say as you fix
> my pupil with your pupil blue
> What is poetry? And you are asking me?
> Poetry... is you.

With the passing of Bécquer came the arrival of Machado, two of them in fact. The brothers would revive the name of Sevilla amongst the literary inclined and come to symbolise the tragedy of their era. They may have belonged to the literary movement of the *Generation of '98* but they were unfailingly the artefact of the Spanish Civil War. The split in the nation was mirrored by the family division between Manuel and his younger sibling Antonio. Their differing political convictions were replicated in their writings and ultimately on which side of the Spanish border they would end their days.

Manuel Machado sided with the fascist rebel forces and wrote panegyric poetry in honour of the regime such as '*The Sword of the Caudillo*' as well themes heavily influenced by his rediscovery of his Catholic faith. His more noteworthy brother came down in favour of the Republic and eventually escaped to France. He spent his last months in the alluring coastal town of Collioure, near the Catalan border where he is buried. He veered towards poetry after a brief stay in Paris during his youth where he met amongst others Rubén Dario and Oscar Wilde. His most celebrated works are *Soledades* and *Campos de Castilla*. It is impossible to reside for a prolonged interlude in Spain and not come across the name of Antonio Machado at some point during your sojourn.

The Sevillian poet Luis Cernuda (1902-63) is another name that will also sound familiar to the long term resident. In addition, he is another of the countless victims to have been exiled at the end of the Civil War. He worked at Cranleigh School in England, Holyoke in the US and ultimately in Mexico. His outstanding accomplishment was *La Realidad y el Deseo* (Reality & Desire), and together with the corpus of his work he has been remembered for his pioneering efforts in the name of homosexual literature in Spain.

Recognition of Sevilla's contribution to the art of the written word was made official when another of its modern poets Vicente Aleixandre (1899-1989) was awarded the Nobel Prize laureate for Literature in 1977. He belonged to the literary movement the *Generation of '27* and his often surreal work was primarily concerned with the magnificence of nature, especially the earth and sea, and marked by his sorrow for people's lost of passion and naturally free spirit. He had begun his life as a lawyer but his career was cut short when TB left him infirm for life and unable to continue his profession. Then he began his time as a poet, greatly influenced by the work of Freud. He was trapped in the fallout of the Civil War and had to readjust to living in fascist Spain. At odds with the radical right-wing regime his work was censured by Franco's administration. To compound his adversities his weak health hindered him daily and he once commented on it by saying,

"Hours of solitude, hours of creation, hours of meditation. Solitude and meditation gave me an awareness, a perspective which I have never lost: that of solidarity with the rest of mankind."

- QUINCE -
EXCURSIONS: ¡VÁMONOS!

What should I have known or written had I been a quiet, mercantile politician or a lord in waiting? A man must travel, and turmoil, or there is no existence.

Byron

Sevilla is not as fortunate as Madrid in having so many excellent sites at such close hand to visit. But if you are prepared to make a little effort to go the extra kilometre then Sevilla will connect you with scarcely populated mountain *sierras*, hidden white villages, exotic Moorish monuments, landscapes of enormous proportions and individual character.

Not too far from the city and you can immerse yourself in carnival, horse racing on the beach, the world's oldest and Europe's biggest open-cast mine, Europe's most diverse wetlands, views across the straits to Africa and into Africa herself as Morocco stands beckoning. You are able to go skiing, diving, watch killer whales and dolphins. You may trek off into the unknown, go rafting or discover prehistoric caves. Europe's only desert lies east at five hours drive. Beaches, unique *fiestas* and the wilderness are also easily accessed in this part of the world. Historic towns proliferate a land filled with interesting locations.

The first port-o-call for anyone in Sevilla is the province's most elegant town, Carmona, located 30km to the north on the NIV motorway which leads onto Córdoba and all the way to Madrid. If you were to follow it past Córdoba, it would lead you through a winding mountain pass and out the other end onto the characteristic flat plains that are dotted with old windmills of Don Quixote fame. The arid land of Castilla-La Mancha is another journey though.

Carmona not only has a delightful name but also aspect. It is unostentatious in its aspirations but its laidback appearance is deceptive. As you drive through the new part of town you will find a replica of the *Giralda* tower in Sevilla, known as *La Giradilla* but built between 16th and 18th centuries. To its right is a pleasant park for the strolling locals, which commands a view of the outlying plains and old quarter of the town. The park is also reminiscent of details found in *Parque María Luisa* in Sevilla. Turn the corner and you are met by an unforgettable sight. You will have to pinch yourself to remind you that you are in Spain and not North Africa.

The *Alcázar Puerta de Sevilla* is as Arabic as any structure on the Peninsular and marks the southern entrance to the city. Part of the old city walls still stand to the left of the gate. Pass through it and you enter the familiar narrow streets of any Spanish town but here the similarities end.

The higher you climb into the town the more its character changes and takes on that particular to Carmona. The seigniorial houses, imposing in their stone and aristocratic patronage are not over imposing in their scale, tucked as they are among the pinched streets. Nearly all the houses in Carmona's old town are fronted by huge wooden, brass-studded doors. Inside, *patios* are frequently open to the eye of the real estate *voyeur*. The unpretentious façades only give away the fact that they have paradisiacal interiors through the attractiveness of their triumphal entrances built of contrasting stone. Carmona is littered with such residences, all bearing ancient coats of arms long past their status date. Among such serenity stand the darker shades of the churches, their graceful towers and convents. The religious buildings are so spaced that they thankfully break up the long lines of white. At every corner there is something new to surprise you without interfering with the balance between stone, craftsmanship and the historical spirit of the town. The two *plazas* of note here are *la plaza de San Fernando* and *la plaza de Abastos*. Both offer a retreat for those looking to rest their pins and see where the local Carmonans come to meet. The *patio* of the church *Priorial de Santa María* is part of the original erstwhile mosque.

The town was founded in Neolithic times but was given its present importance under the Carthaginians. Then came the Romans who really put the *urb* on the map. To this day Carmona retains Spain's biggest Necropolis, which stands near the open and flattened remains of its amphitheatre, which can be viewed from the road.

At the far north of the town is another jewel in its architectural crown. The defensive walls that remain are the oldest of their kind in all of Peninsular Spain and were erected by the Carthaginians. (The oldest defences in Spain are Phoenician and found on Ibiza) Removed from the walls to the extreme left is the gate that once acted as the principal portal to and from Córdoba. *La Puerta de Córdoba* is Roman in origin, later added to by the Moors and finally crowned by the Christians like all Moorish monuments in Andalucía. Connected to the ramparts is an impressive castle now one of Spain's most impressive National *Paradors* - state run hotels, *El Alcázar del Rey Don Pedro I*. The regal courtyard, entered through a fortified gate with the arms of *Castilla y León* standing out proudly, is well worth the visit. Once there you might as well go in and have a drink from its small bar and venture out onto the balcony overlooking the vast plains below. In the foreground one will see the remains of a Roman bridge which once formed part of the *Vía Augustus*. The setting is impressive but mercifully the same cannot be said of the price of drinks. The castle was enlarged by Pedro I when the city was blessed with his royal patronage. The castle today is a resplendent four star hotel with a sumptuous *mudéjar* dining hall. It is not the only four star hotel in the small town; there is another and a five star hotel as well. If the balcony in the Parador is closed or full, just outside is another bar and restaurant where, weather permitting you may enjoy an unblemished view of the plains near an old, precariously positioned Moorish tower, while coffee is served. It is hard to grow tired of returning to Carmona.

The town, however, does not hold the nearest monument worth visiting. That privilege falls to Santiponce, 5km to the south. Situated there is the original and eclectic looking *monasterio de San Isidro*, built by Guzmán el Bueno in the fearsome times of the 14th century. He won the name of *el Bueno* - the good, after his son was taken prisoner by the Moors besieging Tarifa and he preferred that the invaders killed his offspring rather than surrender the townto them. It was declared a national monument as early as the first half of the 19th century when it became a family home. But the town is known above all else for the ruined town of *Itálica*, which in its heyday was one of the principal Roman towns in Hispania. Today many mosaics are still in place as well as an impressive amphitheatre. However, few walls are still standing. The majority of the statues are now in the Archaeological museum along with some of the mosaics. The rest were removed long ago and made their way into seigniorial houses in Sevilla. The site on the hill planted with cypress trees is well preserved and set apart from the modern world.

Back in the main part of the town of Santiponce is the restored Roman theatre. The best Roman ruins, though, are to be found in Mérida, two hours west from Sevilla in the region of Extremadura. If time is not on your side to make it to Mérida then perhaps *Itálica* will stand in as a good, if lesser, substitute.

Excursions: ¡Vámonos!

A little further out and removed from the city bustle is the sleepy town of Salteras where the city-dwellers escape to for their Sunday lunch. The town lives off the restaurant trade at weekends. In the green fields on the way out there are the caves at Guadalcanal and the dolmen burial-chambers of Castilleja de Guzmán as well as those of Valencina. They are well preserved and the key can be obtained by phoning up the Town Hall in advance. It is a step back to the Copper age.

More escape routes from the city are found in the *Sierra Norte de Sevilla*, which forms part of *La Sierra Morena*, a natural barrier between Andalucía and central Spain. Forty-five minutes and you are surrounded by countryside among gnarled olive trees, red Martian earth and white houses eking a living from the land. As the road winds through ancient forest, black Iberian pigs collect the latest harvest of acorns that have fallen. Metal plaques painted black and white, signal the limits of private hunting estates, warning: *Privado. Coto de Caza*. The dense vegetation offers good cover for hunters, wild boar and deer; but it also means those who come seeking peace and quiet can't see them either. Hunting is big in these lands and it is not uncommon in bars to see hunters march in and sell their 'bag' to the owner. There is no doubting the freshness of rabbit or partridge around here; just don't swallow the buckshot.

Large, sturdy, whitewashed gateways dot the roadsides, marking the entrances to the sizeable farming estates hidden from view and secure in their isolation. You can sense the remoteness among the olive and cork trees, the greenery and impenetrable landscape. Here there is a different rhythm of life and alternative priorities from those of the modern city.

The principal town here in the *sierra* is Cazalla, known for its aniseed and it offers a village version of city night-life. In an area seemingly forgotten by people and time we would occasionally meet up at a friend's modest country retreat, cut off from everyone and everything. The house was surrounded by olive groves and rugged hills. It was the perfect place to park up, get the barbecue blazing and spend some time out with friends soaking up the sun and untainted country air. As usual the drinking and eating only stopped for sleep.

To own *un cortijo*, or *hacienda* - farmstead, is the dream of any *andaluz* with social ambitions. It is to the locals what the country mansion is to the English and ranch to the American. It combines its working facilities with its living quarters while always emphasising the aesthetic. Thick walls breathe in summer and insulate in winter. Antique Spanish furniture rubs shoulders with old English cabinet making. Spanish saddles hang above English riding boots and ornate architectural details stand against the complexity of nature. Some *cortijos* have been abandoned, others turned over to tourism, but the majority of the estates still work the land as they have always done.

El Cortijo 'El Esparragal' in the town of Gerena near Sevilla is a classic example. It not only takes in guests, stables fifty head of pure bred white Spanish horses, breeds Spanish and Hereford bulls but also produces fresh milk. The English style of the interior is clear to the eye and the oleander growing against the house with its *'mirador'* tower overlooking the landscape and swimming pool is 100% *andaluz*. It is the Andalusian country ideal in all its glory.

The nearest city to Sevilla is Huelva to the west. Spain was made for driving around but not its cities. The first thing you will notice out on the open road, especially if you head along the A47 to Huelva, is that the central reservations are planted with oleander bushes that blaze a bright and colourful trail across undulating open land to your next destination. Huelva may not be much but its surroundings are everything.

To the north of the city in the province of the same name and crossing over into Sevilla in *La Sierra Morena* is *La Sierra de Aracena*. Grand Canyon-like views are possible at times over a land heavily planted with eucalyptus trees to resist the spread of fire. The capital of this *sierra* is the town of Aracena. White, peaceful and pleasant, like all the towns of these hills. Aracena is watched over by an impressive church and castle on the high hill battling against the gusts of *sierra* air. This place has had its fair share of history. Romans and Moors have been through here and it was briefly in the custody of the Knights Templar. Today the local people look after their own affairs.

The principal attraction, though, is *La Gruta de las Maravillas*, the limestone caves which are the biggest of their kind in Spain. Containing twelve underground lakes, it has been the setting for several films including *'Journey to the Centre of the Earth'*. Nearby is the small town of Jabugo known all over as the *Jamón Iberico* HQ. This is where the best of the best cured Iberian mountain ham - *jamón serrano*, is produced and is a Mecca for *jamón* lovers.

The village of Carboneras has one bar to its name and that's it, no shops, no bus stop, no newsagent's. It is a typical example of the area. The road that leads to the sleepy hamlet takes you past the village and out to a reservoir where wild horses run free. Back in Carboneras the *sierra* character is clearly identifiable in its narrow cobbled lanes, the abundance of water in its fountains and streams, the open air public laundry and houses that face south so their balconies, *solanas*, allow the sun to dry fruit, herbs and spices. Today many are overhung with flowers. Vegetation sprouts from all angles and provides the fortunate visitor with a welcome escape from the urban jungle.

Here everyone knows everyone else's comings and goings. Higher up the hillside, and blessedly out of sight, are more modern dwellings even more remote than the villagers below. The majority belong to Germans and locals of the village who once left to go abroad and have now returned home after making good.

All around the area dirt tracks disappear into woodland which swallow up travellers as they make their way to their hidden nests. Houses are the very definition of earthiness with their heavy walls, sturdy beams, huge flagstones and a toilet in the old cellar, which leads out to the street. People gather around their large open hearths, where meat is cooked on the spit and eat, drink, sing and dance. This is rustic Spain at its simplest and most endearing.

You don't have to go far here to be out of your depth language or culturally wise. Leave the city boundaries and you will soon find yourself among a barren landscape or deep hills that close in and overawe you. This is still a very wild country with villages concealed from intruders for most, if not all, of the time. There is not only another way of life but also a different accent once outside the city limits. The *andaluz* of Sevilla sounds refined when compared to its rural counterpart. If you thought you had trouble understanding people in the big city don't even bother asking someone directions out in 'the woods'. You won't a get a word of it and that is *exactly* why you just have to wind the window down and give it a try. It's good to be reminded that you are out of your comfort zone.

Red wine here is not known as *vino 'rojo'* but as *vino 'tinto'*. *La Gruta de las Maravillas* may be nature's best underground work of art in the southwest of Andalucía but man's worst overground creation is also here in the province of Huelva. The Riotinto mines have been in constant use for over 5,000 years thereby making them the oldest mines in continual use in the world. *La Corta Atalaya* in Riotinto is also the largest open-cast mine in Europe. *"A huge crater, with stepped sides dwarfing an acid-red lake is an awesome sight - a man-made Grand Canyon in the middle of Huelva."* It is over 1 km long, almost as wide, 300m deep and at its base the area now occupied by water is big enough to hold 2 football pitches. The mines contain the largest known quantities of copper pyrites anywhere. The river called Riotinto is the best named in all of Spain, because it really does run as red as *Rioja* wine. The area has been mined by foreigners until very recent times. The Phoenicians started the mining here, followed by the Romans, Moors and the mine was later bought by a Swede in the 18th century. But things didn't get going here big-time until the British bought the business in 1873 staying until 1954. By 1887 The Riotinto Company Limited was the biggest in all Spain producing 40% of the country's copper. The mines and adjoining residences covered a total of 24,700 acres. There were 130 locomotives transporting ore to the port of Huelva. Not all was a bed of roses as the harsh working conditions and subsequent pollution from the mining caused strikes, which were severely repressed and where 200 people died, yet the officially recognised figure was just 13. At one time the British company employed as many as 19,000 people from as far afield as Galicia and Asturias. When these miners returned to their native lands they took Flamenco with them and to this day many songs in the north contain lyrics of miners' strife.

The Spanish had to adapt to British ways including celebrating the *fiesta* of Queen Victoria's birthday, decking the area out in bunting. The first football match also took place here in Riotinto and thereby established the game in Spain.

The directors of the mines lived in the hilltop residency of *Bellavista* - Beautiful View, in the *colonia inglesa* while lesser employees took up lodgings in the *Reina Victoria* district in the heart of Huelva city called *el barrio inglés* by the local people. They were built in colonial style and a few homes still survive. The style of living was based on the Victorian mode of the time with its gardens and social club, cricket club and tennis courts. It had its own Presbyterian church and pastor, Protestant cemetery and of course schools. The Spanish employees did enjoy some things, however, not available to them elsewhere in Andalucía, such as hospitals and being paid weekly. The inward looking idyll reminiscent of The Raj was disrupted one day when three doctors refused to pay the traditional fine of a bottle of whisky for having entered the club house with women. They were thrown out of the building as a result and then they took the company to court in Huelva and won.

But the true importance of the mines to most Spaniards today is that this was where football was first introduced when the locals saw the British miners kicking a ball about. Two teams were organised in 1879. Huelva Recreational Club - *Huelva Recreativa*, and Riotinto F.C. The first game was played between the Spanish workers and the British engineers.

In 1954 the mines were eventually sold back to Franco who had referred to them as *'An economic Gibraltar'*. The last of the British workers left in 1970. Today, after years of decline, the mine is used more as a museum, entertaining foreigners and school trips alike. The present director stated that, *"There is no other place like Riotinto in the world as it is 5,000 years old, so all humanity's imprints from the beginning of its civilisation are to be seen here."*

Huelva still holds more for the visitor and another first in Europe. Tucked away in its south eastern corner, hemmed in by the Atlantic and the delta of the river Guadalquivir is Europe's largest wetland reserve, officially protected since 1969. It covers a total of 247,105 acres and has been declared a World Heritage Site and Biosphere Reserve. It is a National Park and Nature Park, noted for its biodiversity of flora and fauna. 300 species of birds use this watering hole as a stopover between Europe and Africa and flock here by the thousands. Red deer, fallow deer, wild boar, a wide variety of waterfowl and horses spend their days here. The rare Imperial Eagle and the largest number of Iberian Lynxes are of particular note. Swamps, rice fields, marshes, 3 types of dunes, forests. beaches and *corrales* make up the landscape. Doñana can be visited on horseback, in horse-drawn carriage, by 4X4, on foot or by hot air balloon at dawn.

In Palos de la Frontera, a small town near Huelva, at the opposite end of the park, is the perfectly proportioned and contemplative structure of the *monasterio de la Rábida*. Preserved as a national monument, it contains some of the personal effects of its most illustrious guest: Cristóbal Colón (Christopher Columbus) just before he left for the New World. Replicas of his ships, *La Niña and Santa María*, are anchored nearby. Within the park, on the edge of the marsh overlooking wading birds, foraging flamingos and wandering horses is the famous sanctuary of El Rocío.

The longest foreign influence in Spain has always been in Andalucía and one town to have been in part moulded by that incoming contact has been the city of Jerez de la Frontera. English wine merchants arrived in the area in the 14th century. In the 1530's they formed the Andalusian company known as The Brotherhood of St. George. Chaucer made mention of the sherry of Andalucía in his Canterbury Tales *'the fumositee'* - fortified strength. As early as 1519 'sack' wine was imported to England from *Las Islas Canarias* via Bristol. The importers faced hard times when Spain eventually confronted 'heretical' England. By the 1870's the English wine barons were entirely integrated into local society; but the Anglo-Spanish 'Lords of Jerez' were easily recognisable, as today, by their English attire and aristocratic lifestyle. The sack region was sherry's 'golden triangle' of Jerez, el Puerto de Santa María and Sanlúcar de Barrameda, which also produced brandy and Manzanilla. The exceptionally hot sunshine ripens the grape with a higher than usual sugar content ideal for making sherry. The wine *bodgeas* of Harvey and Osborne were English, Terry was Irish and Domecq French. The Englishman Robert Blake Byass set up a bodega with

Manuel González a bank employee who invested all he had in the company plus a loan from his uncle José who he immortalised in his sherry Tio Pepe - Uncle Joe.

> *"A good sherris-sack hath a twofold operation in it. It ascends me into the brain; dries me there all the foolish and dull and crudey vapours which environ it. The second property of your excellent sherris is, the warming of the blood; which, before cold and settled, left the liver white and pale, which is the badge of pusillanimity and cowardice."*
> Sir John Falstaff, Henry IV part II

Jerez has more up its sleeve than just its wine *bodegas* which can be visited free of charge. Take a trip round the historic and impressive wine cellars and finish off the tour with a more than generous sampling of the sherries offered to the visitor in one of its beautiful patios. Jerez is also the home of the Royal Andalusian Riding School - *La Real Escuela del Arte Equestre Andaluz*. The impressive riding installations, including one of the few buildings created by Charles Garnier - architect of the Paris opera house, can be visited while taking in the riding exhibition of the pure-bred white Spanish horses. Jerez also has a superbike circuit and a clock museum that warrants great praise.

Huelva may be the nearest city to Sevilla but the nearest city to inspire the visitor is without doubt Córdoba. An hour and a half north on the road to Madrid, it stands at the foothills of a *sierra* with its Moorish mosque in the old Jewish district and still dominates the city skyline. Roman and Visigothic cultures flourished here but it was the Moors who really made the city burn bright, becoming an independent Caliphate in 756. It was the centre of learning in the 9th and 10th centuries in Europe. The mosque – *mezquita*, is beyond doubt one of Europe's architectural jewels. It was listed as a World Heritage site in 1984. It was begun in 785 and added to for centuries until it was finally left in peace in 1776. Inside its labyrinth of 110 pillars it is impossible not to think of Minotaur mythology. But as with all Moorish monuments the Christians crowned the Cordoban *mezquita* by leaving their imprint upon it. But before the building was affected by Christian interference the architects faced the anger of the local population of the time, who objected strongly to 'their' mosque be altered in any way. The Jewish quarter, established in 1315 has some of the most constricted streets in Spain and one of the few surviving synagogues. In the river are hundreds of birds' nests nestling like buds of cotton in the trees and the remnants of Moorish mills still resist the currents of change. The Roman bridge with its 16 arches leads a triumphant road across the river and into the mosque.

Eight kilometres from Córdoba is Madinat al-Zahra - the ruins of what was the Caliphate's most lavish palace in *al-Andalus*, now undergoing restoration. Built in 400 of the Hegira epoch and 1010 of the Christian era, it was only inhabited for 65 years after taking 25 to build it. It then suddenly fell into ruin after being sacked by fanatical Berbers. Not all al-Andalus was a period of enlightenment. It was then swallowed up by the mists of time, and above all the mud washed down from the *sierra*. It sat untouched, awaiting to be rediscovered, which happened in 1910. Until then scholars had doubted the claims of the palace's lavishness. There was too much material for a museum, so they decided to solve the problem by rebuilding the grand palace with the remaining stone found in situ. The area so far uncovered is vast, but it only constitutes 10% of the original palace.

At the entrance to the Mediterranean stands the ancient port of Cádiz, Europe's oldest town. Apart from its irresistible similarities to Cuba's capital *La Habana*, its most outstanding feature is its carnival and quiet central streets, when the local *gadetanos* are not out hell-raising. On its eastern outskirts towards San Fernando the road passes through a strange landscape. Deserted salt mines, abandoned buildings and wetlands create a home for wildlife and flamingos, which are often seen sifting through the mudflats. The forest *Los Alcornocales* is considered by many to be the best in Spain, referred to as the 'Virgin forest of Europe' and claimed to be the most beautiful ever seen by at least one visiting German biologist.

Further down the coast is Málaga, thorn in the side of Sevilla's aspirations to remain the capital of Andalucía. Its summer fair, in the city streets by day and then in its fairground enclosure - *el real*, by night is all on a grand scale. The modern capital of *La Costa del Sol* maintains its historic roots where its *Alcazaba* and castle of Gilbralfaro are stunning Moorish remains.

Southwest of Sevilla is a chain of white towns famed for their colour and character - *Los Pueblos Blancos*. Ronda not only has the oldest bullring in Spain, but it was also immortalised by the romantics for its bandit -

bandoleros - country. Many writers have passed through this town to see it for themselves. Hemingway was a keen enthusiast of the place. Juan Goytisolo described his arrival there: *"We caught sight of Ronda. It was perched in the sierra like a natural extension of the landscape and, in the sunlight, it seemed to me the most beautiful town in the world."* Its famous New Bridge, finished in 1793, links the town across the attractive gorge that brings in visitors up from the *costas*. The 330ft-deep narrow valley winds on for about a quarter of a mile where it can be descended by some 365 steps. Many claim Ronda to be the most beautiful town in Andalucía.

The cliff-top town of Arcos de la Frontera never fails to impress. In its *Parador* you can drink coffee while reclining in an armchair with the edge of the rock face right at your feet and birds of prey hovering jealously outside your privileged eerie. The driver will sweat as their car strains to avoid scraping its sides in the slender streets, barely designed for carts let alone motorised comfort; but the view is rare and the exploring well rewarded.

Another white town in the area is Grazalema. The road snakes a narrow and tortuous route up toward the village hidden in the palm of the *sierra*. The road surface maybe newly laid but it is still only wide enough in places to allow a mule past let alone the bus coming confidently in your direction. Somehow people avoid hitting each other and the drive up is a incentive in itself. Cork trees line the route with their trunks stripped bare. They stand in the countryside like T-shirt toting toddlers bare bottomed at the beach, naked from the waist down. From behind the trees the jagged outline of the mountains and sunshine blinks through their branches streaming past the car window. The town is compact, white as promised and remarkably well-kept. Closed off from the outside world it is another example of the impossible. How can they maintain themselves here? What do they do for a living these people? At every turn the walls gleam, the doors are grand and the windows are all fronted by pristine wrought-iron grilles. Noble stone entrances are plentiful and the manicured nature of the buildings does not fail to amaze. Villagers stroll through the squeezed lower streets where tourists sit under parasols enjoying the relative seclusion afforded by the intimate alleyways. Cragged tops of rugged rocks peer down on the village. White walls shine as the paint, which looks recently applied to the whole village, earns its money by reflecting the heat. The view offers an escape into the open valley below. Higher up, an open swimming pool looks over the landscape from another vantage point in the town. Drinkers there while away the time in a thatched bar and bathers float past enjoying the blue sky above, the mountains behind and the distant scenery in front of them. If you're ever in Ronda, a trip up here afterwards will complete your day nicely; but don't say you haven't been warned about the road.

Of course *THE* monument of Spain is not Spanish but Arab. In Granada one of the modern world's wonders is the *Alhambra*. This lavish palace, dating from the 13th century is unequalled in Europe as is its position, set as it is against the white summit of Sierra Nevada's emblematic mountain *el Pico de Veleta*. It is not the highest, that claim goes to *El Mulhacén* next to it, the biggest in the Peninsular and named after the father of Granada's last Moorish ruler. The promontory between the mountains and the Jewish quarter is entirely taken up by the sprawling palace. At its feet flows the Darro. Inside its walls are towers, balconies, patios, domes, intricate artisanship, gardens, fountains and streams. The word 'Granada' for the curious means 'pomegranate' and is the symbol of the town. The fruit also puts in an appearance on the Crown's standard.

Its most beautiful district is the old quarter of *el Albaizín*. Private houses with gardens and cypress trees fill the hillside. The area now has a new mosque, the first in the city since 1492. It is not the first in Spain opened since the arrival of democracy but it is certainly the most symbolic. After 507 years, Islam has an official place of worship in what had been the Nasrite kingdom and the last vestige of Medieval Islamic culture in Europe. The mosque now looks back at the Alhambra.

The most famous neighbourhood in the city, though, is Sacramento, the Gypsy *barrio*. Behind the Alhambra in the hills are the old cave dwellings of the long established community now home to the Flamenco shows that entertain visitors and allow the Gypsies a decent standard of living.

Andalusia's most isolated city is Jaén. The interior of the province of Jaén is an enormous sea of olive groves. From a high vantage point in the centre of the city stands the Moorish fortress now fully restored as a National *Parador*. From here it is possible to look out over the plains and down onto the Baroque cathedral in the heart of the rural town. It is a unique sight. Also in the province are the Renaissance towns of Baeza and Úbeda, recent additions on Spain's long list of monuments considered by UNESCO as part of the world's heritage. Both towns competed for status as their nobles opened their purses and brought in architects to raise edifices to glorify their achievements.

From Úbeda it is possible to see a small town nestling in the folds of distant mountains. The town of Cazorla is a base for those wanting to venture into its national park and reach the spring of the Guadalquivir. The park is overflowing with wildlife. The rural town moves at a different pace, whose overhanging cliffs are home to a population of vultures forever circling the skies - possibly on the lookout for lost tourists.

Almeria is the most easterly city and sits south of the only desert region in Europe. She rests by the Mediterranean with her impressive Moorish fortress high on the horizon and her summer *Feria* well attended. Set in the north of Almeria province, in the parched yellow earth and Europe's only desert, is the cowboy town of Tabernas, where Sergio Leone's Spaghetti Westerns were filmed and open as a touristic attraction today.

One trip you won't be making on foot is to the north of Spain. The typical route of the world's oldest pilgrimage route is from France across the north of Spain eastwards to its sanctuary and destination in Santiago de Compostela. Possibly the most forgotten route though to Santiago is that which starts out from Sevilla along the *Ruta de Plata* once known as *el Camino Mozárabe*. A trek of about a thousand kilometres. The journey starts in the cathedral in Sevilla. Here homage is paid and, more importantly, the document acquired from the church which will allow the pilgrim to take advantage of special hostels along their route. Hostels and refuges that offer free board in many cases and others where only donations are required. Beginning at the gate of the cathedral, the yellow arrows painted at intervals on the curb, take the pilgrim out across the bridge in Triana, into the countryside and onto the old Roman route north past Itálica, Mérida, Salamanca and eventually crossing the green hills of Galicia. The route is maintained by a group of *aficionados* who, with the collaboration of the various Town Halls on the way, keep the arrows and paths intact. In 1992 only 30 made the journey but the numbers, like the pilgrims' progress, have been climbing steadily.

All the major cities of Andalucía excel in the celebration of the essential characteristics that make Andalucía a unique region in Europe. All have their Moorish ramparts, their *Feria* and *Semana Santa*, their olive oil and wine production as well as Flamenco and the Spanish horses. But they all shine in varying intensities. For the Moorish and Flamenco heritage you should go to Granada, for the olive oil to Jaén, for the *Feria* and *Semana Santa* visit Sevilla. To see the best of the Spanish horses and wine *bodegas* Jerez is the very pinnacle. To spend time in lush green rolling hills then Aracena beckons and for rugged landscapes and white villages Ronda and *Los Pueblos Blancos* stand out from the rest. But good food, inexpensive wine and even greater cheer is found everywhere in equal measure. After all, that is why you have come to Andalucía.

- DIECEISÉIS -
FIRST IMPRESSIONS

As the Spanish proverb says, "He who would bring home the wealth of the Indies, must carry the wealth of the Indies with him." So it is in travelling; a man must carry knowledge with him, if he would bring home knowledge.
Samuel Johnson (1709–84)

An alternative perspective is often just the ticket when trying to decide whether another's opinion has some validity to it or not. Here are a traveller's first experiences and impressions of Sevilla...

My Spanish is extremely limited, even when not in a pressure situation such as trying to make myself understood on the street or in a bar in a busy city like Seville. Faced with the need to ask for something or, worse still, answer a question or follow directions from a local, I found myself almost totally unable to make myself understood. As often as not I would blurt out a bizarre blend of Franglais and Spanglish. It confused me, so it couldn't have been - and was not - comprehensible to the listeners.

You can imagine then, that I had a pretty difficult time in Sevilla. And you'd be completely wrong, *amigo*. I had some of the most enjoyable days I can remember. I will return to do it all again as soon as possible.

The main reason for this trip was in the crowd of waiting meeters and greeters. He stood out head and shoulders taller than the throng and, in contrast to the locals around him, very blond. My son, Mark. We hadn't seen each other since my emigration down under. Seven years before.

We took a taxi into to town and as we neared the heart of Sevilla, I began to realise why he is so pleased to be living there. It is a beautiful old place of cobbled streets, many of them very narrow, plenty of *plazas*, countless little - sometimes very little - shops, among many fine buildings large and small. It is, in a word, charming.

And its proportions are so very human. I learnt later that no building can be taller than the local landmark - La Giralda. This is the square tower of the city's old, very old and huge cathedral. What's more, the city is flat and covers a comparatively small area. I have no real notion of actual size; but had no trouble getting around the centre on foot and I saw most parts of it at least once. Five of the seven days I was there, were spent strolling the streets and innumerable narrow alleyways in this central part of the city.

My favourite part of town was the tiny Barrio Santa Cruz, the Old Jewish Quarter, I believe. It hugs the high wall on one side of the Real Alcázar and is a maze of the narrowest streets with many interesting small buildings and pretty little squares. As we turned one of its myriad sharp corners we saw, through a slightly open gate, one of the most attractive little (there's that word again; but it's simply unavoidable in this place) restaurants in a minute courtyard. I went back a day or two later, only to find the gate firmly shut.

Like all the best places, Sevilla has a river, the Guadalquivir, dividing it. Triana, where I stayed for the week, is on the opposite bank to the heart of the city. This is a district, which is famous for its ceramic tiles. Although evidence of this is brilliantly displayed everywhere in Sevilla and the few other parts of *Andalucía* which I visited, there were no obvious signs to my eyes that Triana was the heart of the trade. There is only a very old factory, now more a museum, as far as I could tell (it was closed when I visited it). Perhaps I wasn't looking in the right places.

For lovers of old, fine or fine old buildings, Sevilla's an absolute must. They range from its Moorish Royal Palace Buildings - Reales Alcazares, and Cathedral through architecture from every era to the super-modern structures of the pavilions of the 1992 World Expo on the Isla de la Cartuja.

Probably the most striking structure in the city is the Plaza de España. This is an enormous crescent of a building, combining Baroque and Renaissance styles, built mainly of brick in the 1920's and beautifully decorated with motifs and murals of local ceramics. It also contains a canal with bridges that can only be described as Venetian. It's quite a hybrid and a definite must-see.

Then there is the twelve-sided Torre del Oro on the banks of the river, close to the splendid bullring: plus the museums, the embassy buildings in their various styles and the never-quite-finished city hall, *Ayuntamiento*. The list, as you can imagine, is almost endless.

Food formed one of my abiding memories of Sevilla. I was introduced to a special kind of continental breakfast at my son's flat. He keeps a small, narrow-necked bottle of olive oil flavoured with chopped garlic. This is spread on toasted slices of local bread and finished with a thick coating of tomato paste. Very tasty and probably equally healthy. Apart from this great start to the day, we ate mainly in bars large and small, scattered all around the centre of the city. I'm not a city dweller at all; but tapas bars are one aspect of this city's style of living of which I heartily approve. We enjoyed so many different small dishes that none of them stand out in my memory. I enjoyed every one of them.

My trip happened to fall at Easter. Not planned that way for any particular reason. It turned out to be an excellent piece of timing, though. First there was the weather - perfect the entire trip after what had just been a pretty damp spell. Then there were the processions. They simply have to be experienced to be believed.

Semana Santa, Holy Week, is supremely important to all Christians, Catholics especially, but none more than the Spanish, I'd guess. The entire population appears to be caught up in it, if Sevilla is typical. And I believe it is. Religious displays concerning crucifixion and/or the Madonna abound in growing numbers of shop windows as the week progresses.

Then the processions begin. Each parish church possesses one, or sometimes two, life-sized, usually extravagantly ornate icons in the form of a statue of The Virgin, Christ on the cross or a scene from the Easter story. This is often under an elaborate canopy, probably surrounded by candles and mounted upon a float the size of a truck. It is paraded through the streets from its home to the cathedral and back, escorted fore and aft by scores of robed and hooded 'penitents' also often carrying tall candles. A band goes along as part of the action. Each church's brotherhood of penitents has its own colour scheme of robes and regalia, making it a fantastic experience of sight as well as sound. The costumes looked sinisterly like coloured versions of the KKK to my uninitiated eyes. Some of the processions involved as many as six hundred.

The most striking aspect of all this for me, was that the floats, which must weigh tonnes each, are carried on the shoulders of men both young and old who are all but hidden behind velvet curtains draped around the bases. Their feet are all that can be seen, shuffling along over the cobbles. There are tiny, mesh-covered peep-holes at the front to give the lead porters some view of where they are going; but, for the most part, instructions are shouted to them from outside. These objects are not small and the narrow streets, filled with the thronging thousands of spectators make the business of negotiating the many tight bends on their route look none too easy. Distances travelled vary, of course, depending upon each church's location.

First Impressions

The longest of them take many hours and they don't all happen during daylight hours.

I was privileged to witness one from the vantage point of a balcony overlooking a church from which it began its pilgrimage in the beautiful Plaza del Museo. Below us the small square was packed tight with onlookers, as were the streets along which it would pass. At about nine (p.m.) the penitents began emerging from the building. Hundreds must have passed through the excited crowd before there was a sudden and complete hush. The float, with its crucified Messiah was about to emerge. Slowly and laboriously as it happened, because it was too tall for the bearers to carry it through the doorway standing. They must have been almost crawling with it on their backs until it was fully out when they rested briefly and caught their breath. There was then a sharp rapping from the 'captain' of an ornamental door-knocker mounted on the front of the float. This alerted the bearers to be ready to lift on his command. As they did, it rocked unsteadily while they settled their heavy burden and a huge round of applause went up from the crowd. They seemed relieved that it had been achieved safely. Or perhaps they were simply pleased that things were finally on the move. More hooded figures stepped into view, followed by the band and they slowly wound their way around the palm tress in the *plaza* and finally out of sight (though not sound) of our balcony. It had taken two hours for them all to pass through the church and they were not expected to complete their round trip before three a.m.

So many of them are involved that timetables are printed and distributed to let everyone know which streets will be affected and when. The disruption to traffic is immeasurable and finding a parking space in the city centre during this time can take hours unless one is lucky - very lucky.

A year has passed and it's *Semana Santa* again. Doubtless the brothers will be donning their hoods once more to carry and escort their magnificent floats through those narrow streets to the delight of the admiring crowds. Carpenters will be busy erecting yet another temporary masterpiece to herald *La Feria*. I'm not there to see, hear and experience any of it. The memories are unlikely to fade and there is always the hope of returning one day.

In the meantime at home, close to the toaster we have a small tapered bottle of garlic-flavoured olive oil and in the fridge, a jar of tomato paste.

- DIECISIETE -
HASTA LUEGO

Despite its 16th century chauvinism and acute civic pride,
the atmosphere in Seville is irresistible.

Sevilla, and Andalucía, surprise the visitor by displaying an abundant culture and history which is palably alive in their daily fabric. Sevilla is a city tantalisingly placed between exaltation and disillusionment; between ecstasy and tempered reserve. But that is the essence of Spain's ironies: the bitter sweet. The bullfight is *a fiesta* of cruelty and death to accentuate the sense of life and is Spain's quintessential spectacle. But this is Sevilla: Spain's archetypal city.

In these pages we have been under the sun, gazed upon ancient foundations and Moorish architectural marvels. We have tasted the fat of the land and savoured its spring fragrances. The river has guided us through a land's history and its people have displayed a culture which has been exported around the world and which has inspired many a writer, thinker and dancer. Its humanity has soared to great heights and plunged equally as great depths, having been host to great artists and writers as well an intolerant Inquisition. Its two selves stand in contradiction but next to one another: secular liberation in *La Feria* and religious duty in *Semana Santa*. We have known what it is to feel another people's preoccupation with death and their love for life. Being never far from death in their local culture is what gives them such a thirst to live. Just as if you had a scrape with death you would come out from it with a greater appreciation for the time you have left. It may be important to buy a house but there is no need to wait until the mortgage is paid to start enjoying yourself. Plan ahead by all means, but don't forget to live the day that is upon you.

Sevilla symbolises, through its striking identity and sharp authenticity that you can choose the way of life and the city you most desire. Things do not have to be the way they are, they *can* of course be changed. It all depends on your priorities: what do you want from life?

The Spanish are a rare breed in today's cynical world, and the *andaluces* and *sevillanos* especially so. They are *actually* happy with their lives, no matter how imperfect it may seem to others. They are content with their lot. They do not need visits to the shrink or aspire to travel the world. A few *tapas*, drinks with friends, have their family around them, enjoy their *fiestas* and spend the summers by the beach is, for many, their recipe for 'success' in life. The modern world searches for happiness while here they seem to have found it already.

We have created the world we live in. It was not preordained when we arrived on this planet that traffic jams and street crime would be waiting for us. They are of our own doing. The great variety of different cultures lets us know the route that each people has chosen to take. The route that Spain went down, and Sevilla in great part led, has attracted many intellectuals and travellers in its wake.

There are certain human characteristics that bind us all, but each culture has taken these mores, morals, ethics and emotions and moulded them through their own best judgement. Then they have applied a good coat of pride and prejudice and then sealed them in tradition.

Anything that might have changed your perceptions is to be commended and not feared and this book has attempted to act as testament to the *sevillanos'* vision and recipe for living. After all, this is a city whose passion for death is only matched by its lust for life.

'My time has been passed viciously and agreeably; at thirty-one so few years, months, days, hours or minutes remain in that "Carpe Diem" is not enough. I have been obliged to crop even the seconds - for who can trust to tomorrow?'
Byron

While *Carpe Diem* is important the Spanish have perfected the art form of 'seizing the day' while also living for tomorrow. They live today's *fiesta* with intensity but they will be up early tomorrow to start planning ahead for the next celebration. There's no time to lose.

Perhaps every time that a peice of travel writing takes you off to a sunny country, it loses itself in all the positive feelings brought on by the change of climate. As a result we want to see everything through rose-tinted glasses. It is hard, however, to avoid such a feeling of positiveness which wells up here in Sevilla and positively bursts into life during its *fiestas*.

Sevilla is hot, traditionally minded, *alegre* and a great place to live a leisurely urban life. It could even be a great place to end your days (if such a place really exists) but Sevilla would be one of the worst places to pass away from. Leaving this world is one thing, but having to do it in a place where all around you are in joyous spirits would be even more annoying. However, the lyrics from a *Sevillanas* tell us: *'En Sevilla hay que morir'* - You have to die in Sevilla.

Sevilla, as in the rest of Spain, has built that appreciation into their daily psyche which they contemplate in their *Flamenco Cante Jondo*, *Corrida* and *Semana Santa*, and which they liberate in their *Flamenco Alegría*, *Feria* and *Romería* to *El Rocío*. Sevilla is always true to herself, correct to the extreme on occasion, well-intentioned and keenly proud of its place on this earth.

Its citizens are not afraid of their emotions and certainly not scared to let them surface through the skin. It is this that has forged their music and *fiesta* and set their sights on the future. It is also this living and fearless expression that brings people together and draws those of us from abroad to join their number. We are not just here to eat and look up at the balconies. We spend most of our time looking around us seeing what the *sevillanos* will do next.

Any book on Sevilla has to cover religion, its history, its idiom, dance, song, its cuisine, *fiestas*, customs, art and architecture. This is a great part of its attractiveness. There are *fiestas* in all of Spain but those here are very much *sevillano* in nature. There is bullfighting throughout the peninsular but here it takes on a different character. Architecture abounds in this country but Sevilla has a style and collection of great personal note. It has its own music, its own vision of Catholicism and its own identity. Sevilla is a riddle wrapped in *Andalucía* inside *España*. One day the answer may come out but hopefully not just for the moment.

To swagger through the cobblestone streets of old Seville in well-dressed, *alegre* Spanish-eyed company; to feast the senses on its exotic cocktail of Roman, Jewish, Visigothic and Moorish history; to be touched by its song, suns, swooning heat, feminine guile and join family gatherings is the stuff Hispanophile dreams are made and the experience of anyone who has stayed long enough in the city.

To leave *Andalucía* is to leave the *Fiesta* and your life will from then on always feel as if it is lacking something. Unless of course, you move to a corner of the world with a calendar as exhaustive as here, and that really *is* saying something.

So, if you are already in Sevilla while reading this then you are by now enjoying the city as much as the natives, and if you have yet to come out here and experience the capital of Andalucía for yourself, then as the title of this closing chapter suggests… until later.

"Twenty years from now you will be more disappointed by the things that you didn't do than by the ones you did do. So throw off the bowlines. Sail away from the safe harbor. Catch the trade winds in your sails.
Explore. Dream. Discover."
Mark Twain

Printed in Great Britain
by Amazon